The Angel of the Countenance of God

The Angel of the Countenance of God
THEOLOGY AND ICONOLOGY OF THEOPHANIES

VLADISLAV ANDREJEV
Translated by Alex Apatov

Angelico Press

First published in Russian as *Angel Litsa Bozhia*
by I. V. Balabanoff in 2011
© V. Andrejev, 2011

English edition © Angelico Press, 2021

All rights reserved:
No part of this book may be reproduced or transmitted,
in any form or by any means, without permission

For information, address:
Angelico Press, Ltd.
169 Monitor St.
Brooklyn, NY 11222
www.angelicopress.com

ppr: 978-1-62138-729-9
cloth: 978-1-62138-730-5

Book and cover design
by Michael Schrauzer

Table of Contents

Prologue. ix

1 The Mirror of God's Actions. 1

2 Mythology and Faith 11

3 Theophanic Religion in Myth Images. 27

4 Manifestations of Jehovah in the Likeness of an Angel: The Old Testament 43
    The Patriarch Abraham 45; *The Patriarch Isaac* 49; *The Patriarch Jacob* 50; *The Prophet Moses* 53; *Joshua and the Prophets* 62; *The Prophet Daniel* 69; *The Prophets Zechariah and Malachi* 71

5 Iconological Images of Theophanies. 75
    Memrah-Logos-Word-Speech 77; *The Son of Man* 86

6 Names of God. 89
    Hypostatic Names of God 98; *Prosoponic Names of God (by the Image of Action of God)* 104

7 Logos—Miraculous Angel in the Manifestation of Energies: Shekinah, Sophia, and Agape 109
    Shekinah—God's Dwelling Place 113; *Sophia—God's Wisdom* 119; *Sophia in the Speculations of the Church Fathers* 126; *Iconography of Sophia* 138; *The Doctrinal Meaning of Sophia* 143; *Agape—God's Love* 153; *Love Images in Mythology* 157; *The Theme of Love in the Song of Solomon* 165; *Images and Types of Interpretation of the Song of Solomon* 169; *Seven Interpretations of the Song of Solomon* 173; *Iconology and Iconography of the Song of Solomon* 192

8 Continuation of the Song of Solomon:
   Theophanies of Agape in the New Testament. 207
   *The Hymn to Love by Symeon the New Theologian, Homily
   53* 228; *A Word on Love by St. Maximus the Confessor* 246;
   Life as Love. The Story of Peter and Febronia 252

9 Theology and Iconology of Theophanies in the
   New Testament 261

   Epilogue 287

Prologue

*For there stood by me this night the angel of God,
to whom I belong, and whom I serve,
and said, "Do not be afraid."*
Acts of the Apostles 27:23

THIS BOOK IS DEDICATED TO THE RESEARCH of questions about the iconology of the epiphanies of God. The interest in iconology as a theme closely tied to iconography has recently become a prominent topic of discussion in spiritual literature. In the book, we offer an analysis of the biblical theme of the "Angel of Jehovah," trying to understand it from the point of view of iconographic practice. The main characteristic of the book is the attempt to differentiate between the nature of the "created angel" of the Heavenly Hierarchy and the "uncreated Angel" of Epiphany. This difference is essential to both the practical and theoretical development of the iconographic culture which inevitably corresponds to dogmatic theology. The research itself refers to the task of an iconological course and presents an important question: what is the essence of the icon when regarded as an epiphany of Life?

Our research reveals that the icon written on a board is only the external, spoken visual word. The significance of the true meaning of the icon is within each person created "in the Image (Greek, *Eikón*) of God" (Gen. 1:26). In other words, man himself is the living Icon of the Image of God. Furthermore, the Image of God is the immaterial, essential Light of God by means of which "actions" of God are depicted and made visible. Therefore, it is said that icon-writing is the method of "symbolic realism," and while it is not capable of depicting God, it is fully able to depict the image of His actions, in other words the Divinity of God.

"Iconology" is the study of the Icon of Divine Presence in the inner man. Man is Icon, and religion being the method of God-knowledge cannot survive without its visual incarnation through art. In turn, art must be abundant in religious meaning. The unity of these cultural "beginnings" creates a bond between "outer" and "inner" life ("matter" and "spirit").

We present biblical occurrences of Epiphanies as iconographic appearances of divine Light, in various forms like divine "signs." For example, in the Bible they are described as clouds, dew drops, fire, doves, crosses, etc. Alongside these symbols, the icon-writer is intrigued by the numerous phenomena of Divinity as the image of the *uncreated* Angel, identical to God in the nature of Light. A vivid example of this is when Moses saw the divine Angel in the flames of the Burning Bush. Likewise, the Christian tradition has the icon of the royal Maiden Sophia, the personification of the Wisdom of God depicted as the Angel of divine nature.

Rather than being viewed as theological research from a scientific point of view, the theme of the uncreated Angel, the direct messenger of God to the world, is observed from philosophical-anthropological and religious-theological positions that correlate with iconography. We do not lay claim to *academic* accuracy in this study. The work before you is the result of an icon-writer's in-depth meditation. His findings are based on extensive practice that aids the development of iconography with an accent on the symbolic interpretations of God's Epiphanies.

This book, presented in the form of an "hypothesis," is a unique "theologoumenon" of the relationship between the dogma of faith and the icon. The text is structured in the style of "free narration" and does not carry with it any strict scientific or theological aspects. The citations throughout are not used for the purpose of proving a right or a wrong, but rather as an addition to and an amplification of what is being said. In providing citations, we acknowledge the fact that even the clearest of interpretations are greatly dependent on the translation. Therefore, footnotes or references with exact page numbers for the citations are generally not included, and for that we apologize.

Faith is not only a learned dogma, but even more so it is Life with a capital letter, and the life of a person is the Icon of symbolic realism. Iconography is creativity that has been absorbed through the

Prologue

experiences of various steps of the contemplation of Epiphanies. In this way, all the "phenomena" of life can be regarded as a relationship between "Man" and "God."

This book is written based on forty years of the icon-writer's personal experience in researching the questions and tasks of the icon, as posed by both ancient and contemporary culture in the realm of art, religion, and icon-writing.

V. L. Andrejev
*Founder and Director of the Prosopon
School of Iconography and Iconology*

THE MIRROR OF GOD'S ACTIONS

1
The Mirror of God's Actions

*I, Jesus have sent Mine angel to testify
unto you these things in the churches.*
Book of Revelation 22:16

THE DOCTRINE OF ANGELS—ANGELOLOGY—is not only a body of knowledge about immaterial beings of the celestial Hierarchy, with its nine orders. The angelic world invisibly participates in the lives of people, strengthening their faith and inspiring them to know God. Angels stand facing those who keep their prayer rules, being "secondary lights" and, in essence, *minds*, heavenly powers that help people open the heart's mind and restore their noetic (spiritual) nature. Through the angelic light, people are moved toward opening their heavenly image, where the Logos—God's name—is imprinted as in a mirror. The angelic light makes your sensual heart so clear and transparent that you can see yourself in it, as an *icon* of the image of God's *actions*. In this sense, icon painting, as the sacred art of symbolic realism, can be one of the ways for the soul to ascend to the Image of God.

Angels teach faith to people, elevating their heart energy and minds to the contemplation of the Kingdom of Heaven; and on the ways of this anagogic ascent, the soul, while still in the body, can know God. In the New Testament tradition, angels act not only as "ministering spirits," messengers who bring tidings from God to humans:

> In communicating illumination to each other, the angelic powers also communicate either their virtue or their knowledge to human nature. As regards their virtue, they communicate a goodness that imitates the goodness of God, and through this goodness they confer blessings on themselves, on one another and on their inferiors, thus making them like God. As regards their knowledge, they

communicate either a more sublime knowledge about God—for, as Scripture says, "Thou, Lord, art Most High for evermore" (Ps 92:8)—or a more profound knowledge about embodied beings, or one that is more exact about incorporeal beings, or more distinct about divine providence, or more precise about divine judgment.[1]

Some of the angelic hosts serve together with priests at every Divine Liturgy and offer, together with worshippers, prayers to God, as it is said "Who art in Heaven," i.e., in the Kingdom of the Celestial Hierarchy. So, angels' participation in the affairs of earthly piety and faith forms the uniformity and fullness of the heavenly and earthly Church. The idea of "God's Image"—which is embodied in the actions of Man's body, soul, mind, and spirit—is directly related to the actions of the angelic light, which is directly indicative of the uncreated divine Light.

Immersed in sense impressions most of their lives, people still must restore their noetic nature and, having cleansed it, reunite with the center of their souls, just as clay unites with gold in icon haloes. Reunion of the heart's mind (clay) and the angelic mind (gold) is an indispensable condition for the stability of faith in different situations. By the heart's mind, we understand a preliminary (i.e., on the way toward restoring the Image of God) reunion of the five human senses, whose center is intelligence: the sixth sense resulting from the five senses and leading to their unity. This is what is called "wisdom" in Man.[2]

Angels are intermediaries for the fulfillment of Divine Providence in the material Cosmos, and sacred history tells us about their participation in the ways of Man's God-knowing experience (they are *messengers* to the same extent as they are *viators*). The Bible describes a sufficient number of instances of God's manifestations in the form of an angel, which make us reflect on and try to discover the deep meaning of "God's actions" as depicted in

---

1 St. Maximus the Confessor, *The Four Hundred Chapters on Love, Third Century*, 33.
2 See *The Nativity Troparion*: "the Light of wisdom hath shone forth upon the world."

icons. The Old Testament salvation history begins with Abraham's meeting with the three angels, while that of the New Testament begins with the appearance to the Virgin Mary of the Archangel Gabriel who announced, "Today is the beginning of our salvation and the revelation of the eternal mystery!"[3]—the revelation of the Son of God on earth. Those appearances were quite different. The first instance describes the appearance of divine angels. The second one deals with a created angel, but Gabriel brings the news of the birth in this world of Christ, God's Son and Logos, who is the "Image of the invisible God." It was the birth of the perfect Man in human flesh—God who became the Icon of humanity. That was the starting point not only of theology, but also of the iconology of the ways to salvation. Bearing in mind that God is invisible and unknowable by essence, while professing the Church Fathers' doctrine of uncreated energies of the divine Revelation and Oeconomy, we can assert the existence of iconology—the "figurative" science of God's so-called "Appearances" out of His inaccessibility. These are the Theophanies illuminating Man's spiritual ascent *in the commandments, the doctrines, and the faith.* For, according to St. Maximus the Confessor, "these are the three objects of the Christian's philosophy."[4] Iconologically, Man before God is His Icon imprinting the Revelations of historical and mystical events, rather than one of the characters in the picture of cosmic events. Meanwhile, angels are secondary lights who open the possibility of iconographic depiction of God's *actions*, Theophanies. Through participation in the angelic light, the human soul is iconographed, gaining the ability to contemplate Theophanies.

With the birth of Christ, it is not only in the soul that the opportunity to embody iconological ideas arises. Iconography receives its visible representation in human life. It becomes possible to express faith in the religious creation of "manmade" icons. In the New Testament, the icon becomes a sign of holiness and a dogmatic symbol of the Incarnation of the Son of God. It is a sacramental decoration and a criterion for correspondence with the Church's *image of*

---

3 *The Annunciation Troparion.*
4 St. Maximus, *Chapters on Love, Fourth Century.*

action, because iconography and iconology are a liturgical theology in image. This liturgical correlation of the *image and the logos* (*the word*) can be defined by the term "orthodoxy"—a doctrine that is *true* in terms of the *image* of faith and the *logos* of the confession of the Trihypostatic God. Being the banner of contemplative faith, the icon not only illustrates a liturgical event, but also unites two prayerful actions from the visible and invisible worlds into a single Liturgy. In this regard, accuracy and further development of the iconography of angels is vital not only for icon painters, but also for all members of the conciliar Church of Christ, which in the present period of its existence expresses the state of "earthly" and "heavenly" faith. When considering the iconography of Heavenly powers, it is necessary to proceed from the basic tenet of its teaching: angel is the name of their *office* and *action*, not of their nature.

"The name ἄγγελος refers more to service than substance."[5] "Angels are depicted in a form that corresponds to the action of the forthcoming achievement."[6] According to St. John of Damascus, Man can see "an angel's image rather than essence, because an angel's nature is not visible to bodily eyes."[7] In addition, Dionysius the Areopagite testifies that angels, as immaterial minds, do not have their own image by nature, and yet they are depictable by their actions, although through befitting and understandable symbols, in the images of the visible world.

> The loving Source of all mysteries ... depicted those supercelestial Intelligences in material images in the inspired writings of the sacred Word so that we might be guided through the sensible to the intelligible, and from sacred symbols to the Primal Source of the Celestial Hierarchies.... The exposition of the hidden Mysteries by the use of unlike [in terms of naturalism] symbols accords more closely with That which is ineffable. Accordingly, this mode of description in the holy writings honors,

---

5 St. Cyril of Alexandria.
6 St. Maximus the Confessor, Comments on *The Celestial Hierarchy* by Dionysius the Areopagite.
7 St. John of Damascus, *Apologia Against Those Who Decry Holy Images*.

rather than dishonors, the Holy and Celestial Orders by revealing them in unlike images, manifesting through these their supernal excellence, far beyond all mundane things.[8]

Angelic images are certainly no figment of Man's rational thinking. They are directly granted in revelations and contemplations: as it is written, "the original and super-original gift of Light of the Father who is the Source of Divinity... shows to us images of the all-blessed Hierarchies of the Angels in figurative symbols."[9] Being "secondary lights," angels directly carry the divine Light. In Church tradition, the Heavenly Hierarchy's orders are classified into three ranks (lower, middle, and upper), "whose appearance corresponds to their order."[10] In accordance with this tradition, all nine orders of angels can also be iconographed in the style of symbolic realism in icon *pattern, color, and light*.

In their literature, angelologists often note that there are very few research papers that comment on the appearances of angels mentioned in the Bible and explain their meaning. In Orthodoxy, where the Icon is revered on a par with the Gospel and the Cross, the iconography of the angelic hierarchy has not yet been fully developed. Basically, books on ancient iconography contain descriptions of only two angelic orders (guardian angels and archangels), with prevailing descriptions of Heavenly hosts generically called "Angel of God." As for the order of archangels, there are many icons depicting archangels Michael and Gabriel, but images of archangel Raphael can be found very seldom (even in later versions) and there are absolutely no really serious works related to the images of five other angels — Uriel, Salaphiel, Jehudiel, Barachiel, and Jerahmiel. Even though the church and prayer tradition mentions all archangels with prayers said to each of them, iconography of most of the angelic orders has not yet been created. In angelology, many iconographic issues should be further deepened and solved, which will also open new opportunities for the development of icons in the modern perspective of an ever-increasing interest in them.

---

8   Dionysius the Areopagite, *The Celestial Hierarchy*.
9   Ibid.
10 St. John of Damascus, *Apologia*.

THE ANGEL OF THE COUNTENANCE OF GOD

Alongside the general issues relating to the liturgical connection between the Celestial Hierarchy of angels and the earthly Church, the appearances of the Angel of Jehovah described in the Old Testament are of special interest; these cannot be understood or explained solely in terms of angelology, because they in fact are of a higher theological order. Having special powers, and not chosen from among the created orders, the Angel is very clearly and quite frequently mentioned in the Bible, although its images are extremely scarce in the history of iconography. Biblical science tries to penetrate the mystery of the "Angel of the Countenance of God" (Is 63:9), with many exegetes noticing a certain specific difference between this Angel and the orders of the Celestial Hierarchy. All biblical descriptions, and many utterances of the Holy Fathers of the Church, give reason to consider this Angel to be *special* and uncreated: "From among angels, the Old Testament distinguishes the Angel of Jehovah's Face, or the Angel of Jehovah, who not only represents Jehovah, but is Jehovah."[11]

Stating that angels as God's *messengers* are determined by their actions corresponding to their service of God rather than by their nature or essence, the Bible associates their appearances to people with the history of salvation of the chosen people. But who can the *uncreated* messenger be then? This question brings together the theological *word* and the iconological *image* in such a manner that it should be clearly answered by both theologians and iconographers. The difference between the nine orders of angels is in the various degrees of light transmission ("God's gifts of light") and God's Revelation ("theurgic knowledge").[12] But is not the *Revelation* itself, the uncreated *Light* itself, the wonderful Angel who directly—"not an ambassador, nor a messenger, but Himself saved them" (Is 63:9, according to the Septuagint version)—carries God's Will, Wisdom, and all-transfiguring Love? Maybe this "Supreme Angel" is the Logos of God's Kingdom who creates and thinks about every creature? That is what we shall try to reflect on, having examined the Old and New Testament Theophanies revealed not through created messengers carrying God's Word through the heavens, but directly through

---

11 Alexander Glagolev, *Angels in the Old Testament.*
12 Dionysius, *Celestial Hierarchy.*

The Mirror of God's Actions

the image of the uncreated Light, which is named the "Angel of the Countenance of God" in the Bible.

Throughout the sacred history, from ancient times to the last Old Testament prophet, we find descriptions of appearances of the Lord of Sabaoth's messenger who is directly vested with power and authority by Jehovah himself—the Maleach Jehovah or the Angel of the Countenance of God. In the Greek version of the Scriptures, the notion "countenance" is denoted by the word "prosopon" (πρόσωπον), so it would be quite correct to use the name "Angel of God's Prosopon," or "Angel of God's Kingdom," considering that God's "Prosopon" is directly related to God's Divinity. Iconologically, such a "wonderful image" must be notable for its specific pattern, color, and light. It should be kept in mind that the iconography of such appearances portrays God by essential *energy* knowable through God's "image of action," rather than by essence or nature. But God's actions are always the *power and sense* of theology and the *beauty* of iconology that can be read and seen. Considering that the uncreated Energy is called the Divinity in the Orthodox tradition, the Angel of Jehovah can be understood as the "Angel of God's Divinity."

According to the Holy Fathers Gregory the Theologian, John of Damascus, Maximus the Confessor, and especially Gregory Palamas,[13] God's iconological actions, as Revelations, can be classified into *direct* appearances (where God Himself in His essential action, i.e., in His light energy, assume the form—*eidos*—of the Angel) and *indirect* appearances (where God shows the way to salvation and speaks his Will through created messengers—angels, prophets, apostles, and saints).

---

13 *The Triads.*

MYTHOLOGY AND FAITH

2
Mythology and Faith

Myth is an absolutely, I must say, transcendentally necessary category of thought and life, there is absolutely nothing contingent, unnecessary, arbitrary, fictitious, or fanciful about it. It is the authentic and most concrete reality.[1]

TO UNDERSTAND THE ENTIRE DEPTH OF DIStinction between "created and uncreated" things, we certainly need to look far into the depths of ancient centuries and to turn again to the history of development of such concepts as "myth" (in pantheism) and "religion" (in monotheism). Angels are mentioned and described in mythologies of many peoples. This makes it possible to trace how appearances of angels affected not only the destiny of the people of Israel, but also the mythological mentality of the pagan world. Religions have different forms, with their specific rituals and cults with different peoples, but *faith* in the existence of an invisible world became the basis for all peoples and was depicted in the monuments of religious art from the time of Sumer and ancient Egypt. As peoples developed throughout their history, faith constantly changed its form in accordance with changes in social consciousness and the Divine Providence. In mythological consciousness, angels, as creatures of special immaterial energy nature, were perceived as "gods" appearing to people from the depths of Space.

In the monotheistic consciousness of the people of Israel, a clear distinction was made between angels and creatures belonging to the spatial dimension. As early as Moses's testament "In the beginning God created the *heaven* and the *earth*" (Gen 1:1), "the earth" is understood as a material form of life, while "the heaven" is understood as "heavens"—an energy, a noetic form of life. According to the Church Fathers, in the beginning God created the noetic (intelligent)

---

1 Aleksei Losev, *The Dialectics of Myth*.

"heaven" with its angelic orders and then He created "the earth," space, inhabited with minerals, plants, animals, and humans. In the Bible, angels are no longer "gods," but ministering spirits, messengers, and heralds of the One God. In numerous hagiographical stories, the mystical experience of the Christian faith gives clear evidence that heavenly beings become not only carriers of divine "ideas," but also active participants of the divine revelation and dispensation. After the temptation in the wilderness, according to the Gospel, "angels came and ministered unto him" (Mt 4:11). This is a quite serious example, because the Old Testament angels brought only news or helped some people, especially the prophets.

Believers clothed in the robe of Christ and baptized in the name of the Trinity have an angelic *spiritual* presence inside them. The angelic presence inside a person who is born again in Christ became a new, qualitatively different state of faith, revealed through Christ in Man's spiritual heart. "The heart itself is but a little vessel, and yet there are dragons, and lions, and venomous beasts, and all the treasures of wickedness; and there are rough uneven ways, there are chasms; there likewise is God, there the angels, there life and the kingdom, there light and the apostles, there the heavenly cities, there the treasures, there are all things," says Macarius of Egypt.[2] After the Incarnation of Christ, Man received all of the essential dynamic worlds created before him, so a physical individual's noetic fleshless nature and life now constitute his *spiritual and fleshly* formation and religious force.

Based on the effect of mutually complementary cognition methods — "science" (in the work of the *intellect* of cosmic forces) and "faith" (an also natural yet noetic *consciousness*), it is necessary to define the structure of levels of *cognition* itself in accordance with its *strength* and *image of action* in different spheres of human existence. The question we are interested in now is as follows: How do we differentiate "faith" correlated with the methods of seeking the only Truth? This is a question to which no direct answer can be given. At this point, we can define four states of active faith (for "faith, if it hath not works, is dead, being alone," Jas 2:17), which should be distinguished yet not separated, because they have common properties

---

2 *Homily* 43.

Mythology and Faith

of cosmic, noetic, and divine powers. The true "golden proportion" of life would be as follows: faith should breathe the Spirit, become embodied and unfolded in virtuous deeds, and be selflessly raised to the level of a perfect iconological image of action.

Faith, as a method of meditation, realization, and comprehension, exists and ascends to its perfection from the initial stages of thought formation, through allegories and comparisons of visible and invisible things, to the direct contemplation of the mystical Reality. Getting closer to the "object" of faith is accompanied by changes in consciousness, in whose fullness faith should become creative work. It should also be understood that the "lower" state of faith, even if minimally, is always associated with the "upper" one. In this sense, "myth," as the subject under discussion, finds its expression even in Theophanies, where "mythological faith" is perfected and its purpose becomes clearer, for, according to Paul the Apostle, now we see only "through a glass, darkly" (1 Cor 13:12).

So, we can distinguish the following levels at which faith is manifested and perfected:

- *Mythology* is a religion where the direction of faith depends on the state of mind and complies with public notions about "visible and invisible" existence; a religion where a "multitude" (a group, a crowd, a people, and a nation) finds its religious ideals in certain "individuals" — powerful beings who possess supernatural powers and abilities (gods, spirits, heroes, persons, and demons).

- *Religion* is a state of "nominal" faith where a "friendly multitude" (individuals) seeks the truth in "The One," cosmologically understanding "The One" as "God" necessarily involved in the life of the Universe. This is what the currently forming cosmic religion of all-encompassing unity will be like. The religion based on the Old Testament and the Gospel of Christ is also addressed to a "multitude" (to nations), but it is not fully included in the Cosmos. In addition, it is singled out from national tones and attributes. The stage of faith having this content still contains the "bridge ligature" (*re-ligio*) principle,[3] as a kind of division into *left-right, top-bottom*, and *back-front* of which the "three-dimensional" consciousness of a nominal

---

[3] Some would derive the etymology of the word "religion" from *religare*, to bind.

believer consists. This polarity of religious division into "mine" and "yours" is overcome in the next stage, in mysticism.

- *Mysticism* is a dynamic state of dogmatic faith of an "individual" (a person) directed toward a "multitude" — the religious life of all planes of created existence, with the Deity itself entering into relations with Man through the Revelations of Light. At the level of mystical faith, individuals feel God's *presence, abidance, incarnation* and *habitation* inside themselves, which makes it possible to correlate the mystically inclined mind to the principles of iconography and iconology. This is the religious plane arisen and "iconographed," becoming visible in the symbolism of the man-made Icon.
- *Theophany* (*manifestation of God*) is a theological state of mystical faith where an "individual" (a hypostatic person) is combined with "The One" in the contemplation of the Trihypostatic God. In Theophany, a believer energically contemplates God in the Trinity "face to Face," or, as saints said, "to see God as He is" — Theoria. This type of contemplation was called "Theology" by the early Church Fathers. At the theological level, contemplation is accompanied by Godseeing and further, to various extents, by deification of the body, soul, and mind until one attains the fullness of knowledge of God.

The above structure shows that mythology is the initial form of any religion. Myths rightfully occupy a certain place in the process of ascending to the summit of faith, and they cannot be regarded only as fairytales (if anything, most fairytales contain elements of myths). In myths, we should find the beginning from which, as history shows, the monotheistic *religion* grows quite naturally. Interestingly, Christianity was easily embraced by those peoples (for instance, ancient Greeks) who created developed mythologies, but had no deep-rooted religious foundations.

From the Renaissance (fifteenth–sixteenth centuries) to nearly the nineteenth century, Europe took a great interest in "myths" — ancient poetic stories, fairytales, and legends about world-governing gods, supernatural beings, spirits, and heroes. In the first half of the nineteenth century, however, science became interested in features that are *common* for many national myths, because mythological systems existed nearly all over the world. Scientific research in world cultures showed that all of them were filled with distinctive myths associated with specific rituals and that, with all their great diversity, quite a few main themes and motifs were in common.

Highly developed mythological systems can be classified as follows: *cosmogonic myths* (related to the origin of the Universe), *anthropological myths* (related to the origin of Man), and *cult and ritual myths*. In myths, the Cosmos is populated by gods and spirits, and people participated in the cosmogonic development of existence, anthropomorphizing the actions and images of gods and the elements. In the human mentality, relations with gods were formed as a *method* of contacts between earthly and heavenly things and of their interpenetrations, which became a characteristic feature of mythology. But myth, as distinguished from religion, regarded "heavenly" things as the "cosmic sky" inhabited by gods, spirits, and demons. In mythology, we can trace two main ideas—*creation* (creationism) and *development* (evolutionism)—that are usually considered to be incompatible: either one or the other. The experience of faith and common religious sense make it possible to see what brings these positions together, while their complementary equivalence can be denoted as "*arising* existence" (creationism) and "*developing* life" (evolutionism). It is important to emphasize myth's consistent development toward ordering the cosmos in the natural course of life, for which reason myth begins to increasingly acquire religious features. As the idea of myth becomes more complicated, mythological images and religious motifs interweave and interconnect, forming cycles where religious rituals and traditions also begin to change; we can observe that different nations have very similar mythical concepts, whose range of subjects already deal with fundamental issues related to the Universe. In national cultures, myth-making forms in three areas: literary, pictorial, and scenes of ritual. The basic principle underlying mythology is *allegorical symbolism*, which makes it possible to treat mythological subjects in terms of anthropology.

Mythological mentality is also characterized by an indistinct discrimination and differentiation between the subject and the object, an object and its sign, and a creature and its name, which results from an uncritical mental attitude toward the polar notions of different planes of existence. In mythology, for example, we can see an interweaving of the natural and supernatural, the historical and eternal, and the rational and emotional. What is logically seen as *similarity* appears as *identity* in mythological mentality. Genetically and structurally, myth is usually associated with rituals and rites, which were characterized by personification of natural phenomena and philosophical concepts. In myth, specific objects and their actions become signs of subsequent events. In mythology, metaphorism may be replaced by symbolism, while one kind of symbolism may be replaced by some other one, to experience ritual events more realistically. In fact, this is what we are interested in in the context of detecting the historical roots of iconography, whose *images* evolved from personifications of the world elements to the symbolic realism of luminous Theophanies. The characteristic feature of myth is a sharp distinction between the mythological period and the present, which found its expression in such notions as *sacred* and *profane*. In the mythological dimension, all comprehensions of heavenly things and their connection with earthly things are based on *paradigm* (from Greek παράδειγμα—"an example," "a pattern," "a model"). That is why myth combines two aspects—a story about the past (diachronic aspect) and a method of explaining the present (synchronic aspect).

People with a mythological mentality perceived all events as a paradigm, as a model for reproduction. The content of myths was perceived as a genuine reality and a necessary emotional experience at the stage of collective consciousness and served as an uncriticizable subject of faith. In this sense, mythology can be considered to be a stage of formation of the principle of connection between the mind and heart; later, this principle laid the basis for many practices of forming religious consciousness. In fact, myth underlies the nascent symbolic thinking that connects the visible and invisible worlds. Mythological images represent personalia in metaphorical form and, therefore, reflect the truth indistinctly and vaguely, because the form in myths may not always be identical to the content. The myth content is viewed by the believer paradigmatically as the "supreme reality." Mythological themes are part of many generations' experience, which is perceived with confidence as a collective tradition and teaching.

The above-mentioned brings us to the issue of relation and connection between myth and religion. Many myths serve as commentaries to clarify religious rites. They include cult myths and rites that are common to all religions and peoples, which make it possible to conclude that they are intrinsically connected with some common archetypal religion that preceded all beliefs. Rites are based on prior experience and usually constitute the most stable part of religion, while mythological images may vary, and acquire more and more new forms depending on the historical period in which a myth was formed.

It should be emphasized that from the modern point of view the personification of the elements, birds, plants, and animals in mythology is not considered to be fully determined by the fear of gods. To a greater extent, this is a certain esoteric teaching associated with heavenly *ideas* and protected by initiates against being profaned by common people who easily turn any theogonic myth into a fairytale.

> The significance of mythology for the self-knowledge of humanity will become self-evident if we regard mythology as a huge stratum of cultural development of the entire humankind and as the most important phenomenon of cultural history that dominated human spiritual life for thousands of years, rather than as "a totality of misconceptions."[4]

But it would also look one-sided if we consider myth only in terms of culture. To fully understand religious consciousness, we should consider mythology to be the "beginning" of formation and development of the future of theology. Theologically, mythology will definitely have a lot of negative aspects (especially with regard to polytheism). But mythology retains something deep that has passed through the centuries, which, in my opinion, should be preserved as a positive phenomenon. Its elements of enduring importance are the high poetry of metaphorical understanding and perception of the Universe, the basis for paradigmatic symbolism that was laid in myths, and, above all, the spontaneous world perception — on the frontier between the mind and heart — that connects the visible and invisible worlds and is

---

4 Sergey Tokarev, *Myths of Nations of the World*.

an essential prerequisite for spiritual experience in any monotheistic religion. In the experience of religious understanding, myth has an important practical function of supporting and developing traditions, while traditions are the basis and foundation for the development of cultural and religious life. "Myth ... is ... seen by primitives as a kind of 'Holy Scripture,' a reality that influences the destiny of man and the Universe."[5]

When considering the issue of the natural transition of myth to religion through symbolism, we can clarify not only the importance of relations between myth and religion, but also the specific nature of *mythological thinking* and its qualitative difference from logical (scientific) thinking, which is quite developed in our modern times. "The prelogical (not 'alogical') character of mythological thinking is manifested, in particular, in non-compliance with the logical law of the excluded middle: objects can at one and the same time be themselves and something else."[6] This consciousness gives rise to a mystical communion of two different sides of existence—exactly this is necessary for the experience of religious faith. In modern times, this is called "antinomy." This prelogical nature of mythology is particularly important to us, because it makes it possible to make myth part of mystical theology, for the presence of natural (like the beginning stage of painting in icon painting) mythological force in the experience of knowledge determines the natural vitality of faith, while faith in the process of awakening acquires a certain intensity that is necessary for ascending to high contemplation.

Especially pronounced in myth is its visual figurative language. This is why we can see a great deal of ancient symbolic drawings where gods and spirits are often depicted with wings. These "winged creatures" became main characters in many national mythologies, which later serve as a basis for the creation of angelology. Approaching the perception of the true monotheistic religion, more developed mythologies begin to distinguish between anthropomorphic gods and spirits, who acquire angelic features in pictorial works.

---

[5] *Myth in Primitive Psychology* by Bronisław Malinowski as paraphrased by Eleazar Melatinsky in *The Poetics of Myths*.
[6] Tokarev, *Myths*.

Mythology and Faith

Mythology, alongside literature and art, emerges as a special form of symbolic culture that can evolve into a different category of consciousness and open a new level of faith. It answers vital questions not directly, but through associations and metaphors, awakening the mind to an interest in symbolic philosophy. In science, this method is known as the method of "bricolage" (French for "tinkering"). But exactly this method is used for the *mythological* reading of the Bible, which represents one of the seven levels of learning its spiritual meaning.

Since the twentieth century, myth has been regarded as a certain way of thinking that is inherent in Man in general, as a certain state of consciousness, and as an essential prerequisite for the development of faith. Mythology begins to describe religious relations between material and noetic things and between created and divine things, whose "images of action" are considered by the mind mythopoetically rather than rationally. "Myth can be found at the highest stages of cultural development. It has been recognized that the figurative and mythological form of presentation of what is revealed in human spiritual experience has several advantages over the rational and philosophical form."[7] Arranging mind-generated general worldview systems into a sequence, we can see that myth will be a vital bond between philosophy and symbolism in the "philosophy — mythology — symbolism" series. Religious experience in myths is somewhat similar to mystical experience in monotheistic religions. However, myth operates at a much lower level of religious consciousness and is formed only by the experience of the created spirit of Man who enters into relations with metaphysical revelations of the Cosmos. Mystical experience, on the other hand, is determined as the communion of consciousness (heart + mind) with the uncreated Spirit, the energy of God Himself. According to prominent mythologist Aleksei Losev, the primary importance of myth is vital rather than cognitive: in myth, we can see coincidence of ideas, *eidoses* (types), and the sensory image (appearance) that determine the power, beauty, and strength of faith, which are essential prerequisites for the knowledge of God.

"From the history of religions, we know that divine triads were put at the head of many national pantheons. Having no direct revelation

---

7   Leonid Vasilenko, *The Concise Dictionary of Religious and Philosophical Terms.*

of the supra-rational Triune Godhead, peoples *naturally* rationalized triunity and triadicity into *three (main) gods*."[8] Giving their dogmas the form of religious myths, symbols, and philosophical ideas embodied in those gods, they formed their lives in accordance with the ideas and eidoses of their sensory perception. Once the Logos was revealed to Adam, his descendants tried to recall the connections and relations between Man and the invisible world. As the arrival of the Savior was promised to Adam right after the Expulsion from Paradise, religion, which served to recover those relations and prepare ways for the Incarnation of the Logos, surely started not from the time of Abraham, but much earlier. Even before His Birth, Christ had been in the process of "continuous coming," which was intuitively anticipated by the pagan world. Zealous missionaries exterminated all traces of ancient religions and cultures, thinking that they did so for the glory of the true God. Now we look at that with regret, because everything that is intrinsically beautiful is "very good." While in our times we have no panic fear of "pagan" things, many modern "fathers" and "teachers" still have panic fear of "cosmic" things. Christian apologists should overcome this fear too.[9] Just as once they overcame the Jewish commandment forbidding religious images on the basis of theological principles (rather than in connection with idolatry), so in the history of mythology we can trace how the mind was forming and opening until it was willing to accept the idea of the incarnation of God. "Who would deny that the apologists and Church Fathers used some *suitable* pre-Christian philosophic concepts in the development of the Christian religious doctrine?"[10] Although many of those who call themselves "theologians" still cannot realize this fact.

Following the iconological formula stating that everything in the Universe is somehow related to God and filled with signs and symbols of God's presence, we can assume that national mythologies reflect some truth, whose prototypes and prophecies were projections of the future Biblical Revelation. The New Testament vitally filled some mythological symbols with a new hypostatic meaning (for example,

---

8 Hegumen Gennady Eykalovich, *The Genealogy of Sophia*.
9 Ibid.
10 Ibid.

the ankh — an Egyptian cross symbolizing life — became the reality of redemption in Christianity). On the basis of the hypostatic faith, for the first time in the history of religions there arose *theology* — not a philosophy of god, not a mythology of gods, not a symbolization of God the Absolute, but a doctrine of Life with the Divinity of the Trihypostatic God.

Summarizing our brief research into the relationship between mythology and religion, let us recall the place of myth in the ladder of "formation" of faith: "myth — religion — mysticism — contemplation (theology)." In this series of ascending forms of faith, it is necessary to identify the positive characteristics of myth itself. Its ability to participate in all kinds of faith and penetrate with sensitive "flair" into religious spheres, filling the heart with natural power for the state of contemplation (θεωρία) of the Reality, undoubtedly makes us pay special attention to peoples' mythmaking, provided that it becomes part of the canons of Christian liturgics (for example, in hymnography).

So, we can note the following positive aspects of myth that bring it closer to monotheistic religions:

- Myth's close connection with rites, religious rituals, and transmission of traditions;
- Mythological thinking is characterized by pre-logical and psychological emotions, which makes it possible to embrace religion with the heart, rather than the intellect;
- Mythology is the oldest form of interpretation and representation of the mysterious processes of spiritual communication of the elements (gods) and their influence on Man's cosmic aspect, which is undoubtedly important for the psychophysical aspect of human existence. Christ said that believers should remain in the world, i.e., in the elements of earth, water, fire, and air. They, in fact, are the chemical composition of the human physical body, but the difference is that those who accept Christ by faith can and must, while "remaining in the world," be "not of this world" (Jn 18:36), i.e., be independent of them;

THE ANGEL OF THE COUNTENANCE OF GOD

- In all historical periods and in all cultures, national mythological mentalities have many analogies, which are particularly reflected in the best examples of literature and art. This entitles us to use them in developing a Christian worldview too;
- Myth is characterized by a desire to harmonize concepts of the Universe and move from the sensory perception of the Universe to the noetic one. Mythopoetical consciousness has no natural barriers to accepting the idea of One God, which was proved by the history of Greece where the seed of Christianity grew directly on the soil of a pagan philosophy and a thoroughly developed mythology.

Based on these points, we can assume that mythology is a certain state of human spirit, with its natural energy and potency of ascending to the highest contemplations. While in ancient myths the ability to create visible images of mysterious Archetypes is just an anticipation of something deeper, in the monotheistic religion this ability acts and is clearly defined as a paradigm, as a relationship between the material and heavenly worlds. In Judaism, it is mythology that serves as a determining connection, a heart paradigm of the Revelation of God, revealing its new meaning: not only a connection between "spiritual" and "physical" things in the Universe, but a relationship between the life-giving Spirit of God and the Universe focused in the mirror of human nature.

To learn how to reliably discern Theophanies in national mythologies and understand them not as ancient peoples' fairy-tale fantasies, we should understand that mythology serves as a kind of Tradition in religion. In seriously developed myths, we can already find the most general aspects of human life, as well as principles that are similar to those that lead to a strengthening of religious feelings in the human heart. Every tradition originates from some myth and is part of a developed mythological feeling. Pushing mythology into the background and neglecting its ontological experience, we cut off some strata of life and thinking, destroying a certain harmony of religious tonality.

Mythology and Faith

Answering our imaginary opponents saying that some doctrinal points having no direct basis in the Scriptures or the Symbol of Faith are determined by the Tradition, we will immediately say that this is true, adding that the boundaries and forms of the Tradition itself are not clearly determined and that even the Holy Fathers of the Church have different opinions about some elements of the Tradition.[11]

Being a product of most peoples of the world rather than some specific people or nation, myth carries the idea of the Presence of God expressed in different mythmaking forms. Consequently, myth is not a fabrication by some poet storyteller, not a fantasy of some writer, but a kind of *description* of real events that occurred on the physical, mental, or cosmic plane of human existence. "And more importantly, myth expresses a sacred and significant event, a primal revelation which serves as an example for imitation."[12]

Myths are the anthropological paradigm of all human activities, because "some aspects and functions of mythological thought are inherent constituents of all human beings."[13] This means that no matter what religious "form" is assimilated by an individual, his/her type of mythological mentality and, therefore, faith is common for all people. The presence of faith is necessary. Primarily, it should be the cornerstone of any religious "building." In this case, this is followed by the emergence and unfolding of the religious question: "What is the truth of this faith?" "The task of apologetics is to correlate what we have gained in Christianity, with what existed before it."[14]

Therefore, the Tradition can be understood as a coherent and continuous alternation of mythology, philosophy, and religion, with none of the links of this chain being belittled. This coherency and connection was emphasized by Paul the Apostle at the beginning of his sermon addressed to the Gentiles: "Ye men of Athens, I perceive that in all things ye are too superstitious. For as I passed by, and

---

11 Ibid.
12 Mircea Eliade, *Aspects of Myth*.
13 Ibid.
14 Ibid.

beheld your devotions, I found an altar with this inscription: To the Unknown God. Whom therefore ye ignorantly worship, Him declare I unto you" (Acts 17:22–23).

The subject of pre-Christian revelation, perception, and attainment of the *only* truth and the very idea of the future Divine Incarnation, does not begin or end only with the Old Testament Tradition. A mythology where even echoes of religion cannot be found is certainly alarming, because "every religious myth — alongside with truth elements expressed in correct intuitions, preperceptions, and anticipations — always contains a lot of materials that are irrelevant, folkloric, theologically neutral, and sometimes false and, therefore, dangerous."[15]

Myth poses the question of existence of *patterns* of life. In terms of seeking the Prototype, however, it gives only initial stages of the path to a life of faith, only slightly opening the spiritual content of the heart mind. Passing through mythology, *images* of visible things find their real prototype in divine Ideas. According to M. Eliade, "The knowledge of myths brings us closer to the mystery of the origin of all things."[16] Every myth contains one or another idea of the future Theophanies. To know myths means to learn how to discern the form of God's Presence in them and, moving from logic to the heart mind, approach the knowledge of God, the Creator of the Universe Whose symbolic image it carries. This is Man's natural development from cosmology to the knowledge of God. As a never-ending mythmaking, the poetry of mythopoetic images will fascinate people in religion too until they know the true reality of God's presence. Until then, there will be no rest for Man. Being interpreted by the ancients as a kind of allegorical symbol, myth in monotheism becomes a Tradition, not a folktale, but the experience of meetings and an understanding of the initial spiritual nature of creation.

---

15 Ibid.
16 Ibid.

THEOPHANIC RELIGION IN MYTH IMAGES

3
Theophanic Religion in Myth Images

> *Behold, I send an Angel before thee,*
> *to keep thee in the way,*
> *and to bring thee into the place*
> *which I have prepared.*
> *Beware of him, and obey his voice,*
> *provoke him not;*
> *for he will not pardon your transgressions:*
> *for my name is in him.*
> Exodus 23:20–21

JEWISH MYTHOLOGICAL CONCEPTS ARE SUCcessively connected with the western Semitic tradition. At their early stage of development, they represented myths revised in the spirit of steadily forming monotheism. In different historical periods, this tradition was naturally influenced by Egyptian, Sumerian, Akkadian, and especially Iranian mythologies. Later, in the post-biblical period, it was influenced by gnostic mysticism. Created over many centuries (thirteenth century BC to second century BC), the biblical books absorbed texts of different natures. Much later, they were revised in accordance with the basic idea of monotheism. In the first Christian century, in rabbinical circles, there arose a tradition of commenting on the biblical texts, which was expressed in so-called midrashim (commentaries), targumim (ancient Aramaic paraphrases or interpretations of the Hebrew Bible), and partly in the Talmud texts. The targum texts were used in the exegesis of the New Testament, especially in the Syrian Christian tradition. The basic content of the Judaic mythology was not so much an overview of the "sacred cosmos" as it was the history of the people who combined the culture of their ancestors (Patriarchs) with the cultures of a vast area of ancient civilizations of the Middle East. The main objective of the history of Israel was to implement the idea of the salvation of the chosen people, who since the time of Abraham submitted itself in obedience to God's will. In connection with this idea, the common mythology of all peoples and nations was freed from all superfluous elements and transformed to express more specifically the *image* of the salvific purpose. It is also important to understand that the chosenness is not about choosing some tribe for "experimental purposes," but about concentrating all cultural polytheistic beliefs in one national mind where they are purified in the fire of the Revelation and coalesced in serving the one God who gave the promise of the coming Messiah. From this point on, the historical reality of "Religion" with a capital "R" penetrates the ancient myth and is harmonized with it. Through Moses, a mythological mentality develops into a religion based on the law of commandments given by God Himself and becomes part of a dogmatic faith in the *existing* God, Jehovah. The original language describing the Revelations and the nature of their perception, which can be called a *mythology of the heart*—"Love the Lord your God with all your heart" (Mt 22:37)—transfers from myth to the Scriptures. The ancient mythological focus on endless metamorphoses, which are inherent to cosmic phenomena ("from a god to a god"), comes to be replaced by monotheistic stability ("from a god to God"). However, myth for a long time remains emotionally colored in the Old Testament and faith slowly develops into mysticism, and especially theology. At first, the mythology of the "Judaic heart" has a difficult time entering and combining Jehovah's ten basic sayings about the creation of the world (and humans) and the Ten Commandments of the law of God given later. Then there follows a long search for the state and place of the internal and external "promised land."

The transcendence and unknowability of God, which became a postulate in monotheism, made Judaists raise and resolve the issue of the "form" of God's *Presence* in the world and the people. Using such concepts as Shechinah (the dwelling of the Divine Presence of God), Memrah (Word, Logos), Chochmah (Wisdom, Sophia), mythology penetrates and fills the anthropology and anthology of the Judaic faith. However, in Israel, for the first time in human history, a foundation was laid for the history of forming monotheism and mystical communications with God through patriarchs and prophets. Thus arises

Theophanic Religion in Myth Images

a kind of "Pascha" of the theophanic transition from "myth — religion" to "religion — mysticism," which is accompanied by the shaping of the basic idea of the New Testament, with a formula that is somewhat new to the pagan world: "The kingdom of God is within you" (Lk 17:20–21). A secret Name, although repeatedly revealed to people in God's power and glory, gradually becomes the key to the Kingdom of God. The depth of faith of Israel was in a new ontological understanding of the name of the future Messiah — Emmanuel ("God is with us"). In this name, they will contemplate all the images of the Revelation. The idea of Theophanies, or, according to the Church Fathers, "Appearances of the unknowable God out of His unknowability," reconstructs the entire pagan mythmaking into a new religious set of views of the world and supreme powers. There arises a new understanding of *intermediaries* between God and the world — Angels, who are not willful inhabitants of the pagan cosmos, but messengers of the Word of God and servants of the Light of God having their own heavenly Hierarchy that is independent of cosmic spirits and souls.

History tells us that all peoples have always believed in angels. In mythology, they were occultly referred to under the names of gods, winged spirits of the cosmos. In the biblical mentality, however, angels are no longer associated with the cosmos, because they arose before the creation of the material universe. They become carriers of the luminous Will of a new dispensation, implementing the idea of the future coming of the Messiah. "Thou, even Thou, art Lord alone; Thou hast made heaven, the heaven of heavens, with all their host... and the *host* (*angels*) of heaven worshippeth Thee" (Neh 9:6). Being the paradigm of all kinds of existence, the uncreated light in angels, who themselves are its reflections and "secondary lights," finds its "representatives," whose manifestations were accessible even to the weak spiritual sight of the old man. The Revelation of God is inconceivable without the notion of "light," and angels are created in the image of God's Light and for this reason called the "sons of the Light." The Revelation of God is also inconceivable without the notions of "consciousness" and "mind," and angels are called "bodiless minds." God manifests Himself to Man in the revelation of *intelligent* Light, and Christ, the Light of Wisdom of the Word, came into the world and became man. Man is also intended to be "a mind and a son of Light," despite the fact that he is thoroughly rooted in the nature of the material world. So, the notion of "light" may be synonymous with the notions of "mind" and "angel," and it is very important to remember this in connection with the subject of our discussion.

The archetype of angels, in accordance with which they are referred to as "minds," is the uncreated Light—the Image of *God*. As an "example for imitation" and a "mirror," it is hidden in the depths of nature of both angel and human. Reflections on the Light of Theophanies bring the mind to a hypostatic distinction between the created angels of the heavenly Hierarchy and the Supreme Angel of Jehovah (Malach Jehovah) who is mentioned in the ancient books of the Bible. Here is what theologian A. Glagolev writes about this issue: "The Angel of Jehovah is not one of the created angels, but the divine Logos in the historical form of His Old Testament action. Therefore, the doctrine of Him is actually part of Old Testament Christology rather than angelology."[1] The Angel of Jehovah is presented in the Bible as a special being of divine nature and dignity, whose actions, properties, and powers are inherent in God alone. The kingly Angel who appeared to patriarchs was repeatedly an object of prophetic visions and contemplations throughout the history of Israel. God the Creator is not closed in Himself. Instead, through energies He is involved in the lives of the people, and the images of His manifestations, understood as God's Divinity, do not impair His Oneness. Expanded and deepened by the Church Fathers, orthodox dogmatics states that in God we can discern:

- *His hypostasis* (mode of existence) and *prosopon* (image of action). Perhaps, this distinction would not be clear, because the term "hypostasis" cannot be found in the Church Slavonic translations of theological and dogmatic literature, which also affected modern Russian translations. So, "hypostasis" is traditionally referred to as "person" (Ancient Greek:

---

[1] Glagolev, *Angels in the Old Testament*.

prosopon). Nevertheless, the Holy Fathers of the Church did make this distinction, although it was specially developed and finally established only in a relatively late period, in the works by St. Gregory Palamas (unfortunately, his works were translated only fairly recently) in connection with disputes over the nature of the Light of Tabor;

- *His essence* (*unicity*) and *energy* (*multiplicity*);
- *His energy* and *name as a "seed" containing the fullness of essential energy.*

These concepts constitute the basis of the principle of New Testament theology and iconology: one God is God in a Trinity (*theology* of the Hypostases) and God's Divinity (*iconology* of the Prosopon).

Studying this terminological order, it is important to focus on the distinction between the energy and essence of God. God's energy, glory, or actions are diverse manifestations of His names, which originate from the single "wonderful" Name concealed in the Angel of Jehovah. According to the Prophet Isaiah, "the Angel of the Countenance of God," who did not reveal his name to Jacob-Israel, is the personified image of the Glory and Light of the Trinity.

The kingly Angel is the manifestation of God's *Light*, whose lamps are "the seven spirits of God" (Rev 4:5), while the Light's essential state conceals the holy *Name* (as it is written, "Hallowed be Thy Name"), the Logos of God. So says the Bible (Ex 23:21, 22). The wonderful name of the Angel, according to the Book of Revelation, will be written by Christ during His Second Coming upon everyone who has overcome worldly temptations, and the Name will have three meanings: "the name of my *God*, and the name of the *City* of my God, . . . and *My* new name" (Rev 3:12). All the heavenly angels are *His powers* and are subordinate to Him as servants of the Name of God, the Son of God and the Logos destined to be incarnated.

In the Russian Bible, the name of the uncreated Angel is capitalized, while the names of created angels are not. The idea that all the Old Testament Theophanies were direct manifestations of the Logos can be found in the works by the early apologists of Christianity and in those by ecclesiastical writers St. Irenaeus of Lyon and Tertullian. This opinion is shared by most of the Fathers of the fourth century who believe that the Angel in the Old Testament Theophanies is God's Word, the Speech-Logos, who later appears in the prophetic books under the name of God's Wisdom (Chochmah-Sophia). So, already here we anticipate the basic concepts of the Christian doctrine: God is one, invisible, unknowable, but the hypostatic Trinity is integrally involved in the dispensation of salvation with the *Image* and *Word*, in other words, with the *Icon* and the *Speech* of the Revelation. Christ said of Himself, "I am the Light of the world," and these words are indicative of Christ's *light-like action* in His transfiguration of the world, rather than of His essence or even Hypostasis.

The ancient rabbinic tradition expresses an original point of view of the Angel ("Prince") of the Countenance of Jehovah referred to by the Prophet Isaiah (63:9). The Talmud associates his name with the teaching of the angel Metatron, who is called "the Prince of His Countenance" or "the Prince of the *visible image*" (Sar ha-Panim) and often identified with the Memrah, i.e., the Word of Yahweh.[2] According to Targum Onkelos, the name Metatron (מטטרון) comes from the Hebrew verb "to guard, to protect," although other sources indicate that it originates from the Latin word "Metator," which means "supreme," or the Greek "Μεθατρονος," that is "the one who sits on the throne."[3] Metatron is God's messenger who is present at His throne or behind it. "The Talmud says that the name Metatron is equivalent to 'LORD,' and he sits in the Holiest of Holies and acts as God's emissary.[4] He is called the 'Angel of the LORD,' 'The Prince of the Universe,' 'The Prince of the Countenance,' and even by the name 'Shechina'—the Presence of God."[5]

The Judaic tradition associates the Supreme Angel of Jehovah with the "image of action" of the Deity: he is the *beginning* of God's creatures, which in the Christian understanding is a direct indication of the Logos ("in the beginning was the Logos") and the Messiah.

---

2 Arseny Sokolov, *The Book of Joshua*.
3 Risto Santala, *The Messiah in the Old Testament in the Light of Rabbinical Writings*.
4 *Sanhedrin* 38b, *Hagigah* 15a, and *Avoda Zara* 3b.
5 *Tos. le-Hulin* 60a and *Yebamoth* 16b, Santala, *Messiah in the Old Testament*.

Theophanic Religion in Myth Images

An interesting confirmation of this assumption can be found in the Zohar, which says that Metatron will incarnate in a mother's womb and assume a human body. As Risto Santala points out in his above-mentioned book:

> Stockholm's erstwhile chief Rabbi, Professor Gottlieb Klein, in a work published in 1898, sets forth Metatron's main features as portrayed in the Jewish literature: "Metatron is the nearest person to God, serving him; on the one hand his confidant and delegate, on the other hand the representative of Israel before God... He sits in God's innermost chamber (*penim*). The numeric value of 'Metatron' is the same as that of *Shaddai*, 'the Almighty' [which is close in meaning to the name 'the Lord of hosts'; see below]. He is therefore the delegate of the Almighty. Shaddai (10+4+300) = 314 and Metatron (50+6+200+9+9+40) = 314."

Professor Klein also shows that there are five such intermediaries between God and Man in the Talmud: "1. Metatron, 2. The Word of Yahweh, Mimra, 3. God's hovering glory, the Shechina, 4. God's Holy Spirit, Rûah ha-Qôdesh, and 5. the Voice from Heaven, Bath Qôl (lit., 'daughter of a voice')."[6] Later, in the Christian era, the Judaic mythological tradition, fearing direct analogies with the Christian Logos, transferred the name "Metatron" to the created archangel Michael, identifying it again with the Angel of Jehovah as the patron of Israel in search of the Promised Land and its development.

The opinion that the biblical Angel of Jehovah is a created angel was strengthened especially in the Catholic Church due to its denial of the Eastern dogmatic idea about *uncreated* energies in God's Divinity and, therefore, its rejection of the distinction between "essence and energy" in God. Ultimately, this view rejects the main Orthodox purpose of salvation—"deification," which is based on the identity of and the distinction between the concepts of "God" and "Divinity," because Man will, naturally, be deified in the "image and likeness" in God's Divinity rather than in God. There are other assumptions

---

6 Gottlieb Klein, *Bidrag till Israels religionhistoria*, 89.

THE ANGEL OF THE COUNTENANCE OF GOD

that the Angel of Jehovah is not even a person that is different from Jehovah, but simply a certain "naturalistic" sign through which God manifests Himself. Modern theology actually poses two questions. "Is the Angel of Jehovah a person, an individual and self-existent being?" And, if he is a person, "What is his nature — created, like that of all other angels, or uncreated, divine?"

Below, we shall discuss some examples of the Angel of Jehovah's manifestations given in the Bible. And now, in an overview of interpretations of his image, we shall just make a brief mention of the church's view stating that God's manifestations are possible in some *Image of Action*. Can we limit the diversity of Theophanies to the concepts of our philosophical rather than theological mind, let alone our discursive intellect? To what extent is the existence of an uncreated, divine Light, as the Angel talking to Abraham, Moses, and Jacob, in the literal rather than allegorical sense, at all possible?

Different theophanic images and forms can be found in many biblical verses. The Supreme Angel speaking as God and essentially concealed by a mysterious *cloud* was seen by Israelites from time to time, and these manifestations are characterized as a certain Presence of the Most High (Ex 40:38). "As Moses entered into the tabernacle, the *cloudy pillar* descended, and stood at the door of the tabernacle" (Ex 33:9); or on Mount Sinai: "And the Lord descended in the *cloud*" (Ex 34:5). Similar images are described in the Book of Revelation: "And I saw another mighty Angel come down from heaven, clothed with a *cloud: and a rainbow was upon his head*, and His face was as it were the sun, and his feet as *pillars of fire*: and he had in his hand a little book open" (Rev 10:1–2). This series of visions, which can be continued, is similar to the appearances of the Angel of Jehovah to the people of Israel in a *cloud and a pillar of fire*. Clearly, the Angel was given the attributes of supreme power and kingly dignity: "the Book of Life held in His hand, a voice as loud as a lion's roar" (cf. Rev 5:5). Christ the Logos — "the Lion of the tribe of Judah"; and "And the Angel... *sware* by Him that liveth for ever and ever... that there should be time no longer" (Rev 10:5–6). But created beings, who have only granted power rather than personal divine power, are forbidden to swear.

Theophanic Religion in Myth Images

God's angel who repeatedly appeared to Jacob (Gen 31:11–13) called himself Ha-El-Beth-El, the God of Bethel, and therefore actually likened himself to the God of Abraham and Isaac, i.e., Jehovah (Gen 28:13). It is characteristic that the Messenger does not speak on his own behalf, but exactly conveys the words of the One Who Sent Him. Besides, the execution of His commands is equivalent to the execution of the *will of God Himself*, and it is God Himself who punishes for disobedience, which is also a strong argument in favor of Their identity. For example, in the passage "For My Angel will go before you and bring you in to the land of the Amorites, the Hittites, the Perizzites, the Canaanites, the Hivites and the Jebusites; and I will completely destroy them..." (Ex 23:20–23), this is evident from the alternation of first-person and third-person speech, where "His voice" refers to the Angel and "I say" refers to God. The same is repeated in the following verse: "But if you truly obey His voice and do all that I say, then I will be an enemy to your enemies and an adversary to your adversaries" (Ex 23:22). Their identity is particularly obvious when Jacob calls down the blessing on Joseph's children not only from God, but also from the Redeemer-Angel who appeared to him in Bethel (Gen 48:15). During that blessing, Jacob recognizes the Angel having a "wonderful name" as a being who is different from God; and, although His actions with regard to Jacob are independent, they are akin to the work of God Himself. This difference is evidenced by His very Name, which indicates not His abstract, but personal and specific relation to the Existing One (Whose Angel?—Jehovah's) as God's *Messenger* and the direct *doer* of God's will. It would be incredible if God's Revelation or Providence could be understood allegorically in the patriarchal era. Obviously, the God of Abraham, Isaac, and Jacob is the personal and living God, who is unknowable by His essence yet knowable through His manifestations and actions (Greek: ενέργεια). No action can be without a certain *image*, for God *creates* darkness (matter) yet *forms* the Light (cf. Is 45:7), i.e., He gives Light an image, making It visible, expressively pictorial, and in some cases angel-like and even anthropomorphic.

The antinomy of simultaneous knowability and unknowability of God should already live, at least embryonically, in the minds of the chosen people, because it provides a basis for faith not just in the "idea" of God, but in God Himself who manifests Himself in Revelations from time to time. Theophanies in all His uncreated energies (manifestations) rather than only through created messengers have always been salvific for the people of Israel. Theophanies in the likeness of the Angel occurred exclusively in the Old Testament and were most typical of the early historical period. However, less explicit examples can also be found in the Gospel — the Angel of the Resurrection sitting on the Holy Sepulcher and the two white-robed Angels at the scene of the Ascension. Let us recall that *"malach"* (the Hebrew for "angel") is a name for action rather than nature or essence, and if an action is of divine origin, the Angel — one of the *images* of this action — will also be a direct manifestation of Jehovah's Light. In the Bible, "the Angel of Jehovah" is mentioned 25 times in the context of direct connection with God. In this case, we may state that the Angel of the Countenance of God is a non-hypostatic person "substituting" God and playing His role, "a character" (one of the meanings of the word πρόσωπον) or the Deity whose origin differs from that of the *indirect* created messengers — "angels of the Lord" — who are mentioned there.

> There is no full or exact correspondence between the Greek "angel of the Lord" and the Hebrew "Angel of God." On the contrary, there is a considerable difference between them. In general, the Greek term "angel of the Lord" denotes some indefinite angel, while the Hebrew "Angel of Jehovah" always denotes a certain angel.[7]

So, to better understand the basic distinctions between the "created" and "uncreated," let us first ask ourselves the following question: "Can the Angel who appeared to Abraham at the Oak of Mamre really be identified with the angel Gabriel who appeared to Zechariah, the father of John the Baptist, on the sole ground that the former foretold the birth of Isaac and the latter foretold the birth of John?" But it is the essential Logos who directly reveals God. If a messenger of a king is his son, he is a prince of the same blood with

---

7 Glagolev, *Angels in the Old Testament*.

Theophanic Religion in Myth Images

his father and an heir of his father. But if a messenger of a king is an elected official, he is something different. The Logos of the Deity is His Revelation. He repeatedly participates in the history of Israel as God "whose voice then shook the earth" (Heb 12:26), and in His actions He appears as the *Angel of the Covenant* in accordance with what was said through the prophets: "And I will shake all nations, and the Desire of all nations shall come: and I will fill this House with Glory, saith the Lord of Sabaoth" (Hag 2:7). At this point, it is appropriate to mention the mysterious connection between the Lord of Sabaoth and the Logos-Lamb, which can be traced in the Old and New Testaments. The King, the Lord of Sabaoth, Whom Isaiah saw sitting on the throne (6:5) is the same one who sat on the throne with the Book of Life in His hand, as described in the Book of Revelation: "And *he that sat* was to look upon like a jasper and a sardius stone... and... stood a Lamb as it had been slain, having seven horns and seven eyes, which are the *seven Spirits* of God sent forth into all the earth. And he (the Lamb) came and took the Book out of the right hand of (*the Lord of Sabaoth*) Him That Sat upon the throne" (Rev 4:3, 5:6, 7). According to the teachings of the Holy Fathers of the Church,[8] the Lord of Sabaoth is the uniform iconological Image of the Presence of the whole Trinity and the Lord of the heavenly powers. In this case, His Angel is the Angel of the Deity, while God's secret Name in this Angel—the Logos—is the lord of the Celestial Hierarchy of created angels. Although God's Angel and Logos are never separate, they are not united and recognizable through distinction, for the Angel is the Image and beauty of God's actions, while the Logos is the Power and mystical content of these actions.

The image of God's Angel and Logos is related to the history of Man's salvation and, therefore, essentially concerns the Son of God, Christ, the Author of Salvation, whom the prophets and the Church Fathers also called the *Youth*, the *Branch of Jehovah* (Is 4:2), the *Angel of Great Counsel* (Is 9:6), and *Emmanuel*. However, the *Ancient of Days* is the Lord of Sabaoth, the single Mode of Existence of the Trinity.

---

8 St. John of Damascus, *The Letter on the Trisagion to Archimandrite Jordanes*.

THE ANGEL OF THE COUNTENANCE OF GOD

In his book about angels, theologian A. Glagolev summarizes a positive judgment about the divine nature of the Angel of Jehovah as follows:

> The Angel of Jehovah identifies Himself with Jehovah when He gives Himself divine attributes and takes divine actions;
>
> The persons to whom the Angel of Jehovah appears consider Him to be a divine Person and, therefore, worship and address Him as God Himself;
>
> The Angel of Jehovah unprotestingly accepts as rightful divine worship honors, sacrifices, and even the right to punish and forgive sins;
>
> The biblical writers directly put Him on a level with God and sometimes call Him Jehovah.

Attributing these appearances to a God-substituting created angel runs counter to the Judaic tradition, because God's messenger cannot be substituted by another created person in appearances characterized by *personal communication*. Otherwise, we would have dealt with deification of creatures—in these examples, angels. Jews were forbidden under penalty of death to honor and worship created angels instead of God. In this context, the Angel's appearances are characterized by the fact that the Angel oftentimes referred to Himself as "I." If a messenger's speech authoritatively begins with this pronoun, this is directly indicative of His uncreated nature.

> In God, there is nothing more majestic than *personality*, and, in accordance with ancient customs, it was considered to be decent not to use "I" when speaking with those who are superior and, therefore, in terms of superiority, using "I" befits one who is kingly and Divine.[9]
>
> In the Holy Scripture, the personal pronoun "I" is one of the most common means of referring to God as a personality. In Genesis, pronouns are used occultly to indicate the Persons of the Most Holy Trinity (Gen 1:26).

---

9 St. Philaret, *Commentary on Genesis*, Part 2.

Theophanic Religion in Myth Images

> According to priest Dumitru Stăniloae, "as existence is not given to God from the outside and He Himself is the source of existence and, therefore, the highest personal reality, He Himself cannot be determined or named in any other way than using personal pronouns."[10]

Interestingly, the New Testament contains a mysterious passage about the strange behavior of soldiers in the Garden of Gethsemane: "They went backward, and fell to the ground," when, in response to their message that they were seeking Jesus of Nazareth, Christ said, "I am he" (Εγώ ειμί) (Jn 18:3–8). Well-known contemporary theologian Metropolitan Hilarion (born Grigory Alfeyev) notes:

> What is the reason for such inadequate behavior on the part of the soldiers? It is assumed that in response to the soldiers' question Jesus pronounced the most sacred name "Yahweh" (literally, "I am"), which was strictly forbidden to utter: having heard this name from His mouth, Jewish men and officers fell down in fear and trembling.[11]

In this connection, let us also recall His words that, in accordance with the Jewish tradition, are directly indicative of the speaker's divine nature: "Before Abraham was, *I am*" (Jn 8:58) instead of *I was*!

Nothing contradicts the spirit of the Bible more than putting a creature into an internal relationship with God or calling it by God's name, because this will certainly violate the principle of monotheism. So, Abraham, having recognized the Angel of Jehovah who appeared with two other Angels, welcomes Him using God's name—Adonai. For comparison, let us have a look at two examples of appearances. The first example is related to an Angel of divine nature—"Behold, *I* send an Angel before thee, to keep thee in the way...; Beware of Him, and... provoke Him not; for He will not pardon your transgressions: for My Name is in Him" (Ex 23:20–21). The second example is related to a created angel messenger—"Behold, Mine Angel shall go before thee... And I will send an Angel before thee; and I will drive out the

---

10   Sergei Chursanov, *Face to Face*.
11   Bishop Hilarion (Grigory Alfeyev), *The Sacred Mystery of the Church—The Holy Name Yahweh in the Pentateuch*.

Canaanite" (Ex 32:34; 33:2). Both messengers are assigned to serve as leaders of Israel, but the first passage deals with a complete personal combination of the Angel and Jehovah (only God can forgive sins), while the second one refers only the angel's action. Although the second angel's connection with God's name can be assumed from the context, it is not expressed in the second example as clearly as in the first one.

MANIFESTATIONS OF JEHOVAH IN THE LIKENESS OF AN ANGEL: THE OLD TESTAMENT

4

Manifestations of Jehovah in the Likeness of an Angel:
THE OLD TESTAMENT

*In all their affliction He was afflicted,
and the Angel of His Presence saved them.*
                                    Isaiah 63:9

The Angel of the LORD *encampeth round about
them that fear Him, and delivereth them.*
                                    Psalm 34:7

THE PATRIARCH ABRAHAM

AN OBVIOUS EXAMPLE OF JEHOVAH'S APPEARance in the likeness of the Supreme Angel can be found in Genesis 18:2, where a meeting between Abraham and three *Men* is described. In the early centuries, the Church Fathers, varying in their opinions, had as yet no precisely substantiated answer to the question regarding who had visited the Patriarch. According to Athanasius the Great and Ambrose, it was the three hypostases of the Most Holy Trinity who appeared as the three Men; St. Augustine, Cyril of Alexandria, and Gregory of Nyssa considered Them to be three *divine* Angels, in whom the patriarch recognized God; while Tertullian, Irenaeus, Eusebius, Hilarius, and John Chrysostom thought that Abraham had met with two Angels and the Lord (the Logos). However, none of them thought the Men to be three *created* angels, although some modern authors still retain this non-church opinion determining Them as archangels—Michael, Gabriel, and Raphael (and even Barachiel). This speculation is false and contradicts all the canons and hymns dedicated to the life-giving Trinity. In addition, it is surely at variance with the traditional iconology revealed in St. Andrei Rublev's world-famous icon

THE ANGEL OF THE COUNTENANCE OF GOD

"The Trinity." By the way, there is also a rabbinic commentary on the meeting between Abraham and the Three Angels as described in the verse: "My Lord (an Orthodox form of address to a bishop), if now I have found favor in Thy sight, pass not away, I pray Thee, from Thy servant" (Gen 18:3). In the Targum Yerushalmi, Rabbi Jonathan ben Uzziel said, "The Lord mentioned in this verse is the *Word* (*Memrah*) *of the Lord*, and it was He Who rained fire and hot stones upon Sodom and Gomorrah."

Let us discuss the events preceding Abraham's meeting with the Trinity. "And when Abram was ninety years old and nine, the Lord appeared to Abram, and said unto him, I am the Almighty God; walk before me, and be thou perfect" (Gen 17:1). Although the verse says that He "*appeared*," the Lord's image remained unknown. However, its direct connection with His future appearance in the likeness of three Angels is obvious. During the first appearance, God changed the Patriarch's name from Abram to *Abraham*, which is indicative of the beginning of a new ministry in a new "image of action." Then the narration continues, as it were: "And the *Lord appeared* unto him in the plains of Mamre: as he sat in the tent door in the heat of the day" (Gen 18:1). The very "word *Mamre* is consonant with the Aramaic *Memrah*, which means *the Word of God*: this is the place where the Lord revealed His Word to Abraham and where Abraham spread the Word of God."[1] The words "the *Lord appeared*" eliminate any doubts about the divine nature of the appearance, because an ordinary angel is not the Lord, but His servant. Abraham sat at the entrance to his tent, and the *tent* certainly has a symbolic meaning: the Aramaic version of the Bible uses the word "Shekinah" — a tent (Greek: *skene* — "tabernacle") — which in the spiritual sense means the Glory of God, the energy and place of God's Presence (refer to the section about the Shekinah, p. 113ff.). Abraham "lifted up his eyes and looked, and, lo, *three men* stood by him." He "bowed himself toward the ground, and said, My Lord," Adonai. This personal appeal to God by His Name means that Abraham — being in the spirit of truth and saying, "pass not away, I pray Thee [singular number] from Thy servant" — recognized one God in the Three Men, and

---

1 Dmitry Shchedrovitsky, *Introduction to the Old Testament. Genesis.*

then "recovered himself": "Let a little water, I pray you, be fetched, and wash your feet" [plural number]. In fact, Christians appeal to the Trinity as a single entity too: "O Most Holy Trinity, Our *God*, Glory to Thee!" It would be quite fair to say that the Theophany to Abraham was actually the beginning of a monotheistic faith and a trinitarian theology, opening the way to the messianic era of the future Revelation of the Trihypostatic God.

The end of this world—"Τέλος is Omega, which St. Maximus the Confessor calls both 'the return of the End to the Beginning' and 'the fulfillment of the beginning at the end'"[2]—is associated with the appearance of the Logos-Christ in the Second Coming in the likeness of the Son of Man and in the power and glory of the whole Trinity. The literal meaning of the Greek word παρουσία ("advent") is close to the meaning of the word *prosopon* ("things visible around the essence"). Παρουσία derives from παρα ("around"; outside) and ουσία ("essence"). As Christ the Lord said about Himself, "I am Alpha and Omega, the beginning and the ending" (Rev 1:8).

Based on St. Gregory Palamas's dogmatically correct doctrine on the essential Energy as "the consubstantial Image of God's actions," we can iconologically regard the three Angels as the action of the Lord of Sabaoth personified in three creative energies: the Logos of Providence (the first Angel), Wisdom—Sophia (the second Angel), and Love—Agape (the third Angel). The Three represent a real mystical, rather than symbolic, *Image* of active theology: the Logos of the Father, the Sophia of the Son, and the Agape of the Holy Spirit—"the consubstantial and indivisible Trinity" in both Hypostases and Energies. This is the thrice-radiant and angelic Image of the Trinity, whose icon will most correctly be titled "The Image of the Life-Giving Trinity."

Again, the three Angels demonstrate Their One Divinity in three Persons: "And They said [plural number] unto him, Where is Sarah thy wife?"; but "And he said [probably, the Logos], I will certainly return unto thee... and... Sarah... shall have a son." He Who earlier, during the first Theophany, promised that Abraham would

---

2 Archbishop Athanasius (Zoran Jevtić), *Protology and Eschatology in the Works by St. Maximus the Confessor.*

have descendants (Gen 17:16) confirmed this promise again: "For I know him, that he will command his children." God commanded and Abraham became the one to be named the patriarch of Israel. The Angel acts personally, saying "I," rather than as an intermediary who refers to God as created angels do. In all His words and actions, He reveals divine power, strength, and dignity.

It is possible that the angel-like Logos stayed with Abraham, while the other two angels—Sophia and Agape—went toward Sodom, where Lot sat in the gate of the city and greeted Them at first as ordinary people, "my lords." But then, when one of the Angels (*Sophia*) said, "Escape for thy life," Lot recognized the Lord, because he said to him, "my Lord." And at the request of Lot, with the power of Jehovah's strength and will, the Angel says, "*I have accepted thee* concerning this thing also." The Three Angels are the manifestation of One God in three *IMAGES of action* in the sense that any visible or invisible Theophany representing an expression of God's Will, for example, God's "voice," is an *action* of God's power that is always manifested in an indivisible and unmerged combination of forces of Light of the Logos, His Wisdom, and Love.

The uncreated Angel appeared again when Abraham was about to sacrifice his son Isaac (Gen 22) and when God tested the power of faith of the future patriarch. That landmark event largely determined the future of the people of Israel and showed them the most extremely intense image of Agape Love in the Old Testament. That event became the prototype of the future sacrifice of the Son of God and, therefore, surely required the Revelation of God Himself rather than that of noetic messengers. We can safely assert that Abraham is allowed again to witness a Theophany by analogy with the previous Theophany in the plain of Mamre, because the Angel who appears to Abraham says directly in the name of God, "That in blessing *I* will bless thee, and in multiplying *I* will multiply thy seed..." and then blesses the patriarch and his descendants and gives him a special promise and protection relating to a victory over enemies, "because thou hast obeyed My voice," although it was the Angel who actually spoke to Abraham. The place of that event was also named after God's "image of action"—*Yahweh-yireh*, "Yahweh will provide." According to St. Gregory of Nyssa, it was God's Logos who appeared in an angelic form. St. Gregory of Nyssa irrefutably confirms this quoting Paul the Apostle. He writes,

> For here the Scripture, putting God's Word in the mouth of the Angel, refers to the voice, "the Angel of the Lord called unto Abraham... and said, by Myself have I sworn... for because thou hast done this thing, and hast not withheld thy son, thine only son" (Gen 22: 12–16) to fulfill everything that will be known through the promises of the Word (the Logos). So, who spoke with Abraham in this case? The Father? But we cannot say that the Father is somebody's Angel. Therefore, it was the Only-Begotten Son, of whom the prophet says, "And His Name shall be called the Angel of Great Counsel" (Is 9:6). Paul, who was permitted to see secrets in Paradise, surely knows that the sacred promise was given by the Only-Begotten, because Paul says, "When God the Logos made his promise to Abraham, since there was no one greater for Him to swear by, he swore by Himself" (Heb 6:13).[3]

So, the interpretation of "the miraculous Angel of Jehovah" seen by Abraham is clearly perceived as a *living icon* of Theophany.

THE PATRIARCH ISAAC

The story of the patriarch Isaac repeatedly mentions Jehovah's appearances. For example: "And the Lord *appeared* unto him the same night, and said, I am the God of Abraham thy father" (Gen 26:24). In this verse, the Angel's image is not clear, although the promises given by Him to Isaac are similar to those given to Abraham (Gen 18:18–19; 26:4–5). The reminder "I am the God of Abraham" is indicative of a direct, i.e., visible, Theophany, which was probably in an angelic form just like in the Theophany to his father, because in Isaac's childhood, when his father was about to sacrifice him at the request of God Himself, a "miraculous" Angel appeared and stopped Abraham's

---

[3] St. Gregory of Nyssa, *The Word on the Deity of the Son and the Spirit and the Praise to Righteous Abraham.*

hand from executing His command "naturalistically" understood by Abraham, so young Isaac most likely remembered the appearance of the Lord's Angel who canceled the sacrifice. In this context, we can surely assume an iconography of God's angel-like appearance to Isaac, which does not run counter to the general line of Theophanies to Abraham-Isaac-Jacob.

THE PATRIARCH JACOB

During his eventful life, Jacob had several meetings with the Angel of the Countenance of God. Among them was a remarkable vision of God's angels ascending and descending the "Ladder to Heaven," above which stood the Lord of Sabaoth Who said, "I am the Lord, the God of your father Abraham and the God of Isaac" (Gen 28: 12–15). Interestingly, St. Maximus the Confessor directly interprets this revelation as a descent of logoi to the material world, which is followed by their ascent to the one Logos-Son. Jacob felt the real Presence of God in that place and named it "Bethel" (*Beth El*, "House of God"). Indeed, in Genesis 31:11–13 it is said that it was God, because later the Angel of Jehovah said, "I am the God of Bethel." In this regard, Theodoret of Cyrus says that the one who appeared was "called both 'Angel' and 'God': 'God' as to his nature, and 'angel' so we would know that it was not the Father who appeared to him but the Only-Begotten Son."[4] Therefore, Theodoret's commentary shows that the supreme Angel was the image of the Son of God in His essential power of the Logos.

The next time the Angel of Jehovah appears is after Jacob, fearing his brother, prayed to God for help, by enumerating all the appearances of the Angel-Logos to Abraham and Isaac. This was followed by a very mysterious event — an appearance characterized by some strange combination of action of the created and uncreated worlds. Jacob felt the power of God not distantly, but, so to speak, physically, while wrestling. During the night, "there wrestled a *Man* with him until the breaking of the day" (this is quite significant, because man was formed and animated at the *dawn* of the seventh Day). Then "He said, Thy name shall be called no more Jacob, but Israel: for ... *hast*

---

4 *The Commentary on the Book of Genesis.*

thou power with God and with men, and hast prevailed." Later, the Prophet Hosea confirms that Jacob wrestled with the Miraculous Angel, saying: "he had power over the Angel, and prevailed: he wept, and made supplication unto Him" (Hos 12:3–5), comparing, as it were, the intensity of Israel's spiritual struggle with the power of a sincere and fervent prayer (cf. Rom 15:30; Col 4:12). When Jacob asked the Angel to tell him His name, the Angel replied: "Wherefore is it that thou dost ask after My Name? It is MIRACULOUS" [Church Slavonic version of the Bible] — i.e., inexpressible for unprepared ears, and this again is indicative of the divine origin of the Angel. "Jacob gave the place the name *Peniel*, meaning 'face [*prosopon*] of God,' and he said 'I have *seen* God face to face, and yet my life has been spared.' The two names *Peniel* and *Penuel* are used of this mysterious nocturnal apparition (Gen 32:29–30). Midrash Rabbah commenting on this says that Jacob '*saw the face of God in the Holy Spirit*' [lit. 'in the Shekinah']."[5]

It was definitely the same Angel of the Countenance of Jehovah, who had given his blessings to Jacob before. "And God appeared unto Jacob again... and blessed him," confirming his new ministry, "Israel shall be thy name." The following verses show that the appearance was not a dream, but real: "And God went up from him in the place where he talked with him. And Jacob set up a pillar in the place where He talked with him." Later "Jacob called the name of the place where God spake with him, Bethel" (Gen 35:9–15).

The Prophet Hosea describes Jacob from two aspects: as an ordinary person having a certain character and such natural properties as cunning and self-assurance, on the one hand; and as Israel who received special *powers* for his asceticism, was transfigured by a blessing from the Angel of Jehovah, and became the patriarch of the twelve tribes of Israel, on the other. The peculiarity of this fight was that the Angel-Logos damaged Jacob's hip. This detail is very important, because the idea of the mysterious fight was to test Jacob before making him the patriarch of the future tribes of Israel. In the person of Jacob there fought the twelve future tribes of Israel, but one of

---

5 Santala, *Messiah in the Old Testament*.

them gave way and was damaged. The Jewish tradition has it that it was the tribe of Dan, from which, according to Christian prophecy, the Antichrist would come. This unusual "wrestling" episode definitely describes an appearance of the eternal Logos who mysteriously pointed to the idea of "preparing" for His future Incarnation. The new name Israel, which means "God fights," shows Jacob was endowed with a special divine power to overcome enemies, which could only be given by the Source of Power—the Logos. Jacob's wrestling gave rise to a "point" where the future and the present combined to implement the dispensation of salvation. The following evidence shows how that *beginning* was important for Israel. When Jacob blessed Joseph's sons, he mentioned the Miraculous Angel who protected him for the rest of his life: "GOD, before whom my fathers Abraham and Isaac did walk, the God which fed me all my life long unto this day, the ANGEL which redeemed me from all evil, bless the lads" (Gen 48:15–16). In the Old Testament, no created being is venerated as highly as God or invoked on a par with Him as the "redeemer" "from all evil." Therefore, Jacob's words about the Angel again prove His divine origin, where the Bible expresses the idea of the Miraculous Angel being akin to God by uncreated nature and essential Energy. According to Metropolitan Philaret, Jacob's word "bless," equally relating to God and to the Angel, shows that the Angel is regarded as having the same rights as God and as being in perfect unity with Him. Based on the distinction between the *essence and energy* of God, New Testament theology states that the *unity of His nature* does not deny the diversity of His *revelations*: God's essence always remains as part of God's energy, while His image of action is highly diverse (as can be exemplified by the Angel). Describing the struggle between Jacob and the Angel, Moses says that Jacob wrestled with "none of created and natural Angels," but asked the Supreme Angel for the blessing, showing "that it was no created Angel, but the Word of God" (the Logos). "For knowing that He is also called the Father's Angel of Great Counsel, he said that none other than He was the Giver of blessings, and Deliverer from evil."[6]

---

6 St. Athanasius of Alexandria, *Third Discourse Against the Arians.*

Manifestations of Jehovah in the Likeness of an Angel

THE PROPHET MOSES

A new period of the doctrine about the Miraculous Angel of Jehovah began with the calling of Moses, who continued with the development and dispensation of theocracy by the will of God, which was described in the events related to Israel's exodus from Egypt. Moses was chosen because he could accept a new kind of revelation from God, "With him will I speak mouth to mouth, even plainly, and not in dark speeches; and the SIMILITUDE [of the Angel] of the LORD *shall he behold*. Why then were ye not afraid to speak against my servant Moses?" (Num 12:7–8) In this iconographical manner, God again begins to act in Israel through Moses, creating the future dispensation of the "Promised Land" by the appearances of the Angel of Jehovah. We can say that iconology really began from the times of Moses, if we consider Theophanies to be the method and sense of the future Incarnation of the Logos of the Messiah, because Christ is the embodied icon of humankind. God forbade the Jews to depict any created beings "up to a certain time," preparing their minds for pure perception and promising to reveal the true reality of Icons in the bodily image of the hypostatic Son-Logos and the prosoponic Angel of God.

On Mount Horeb, "There the *Angel* of the Lord appeared to him [*Moses*] in flames of fire from within a bush," but later the Angel speaks as God: "*God* called to him from within the bush." "Moses saw that though the bush was on fire, it did not burn up." "'Do not come any closer,' God said. 'Take off your sandals, for the place where you are standing is holy ground.'" "Then he [*the Angel*] said, 'I am the God of thy father, the God of Abraham, the God of Isaac, and the God of Jacob'" (Ex 3:2–6). During this event, God acts under His different Hebrew names: "*Jehovah* saw that he had gone over to look" and then "*Elohim* called to him from within the bush." The vision of the burning bush reveals several symbolic meanings. Firstly, the fire in the bush resembles the future "pillar of fire," which will lead Israel to the holy land, and furthermore it is said about the spirituality of the "Promised Land" that it is a holy Place (Shekinah) of God's Presence. Secondly, the Angel of the Countenance of God says, "I am the God of your forefathers." This means that the same

THE ANGEL OF THE COUNTENANCE OF GOD

Angel appeared to Abraham, Isaac, and Jacob, and there is no need to prove the truth about the previous similar facts.

At the end of his days, Moses, blessing the children of Israel in the same way as Jacob had previously blessed the sons of Joseph, confirmed the divine quality of the Angel, "for the good will of him that dwelt [Hebrew: *schocheni*, derived from *Shekinah*] in the bush: let the blessing come upon the head of Joseph" (Deut 33:16). But the Angel who appeared in the fire was not only the mystical "image of God," but also his logos's actions (orders) "thou mayest bring forth My people, the children of Israel out of Egypt" (Ex 3:10); and the people were led by the Miraculous Angel of Jehovah. That is why in the iconology of dispensation, the will of God is expressed directly in the unity of *"image"* and *"action."* Let us recall another mysterious episode from the life of Moses: "And it came to pass by the way, at the inn, that [*the Angel of*] the Lord met him [*Moses*], and sought to kill him" for a longtime failure to abide by the law of circumcision. "Then Zipporah [*the wife of Moses*] took a sharp stone, and cut off the foreskin of her son, and cast it at his feet, and said, Surely a bloody husband art thou to me. So He let him go" (Ex 4:24–26). In this formidable Theophany to Moses on his way to Pharaoh, it is also natural to see the appearance of the Angel of Jehovah. This is indirectly evidenced by the words of Moses's messengers who, after the people of Israel wandered in the wilderness, requested of the king of Edom to let them pass through his land: "And when we cried unto Jehovah, He heard our voice, and *sent an Angel*, and hath brought us forth out of Egypt" (Num 20:15–16). The entire journey of Israel was determined by the leadership of the uncreated Angel of the Countenance of Jehovah: "And the Lord [*Angel-Shekinah*] went before them by day in *a pillar of cloud*, to lead them the way; and by night in *a pillar of fire*, to give them light; to go by day and night" (Ex 13:21–22). Once again, we can find here an analogy with the apocalyptic Angel "clothed with a cloud" who in special circumstances can be seen "out of the midst of the cloud," i.e., out of the sphere of "formed Light," yet is always understood as being present there. This is confirmed by the following verses: "And the Angel of God [*Elohim*] . . . removed and went behind them; and the pillar of the cloud went from before their face... *and it was a cloud and darkness* to them, but *it gave light* by night to these" (Ex 14:19–20).

On Mount Sinai, however, God Himself spoke to Moses with great power using his voice, unlike the way it had been during the appearance of the Angel. As if parallel to the figurative form of Theophany, this verbal form is the *Speech of God*. Through his Speech Jehovah gave the Law to the people of Israel and determined His Covenant with them, and it is not coincidental that the Prophet Malachi calls the Angel the "Angel of the Covenant." To distinguish the Supreme Angel from created angels in a general sense, we can call Him the "Angel of Divinity," because He, being the enhypostatic Image and Light, is the direct and inseparable Messenger of God's Divinity. According to the Acts of the Apostles, the Angel is identified with Divinity: "Moses whom... God did send to be a ruler and a deliverer... This is he, who was in the congregation in the wilderness with the Angel which spake to him in Mount Sinai" (Acts 7:35–38). And finally, Jehovah Himself orders Israel to obey His Angel: "Behold, *I* send an Angel before thee, to keep thee in the way, and to bring thee into the place which *I* have prepared. Beware of Him, and obey His voice, provoke Him not; for He will not pardon your transgressions: *for My Name is in Him*" (Ex 23:20–21).

At this critical moment of the sacred history, the Miraculous Angel is granted the power to forgive sins—the ability possessed by God alone, according to the Old Testament. Christ forgave sins by His divine nature, which the Pharisees did not understand, saying in wonderment and anger, "who can forgive sins but God only?" (Mk 2:7) But the strongest evidence of the uncreated nature of the Angel of Elohim is that the holy Name of Jehovah is at the "heart" of the Angel—as an "atom," a light nucleus of all kinds of forces, images, and abilities—and contains force (δυναμις), energy or action (ενέργεια) and energemas, as a result of action (ενέργημα), which is a necessary condition for the outward manifestation of the essence of God (see, for example, the works by St. Maximus the Confessor). Therefore, God's Name (Hebrew: *HaShem*), always having the meaning of internal habitation, is the essential life-giving Logos—the *Image and Speech* of the Trinity: in the *beginning* (*in the prosopon*)

THE ANGEL OF THE COUNTENANCE OF GOD

was the Logos, and the Logos was (*addressed*) to (*the hypostatic*) God, and the Logos was God (cf. Jn 1:1, Prologue). In these examples, we can see the equality of God and Divinity.

From the messianic time, the Logos directs its attention "to the world" too for the salvation of people, as the prophet says, "Behold, the name of the LORD cometh from far" (Is 30:27). The Name-Logos-Speech is by nature not only the Son-*Hypostasis*, but also the *Prosopon*, the "representation of His being" (*Image of His Hypostasis*) — the Name of the invisible God (Heb 1:3). That is why Christ has two names: *Emmanuel* ("God is with us") by prophecy and *Jesus* (Savior) by Incarnation.

The personified IMAGE and essential Light — the Angel of Divinity — appears to the people as a bearer of the mystical NAME-SPEECH, for the Lord commanded Israel to cherish the Name and worship It in a special place. This is the basis of the Old Testament and Christian traditions for building the Temple-Church. The "Temple" is the symbol of God's Image, while the "church" (believer) is the symbol of God's Speech. Therefore, "unto the *place which the Lord your God shall choose out of all your tribes to put His Name there*, even unto his habitation shall ye seek, and thither thou shalt come" (Deut 12:5). God's *image and speech* really dwells inside Man as the seed of Communion, the holy Eucharist fulfilled in the New Testament. Solomon says, "it was in the heart of David my father to build a house for the *Name* of the Lord God." God did not let David do that, saying to him, "thy son . . . shall build the house unto My Name" (1 Kgs 8:16–20). The presence of the Angel of Light in Theophany certainly differs from His presence in a man-made temple, but here it is written, "the [*uncreated*] cloud [*the Glory of God*] filled the house of the Lord" (1 Kgs 8:10–11). As we remember, the "cloud" is the Angel's "vestment." If the "name" is understood as energy, this example shows not the metaphorical or ideally symbolical, but real Presence "in the Kingdom, and the Power, and the Glory" of God's acting Name; and this internal Name becomes visible in the appearances of the holy Angel. Characteristically, the word "name" in all its meanings, as in "Praise ye the Name of the Lord" (Ps 135:1), is mentioned 642 times in the Bible.

Manifestations of Jehovah in the Likeness of an Angel

Considering the symbolism of the three names "cloud," "Angel," and "Name," we can see some gradual accruing of "concealment": the "cloud" conceals the "Angel," the "Angel" conceals the Name of God, and the "Name" contains God who acts and says, "I am the Lord [Hebrew: *Yehovah*]: that is My name: and My glory will I not give to another" (Is 42:8). Only the essential Logos has the fullness of God's glory; Israel was commanded to revere and obey the Angel containing the Name of Jehovah, which is an example of revelation of the same divine nature. On the other hand, the fact that the Lord sends the Angel of Light containing God's Name shows some differences between Them, which has the same meaning as in the distinction between the concepts of "nature" and "prosopon" (person). The distinction (not separation) is that the Logos is the name of God's Son, the second Hypostasis, on the one hand, while the actual Logos and Speech is the energy of seed and the Divinity, on the other. This *distinction* between the essence and the energy of Trihypostatic God and His productive, life-giving, and creative *power and beauty of the Logos* can be found in the works of such holy fathers as Maximus the Confessor, John of Damascus, Gregory Palamas, etc. The kingly Angel is not an independent entity or a hypostasis, but an enhypostatic, personified, and anthropomorphic Image of Light, through which God reveals His Name-Speech of figurative actions leading to the formation and salvation of the chosen people; whereas in Christ "all the fullness of the *Godhead*" began to dwell "bodily" (Col 2:9).

As the Jews violated God's commandments at the foot of Sinai, Jehovah did not speak Himself in the likeness of the Miraculous Angel, but sent the Angel, as if in space, *instead of* Himself: "behold, mine Angel shall go before thee: nevertheless in the day when I visit I will visit their sin upon them; for I will not go up in the midst of thee; for thou art a stiff-necked people: lest I consume thee in the way" (Ex 32:34, 33:2–3). When the people heard these evil tidings, they mourned, and Moses even pitched the tabernacle without the camp. There, when the cloudy pillar stood at the tabernacle door, Moses spoke with God "face to face." With the boldness of faith, Moses asks God, "If Thou go not up with us Thyself [in the Targums: "If Thy Shekinah go not..."], bring me not up hence." Here, we can see

THE ANGEL OF THE COUNTENANCE OF GOD

the difference between Jehovah and the Angel, while Exodus 23:32 makes no distinction between them. As a token of reconciliation with the people and in answer to the prayer of Moses the Lord says, "My presence shall go with thee, and I will give thee rest [Greek: *hesychia*]" (Ex 33:14). This means that the Angel and the Logos again affected the people with equal Revelation. Recalling the exodus of Israel from Egypt, the Prophet Isaiah says: "In all their affliction He was afflicted, and the Angel of His Countenance [*prosopon*] saved them... As a beast goeth down into the valley, the Spirit of the Lord caused him to rest" (Is 63:9, 14).

The sacred texts related to the Angel of Jehovah have the following specific feature: in some verses, the Angel's behavior does not make it possible to exactly determine whether He is created or uncreated by nature. Somewhat vague are the descriptions of the Angel's appearances a) to the handmaid Hagar, b) to Abraham when he sacrificed Isaac, c) in the episode of finding a wife for Isaac, d) in the story of Balaam and his donkey, etc. Nevertheless, the above logical reasonings and the fathers' statements are reliably in favor of the divine origin of the Angel in all cases. In order not to disrupt the continuous chain of actions of the Angel of Jehovah in the revelation of salvation and for the sake of faith, it will be better to recognize that the Angel who appeared in those episodes was uncreated; although this opinion should be considered to be a theologoumenon. This will be discussed in more detail in the section dedicated to the New Testament. Here, it is important to understand the basic principle of God's theological appearances. One of the difficulties in understanding them is that the Bible sometimes describes an appearance or action of Three Angels (as in the appearance of Three Men to Abraham) rather than one. Therefore, it would not be logical to attribute all Theophanies in the likeness of the Angel only to the Son before His Incarnation. Therefore, Theophanies coming from *one essence* should be distinguished by *multiplicity of energies*.

According to the dogmatic theology of the Church, God is invisible, unknowable, and indescribable in any way. He is omniscient and omnipresent, so it would be a violation of the dogma of the absoluteness of God to attribute movement in space and time to

Him. However, God is knowable, describable, and depictable in the properties-energies of His Presence. God is depictable, because God's Divinity is the IMAGE OF HIS ACTIONS and *Revelation*, which may be in the form of light phenomena, a cloud or fire, a dove, dew, or just a voice from heaven, which are mystical signs, i.e., Theophanies. In special cases, in the context of the history of salvation, incarnation, or resurrection, they acquire specific real form, perceptible by human consciousness. God not only speaks to the people, but also appears before them in the anthropomorphic form of the Angel, including such a significant event as the Incarnation of the Logos and the Son in human form, "And the Logos was made flesh, and dwelt [Greek: *eskinosen*, "settled," related to *skene* or *Shekinah*] among us, and we beheld His glory, the glory as of the only begotten of the Father, full of grace and truth" (Jn 1:14). It turns out that the appearances of the Angel of the Countenance of God were preparations for the reality of Incarnation, and the Lamb of God, Who takes away the sin of the world, was Jesus Christ predicted by the Holy Spirit through the patriarchs and prophets. The Logos, who appeared repeatedly and multivariously in the form of the Angel of Jehovah, was seen physically after the Incarnation, "For the law was given [*by God*] by Moses, but grace and truth came by Jesus Christ" (Jn 1:17).

Both statements—relating to knowability and unknowability of God—must be reconciled by the dogma that God (Θεός) is One by *nature*, the Trinity of the Father and of the Son and of the Holy Spirit by *mode of existence*, and multivarious Divinity (Θεότης) by *image of action*. And there is no God without the "image" of His energies in the same way as there are no "energies" that do not make it possible to see Him. Here, we can obviously see the common principle of Theophanies—the unity and difference between notions without confusion or separation. So, in the appearances of the Angel of God we see the direct Revelation of God's Light, whereas created angels are special messengers, intermediaries, and carriers of God's Light.

Revelation itself can take different forms contemplated by a person who is in the Spirit. So, it is possible to distinguish three main types of acting Energy: the essential spermatic Logos-Light and its two typical life-giving energies—Wisdom (Sophia) and Love (Agape), which

THE ANGEL OF THE COUNTENANCE OF GOD

determine the movement of the mind and heart in Man. These are the three energies in which the Trinity is manifest in angelic form in specific Theophanic events. As "each [*celestial*] order is the interpreter and herald of those above it, the most venerable being the interpreter of God who inspires them, and the others in turn of those inspired by God," created angels of the highest order, "trying to mold themselves to the imitation of [Light] God," are named in accordance with God's uncreated energies whose servants and contemplators they are.[7]

To explain the above, let us give examples that can be attributed to the appearances of the Angel of God, even though this is not immediately obvious. First of all, let us recall the two meetings between the Angel and Hagar in the wilderness: He is called the Angel of Jehovah (Gen 16:7–13) during the first meeting and the Angel of Elohim during the second one (Gen 21:17–19). The first meeting is preceded by the following events. Hagar "despised" her "mistress" and was cast out by Sarai. "The Angel of the Lord found her by a fountain of water in the wilderness … and … said unto her, Return to thy mistress, and submit thyself under her hand." By dignity, this Angel is kingly, because His order (expressing His will as "*I*") for Hagar to return to her mistress, the promise to multiply her seed exceedingly, and the prediction of the birth of a son exactly coincide with the promises given to Abraham. Therefore, Hagar "called the name of the Lord that spake unto her, *Thou God* seest me." "Wherefore the well was called Beerlahairoi [Hebrew: well of the Living One that seeth me]." Contextually, it seems that it was the Angel Sophia, because He instructed Hagar and prophesied. Thirteen years after Hagar bare Ishmael to Abram, "the Lord appeared to Abram, and said unto him, I am the Almighty God" (Gen 17:1). Even though the Bible does not mention directly the appearance of the Angel of Jehovah, we can deduce that from the Lord's promise to Abraham to give him a son of Sarah and from the appearance of the Three Angels in the plain of Mamre. Perhaps in the Angels Abraham recognized the image of the Lord from the first appearance, because he immediately addressed the Three as "My Lord."

Another appearance of the Angel to Hagar occurred when she was lost in the wilderness and wept. "And God [*Elohim*] heard the voice…;

---

7   Dionysius, *Celestial Hierarchy*.

Manifestations of Jehovah in the Likeness of an Angel

and the Angel of God called to Hagar out of heaven, and said unto her, fear not . . . arise, lift up the lad . . . for I will make him a great nation. And God opened her eyes, and she saw a well of water" (Gen 21:17–19). Contextually, it is clear that it was the Angel Elohim, while what he said with power and love — "*I will make him a great nation*" — with reasonable confidence enables us to call Him the Agape of God. It is the God of Love who opened Hagar's eyes, for "living water" is the symbol of New Testament love — let us remember the meeting between Jesus and the Samaritan woman at Jacob's well.

One more time the uncreated Angel appeared to Abraham in the likeness of Sophia or Agape during the sacrifice of Isaac (Gen 22:1–18). God tested the depth of Abraham's faith when He demanded that Abraham sacrifice the son promised by Himself. Abraham trusted God and was absolutely sure of His word (would that have happened if it had been a created angel?), but when Abraham stretched forth his hand and took the knife, "the Angel of the Lord called unto him out of heaven: . . . Lay not thine hand upon the lad . . . for now *I* know that thou fearest God [*Elohim*]." Most likely, that was the Angel Sophia, and "Abraham called the name of that place *Yahweh-yireh*," "Yahweh will provide," an aspect of "multi-eyedness" (from which, according to the biblical etymology, the name of Mount Moriah is possibly derived). The Angel who appeared to Abraham bears a direct resemblance to the Christ-Wisdom who sacrificed Himself. It is also noteworthy that "Solomon began to build the house of [*Wisdom*] the Lord at Jerusalem in mount Moriah" (2 Chr 3:1).

In Genesis 24, Abraham sends his servant to choose a bride for Isaac with God's help. He hopes that "The Lord God of heaven, which took me from my father's house, and from the land of my kindred, and *which spake unto me*, and that sware unto me, saying, Unto thy seed will I give this land; he shall send his angel [*Agape*] before thee, and thou shalt take a wife unto my son from thence" (Gen 24:7–8). Finding a wife for Isaac was important for the entire cause of salvation. Abraham believed that God would help him, and the Angel Agape brought his servant to a damsel who "was very fair to look upon." Pure in her faith and always willing to help her neighbor, Rebekah was symbolically chosen to be the bride by a well

THE ANGEL OF THE COUNTENANCE OF GOD

of water, which is very reminiscent of the description of the first Annunciation to the Blessed Virgin Mary at the well. By faith, not even knowing her fiancé by sight, Rebekah immediately said, "I will go," in the same way as Mary who trusted God without hesitation and said, "Behold the handmaid of the Lord; be it unto me according to thy word" (Lk 1:38). This reveals the deep symbolic meaning of the history of faith of the people of Israel.

The Angel of Jehovah appeared to the Prophet Balaam (Num 22:22–35) too. This story is unusual, because the Angel of the Lord was first seen not by the prophet, but by his ass: "And the ass saw the Angel of the Lord standing in the way, and his sword drawn in his hand: and the ass turned aside out of the way," even though Balaam smote her. The Angel opens the mouth of the ass and she speaks in human voice to make Balaam listen to reason, and Balaam suddenly sees the Angel (*Sophia*) with a sword in His hand. "And the Angel of the Lord said unto him, ... I went out to withstand thee, because thy way is perverse before Me. And the ass saw Me, and turned from Me these three times: unless she had turned from Me, surely now also I had slain thee, and saved her alive." Balaam repented, and the Angel of Jehovah taught him to prophesy in the Spirit. Later, Balaam was named "the man whose eyes are open," which enables us to correlate this formidable Angel, in accordance with His image of action, with Sophia, the Wisdom of God. Firstly, the Angel says "I" as the Lord Himself, while the threat to kill the prophet and save the ass alive, if Balaam disobeys, cannot be made by a created angel.

JOSHUA AND THE PROPHETS

In the Book of Joshua, the Angel, in accordance with the time of war, appears as a warrior to the leader of Israel. Actually, this episode is directly indicative of the Angel of Jehovah. Hieromonk Alexander Sokolov (*The Book of Joshua*), commenting in detail on the description of this meeting (Josh 5:13–15), points out that the Holy Fathers differ in their interpretations of the meeting. For example, Theodoret of Cyrus holds that it was Michael the Archangel who appeared to Joshua. This view is also reflected in the Liturgy.[8] Augustine of Hippo also

---

8 *Canon of Matins*, Ode 6.

Manifestations of Jehovah in the Likeness of an Angel

holds that Joshua met a created angel in whose person he, as it were, worshipped the Lord Himself. However, many exegetes — St. Justin Martyr, Origen, St. Gregory of Nyssa, and others — consider the Angel to be the Lord Himself, and there is strong evidence for this view.

The Angel appeared to Joshua with a sword in his hand: "When Joshua was by Jericho... he lifted up his eyes and looked, and, behold, there stood a man over against him with his sword drawn in his hand" (Josh 5:13). This meeting is very similar to the story of Balaam and also has to do with God's fight against paganism. The "two-edged sword" featuring in the Book of Revelation is the symbol of Christ's Wisdom. When Joshua saw the captain of the Lord's host, he "fell on his face to the earth, and did worship." But let us remember that the Jews were forbidden to worship any creature, even an angel. This means that he understood that he saw the Lord Himself in front of him. Later, the Angel's speech is very similar to what was said to Moses by the Angel in a blazing fire from the middle of a bush: "And He said: put off thy shoes from off thy feet, for the place whereon thou standest is holy ground." Similarly, "the captain of the Lord's host said unto Joshua, Loose thy shoe from off thy foot; for the place whereon thou standest is *holy*." When Joshua asked "Art thou for us, or for our adversaries?" he said, "Nay; but as *captain* of the host of the Lord [*Jehovah*] am *I* now come [*to help you*]" (Josh 5:14). In addition, Daniel mentions the Prince (with a capital "p") of the Lord's host (*Sar Tseva Yahweh*): "he magnified himself even to the Prince of the Host" (Dan 8:11). The Angel calls Himself the Prince of the host of the earth (Israel), but then God too defined Himself as such, saying to Moses, "I may... bring forth Mine armies, and My people... out of the land of Egypt" (Ex 7:4) and in Exodus 12:17 He says, "I brought your *armies* [*tziv'oteichem*] out of the land of Egypt." The captain of the Lord's host said unto Joshua, "the place whereon thou standest is holy," which means that from this moment the people of Israel come into possession of the land promised by God, and the Angel of Jehovah naturally helps His chosen people to win victory over the Gentiles.

In the Pentateuch, as we have noted, the armies of Israel are repeatedly called the Tsevaot of Jehovah. The heavenly Commander who

THE ANGEL OF THE COUNTENANCE OF GOD

appeared to Joshua is an Angel and the Captain of angelic hosts, which for the first time shows the connection between His name and the name of the Lord of Sabaoth; He is the Captain of Hosts and the Lord of Hosts (יהוה צבאות, *Yehovah Tsevaot*). According to the Orthodox tradition, however, Michael belongs to one of the nine orders, the "archangelical order," so he is not the captain of the entire heavenly host of angels. St. Gregory of Nyssa writes about this as follows:

> The prophets testify to this, calling him the Lord of all the armies and Lord of hosts. And to Joshua Nave, the powerful one in battle, he said, "I am the commander of the army [of the Lord]." If we have understood the assistance we receive in battle and the leader of our allies, let us make a truce with him, fly to his powerful aid and become friends in order to secure his assistance.⁹

Let us recall that the liturgical theology of the Christian Church supplemented Isaiah's verse "Holy, holy, holy, is the Lord of Sabaoth: the whole earth is full of his glory" (Is 6:3) with the words "*heaven and earth are filled with Thy Glory*," which have become part of the liturgical canon in this form. Therefore, this is of particular importance for us and for our ascent into the Kingdom of God, which opens with the liturgical name — the Lord of Sabaoth, because the Glory (Shekinah) of God should reside not only in the world of angels, but "on earth as in heaven."

The first mention of the Lord of Sabaoth, in the context of sacrifices, can be found in 1 Samuel 1:3. However, this name was mentioned as naturally as if it had constantly been used by the Jews before. In the Pentateuch, the name is used in its literal meaning to denote "armies" or "hosts." In the times of the prophets, however, the name came to mean the King of God's Glory. So, the prophet David exclaims: "Who is this King of Glory? The Lord of hosts [*Yehovah Tsevaot*], He is the King of Glory" (Ps 24:10). The Prophet Isaiah says about the end times: "Then the moon shall be confounded, and the sun ashamed, when the Lord of Sabaoth shall reign in mount Zion, and in Jerusalem, and before His ancients gloriously" (Is 24:23).

---

9 Gregory of Nyssa, *Commentary on Ecclesiastes*, Homily 8.

Manifestations of Jehovah in the Likeness of an Angel

So, the Angel who appeared to Joshua with a sword in his hand, calling himself the Captain of the Host, was the captain of the angelic, heavenly, rather than earthly host. He was the direct messenger of the "thrice-holy" Lord of Sabaoth. The angelic host is a host of spirits or minds; they are the retinue of the Lord God of Sabaoth sitting in heaven and the executors of His will; they are the Celestial Church of God's children who explore God's ways and judgments in unity and close relationship with humankind.

In the Book of Judges (2:1–4), we can find another appearance of the formidable Angel of Jehovah to all the people of Israel: "an Angel of the Lord came up ... to Bochim." He is the same messenger who brought the people out of Egypt, but in this episode he commandingly warns Israel not to make league with the inhabitants of the conquered land. "But ye have not obeyed My voice.... Wherefore ... I will not drive them out from before you.... When the Angel of the Lord spake these words unto all the children of Israel ... the people lifted up their voice, and wept." So, these verses clearly show that the chosen people saw God's Logos Himself in the likeness of an angel, the organizer of theocracy in their lives.

Theophany continues with the bestowal of special might directly from the messenger of the Lord of hosts: "And there came an Angel of the Lord, and sat under an oak which was in Ophrah." He said to Gideon, "The Lord is with thee, thou mighty man of valor.... Go in this thy might, and thou shalt save Israel from the hand of the Midianites: have not I sent thee?" Gideon asked for a sign and then went in, made ready a kid, some broth and cakes, and offered this meal to the Angel. The Angel told him to put everything on a stone. Then the Angel

> put forth the end of the staff that was in his hand, and touched the flesh and the unleavened cakes; and there rose up fire out of the rock, and consumed the flesh and the unleavened cakes. Then the Angel of the Lord departed out of his sight.... And Gideon said, Alas, O Lord God! For I have seen the Angel of the Lord face to face. And the Lord said unto him, Peace be unto thee; fear not: thou shalt not die. (Judg 6:11–23)

THE ANGEL OF THE COUNTENANCE OF GOD

Interesting is the sacrificial offering under the oak, which recalls Abraham's hospitable meal. The actual justification of His divine gift is given by the Angel of Jehovah in Gideon's miraculous victory over enemies.

Another similar appearance of the divine Angel was to Manoah and his barren wife, when they were blessed to have a son, Samson (Judg 13:3–23). "And the angel of the Lord appeared unto the woman, and said unto her, Behold now, . . . thou shalt . . . bear a son; and . . . the child shall be a Nazarite unto God . . . and he shall begin to deliver Israel out of the hand of the Philistines." Then the Angel appeared again, in a field, and confirmed the promise. When Manoah asked what the Angel's name was, the answer was similar to that once given to Jacob: "Why dost thou thus ask My name; whereas it is wonderful?" [Slavonic Bible version] The Angel's wonderful name is miraculous and inexpressible in the language of reason, because it consists of unspeakable letters woven out of the divine Light and Fire. When Manoah made an offering to the Lord on a stone (like Gideon), the Angel confirmed his words by a miracle: "When the flame went up toward heaven from the altar, the Angel of the Lord ascended in the flame of the altar. And Manoah and his wife looked on it, and fell on their faces to the ground." Then Manoah knew that He was an Angel of the Lord, because He kindled a fire on his offering, which, according to the law, no ordinary person was allowed to do. "And Manoah said unto his wife, 'We shall surely die, because we have seen God.'" So, the Angel revealed one more feature in God's mode of action — miracle-working.

This was the last appearance of the Angel of Jehovah in the pre-Prophet period. After that, Jehovah's visible actions continued no more. For a long time, the Bible makes no mention of Him. Biblical scholars explain this by the fact that "in accordance with the general character of these books, the mediating role in the Old Testament theocracy is now replaced by God's Wisdom (Hebrew: *Chokhmah*)."[10] Indeed, Sophia is the creative energy of the Son of God, and the idea preparing His Incarnation in Israel is formed through the people's relations with God's Wisdom, which gradually ascends from its

---

10 Glagolev, *Angels in the Old Testament*.

Manifestations of Jehovah in the Likeness of an Angel

original concept of "wisdom" in the narrow-minded and utilitarian sense of "cunning" to the heights of theology.

However, mentions of the divine Angel of Jehovah are resumed in the prophetic writings. The Prophet Hosea recalls and gives further evidence of the mysterious Angel who struggled with Jacob: "He had power over the Angel, and prevailed: he wept, and made supplication unto Him: He found Him in Bethel, and there He spake with us. Even the Lord God of hosts; the Lord [*Jehovah*] is His memorial" (Hos 12:4–5). Again, the Angel is identified with the name of the Lord of Sabaoth; the Angel's divinity is confirmed by the prophet: He is the "Captain of the host of the Lord." In addition, the Prophet Isaiah recalls: "In all their affliction He [*God*] was afflicted, and the Angel of His Presence saved them: in His love [*Agape*] and in His pity [*Sophia*] He [*Lamb-Logos*] redeemed them; and He bare them, and carried them [*in the Shekinah*] all the days of old" (Is 63:9). But the Prophet Isaiah not only recalls the "days of old," but also sees a mysterious Angel in the likeness of the Lord sitting in the Heavenly Temple. "I saw also the Lord sitting upon a throne, high and lifted up, and His train [*glory*] filled the temple. Above it stood the seraphim ... and one cried unto another, and said, Holy, Holy, Holy, is the Lord of Sabaoth: the whole earth is full of His glory.... Then said I, Woe is me! for I am undone; because I am a man of unclean lips ... for mine *eyes* have *seen* the King, the Lord of Sabaoth" (Is 6:1–5). Iconographically, this vision is amazing, and it is not clear why art historians still deny the possibility of depicting the King, the Lord of Glory and the Lord of heavenly hosts. Perhaps they do so because they rely on the false identification of Lord of Sabaoth with God the Father in trinitarian theology. In this respect, however, John the Apostle says: "While ye have Light, believe in the Light, that ye may be the children of Light.... That the saying of Isaias the prophet might be fulfilled, which he spake, 'Lord, who hath believed our report?' ... These things said Isaias, when he saw His glory (*of the Lord of Sabaoth*), and spake of Him" (Jn 12:36–41).

> Indeed, the anthropomorphism of the image of the one who appeared and the fact that he saw the King, the Lord

of hosts, i.e., not God face to face but His undisguised Image, brings us to the conclusion that He is the Angel of Jehovah's Face who acted inseparably and constantly with Jehovah in the prior history of Israel.[11]

What Moses saw during the passing of God's Glory was the Image (Prosopon) of Jehovah's actions — it was *God's Image* that was recognized by the bodily eyes of Moses. In addition, based on numerous quotations, St. John of Damascus bears evidence that all the Church Fathers recognize the Lord of Sabaoth not as any of God's Hypostases (especially the Hypostasis of the Father), but as the Image of manifestation and presence of the whole Trinity, because "'Holy' — thrice, while 'the Lord' — once."[12] In addition, the Book of Revelation mentions the Lord of Sabaoth "sitting upon a throne" in His creative power and glory:

> And I saw in the right hand of Him Who sat on the throne a Book written within and on the back, sealed with seven seals. And I saw a strong Angel [probably, *Sophia*] proclaiming with a loud voice, Who is worthy to open the book, and to loose the seals thereof? And no man in heaven, nor in earth, neither under the earth, was able to open the Book [*of Life*], neither to look thereon.... And, lo,... a Lamb [*Logos*] came and took the Book out of the right hand of Him Who sat upon the throne [*the Lord of Sabaoth*]. And every creature which is in heaven, and on the earth, and under the earth... heard I saying, Blessing, and honor, and glory, and power, be unto Him Who sitteth upon the throne [*the Lord of Sabaoth*], and unto the Lamb [*His Logos*] for ever and ever.... Amen. (Rev 4:2, 5:1–14)

This brings the biblical history to its final line, where ultimate completion is attained in the relations between *essence and energy*: God acting in the likeness of the Angel Lamb, the Logos of creative energy — the Alpha and Omega of salvation history.

---

11   Ibid.
12   St. John of Damascus, *Letter on the Trisagion*.

Manifestations of Jehovah in the Likeness of an Angel

THE PROPHET DANIEL

The Angel of Jehovah is repeatedly mentioned in the Book of Daniel. First, there is a recurring phenomenon and bond between the Lord of Sabaoth and the Logos: "And the Ancient of Days did sit, Whose garment was white [*cloudy*] as snow, and the hair of His head like pure wool: His throne [*ophan — an angel of high order*] was like the fiery flame, and His wheels (*merkabah, light energies*) as burning fire" (Dan 7:9). In another vision, Daniel says: "Behold, one like the Son of Man came with the clouds of heaven, and came to the Ancient of Days, and they brought Him near before Him. And there was given Him dominion, and glory, and a kingdom, and all people, nations, and languages" (Dan 7:13–14). The mention of "white garments and clouds" again implies the Angel of Jehovah. The visions of the Prophet Daniel and John the Apostle are indubitably identical and indicative of the essential Logos (addressed to the Lord of Sabaoth) who by flesh became the Son of Man.

The "Son of Man," whose image was seen by Daniel, is the prophetic name of Jesus Christ, Who always referred to Himself by this name. It is this name (*the Son of Man*) adopted by Christ that was especially strongly resented by the Pharisees, because it was mentioned in Daniel's prophecy of the Messiah, while they refused to recognize Jesus, a carpenter's son, as the Messiah. In Daniel's vision, the Ancient of Days is described in the same way as Christ in the Book of Revelation:

> I saw seven golden lampstands, and among the lampstands was One like a *Son of Man*, dressed in a robe [*made of linen*] reaching down to His feet and with a golden sash around His chest. The hair on His head was *white* like wool, as white as snow, and His eyes were like blazing fire. His feet were like bronze glowing in a furnace, and His voice was like the sound of rushing waters. (Rev 1:13–15)

Daniel gives the same, absolutely iconographic, image of the Messiah: "A Man dressed in linen, with a belt of fine gold from Uphaz around His waist. His body was like topaz, His face like lightning, His eyes like flaming torches, His arms and legs like the gleam of burnished bronze, and His voice like the sound of a multitude" (Dan 10:5–7).

THE ANGEL OF THE COUNTENANCE OF GOD

Then, the Logos Son says, "Do not be afraid... Now I have come to explain to you what will happen to your people in the future" (Dan 10:12–14) and gives the Prophet *strength* by touching him. The comparison of these verses shows that the Angel Man described by Daniel (10:5–6) is the same person as the Son of Man. It is also interesting that the image of the Lord of Sabaoth, the Ancient of Days with white hair, and the image of the Son of Man described by John (Rev 1:13–15) are almost identical. The only difference between Them is that the Lord of Sabaoth holds the Book of Life in his right hand, while the Son-Logos holds seven stars which are the seven Angels (uncreated Spirits) of the seven Churches. The third thing that attracts iconological attention is the vision of *two* Angels (Dan 12) who can easily be identified with the images of Sophia and Agape:

> There before me stood two others, One [*the Angel Sophia*] on this bank of the river and One on the opposite bank. One of them said to the Man [*the Logos*] clothed in linen, Who was above the waters of the river, "How long will it be before these astonishing things are fulfilled?" The Man clothed in linen... lifted His right hand and His left hand toward heaven,... and I heard Him swear by Him Who Lives Forever [*the Ancient of Days*], saying, "It will be for a time, times and half a time... all these things will be completed." (Dan 12:5–7)

In Christian iconography, this triple image of the Divine Economy is the Icon of Paternity (Fatherhood), where the Lord of Sabaoth is depicted as the image of Jesus Christ, yet having snow-white hair in the likeness of the Ancient of Days, with His essential Logos Emmanuel sitting on His lap and holding a celestial sphere with His Spirit in a generalized image of an Angel—the Shekinah, Agape, or Sophia.

So, the iconologically manifested Name of Jehovah, in accordance with the prophecy of the Incarnation of the Savior, undergoes conceptual changes, which are reflected in the change in, and transitions of, theophanic *images* from an Angel to the Logos, in accordance with the *action* of the Light, "preparing the Incarnation" but not yet by the mystical meaning of Incarnation itself.

Manifestations of Jehovah in the Likeness of an Angel

THE PROPHETS ZECHARIAH AND MALACHI

The Angel of Jehovah is also mentioned in the books of the later Jewish prophets Zechariah and Malachi. Zechariah describes the Angel of Jehovah as the head and lord of created angels who fulfill the will of the Lord of Sabaoth: "Turn ye unto Me, saith the Lord of Sabaoth, and I will turn unto you." Then the Logos of God is described in the vision: "And behold, a Man riding upon a red horse, and he stood among the myrtle trees that were in the bottom" (let us recall that angels are often referred to as "men" in the Bible, including the three angels who appeared to Abraham). He who stood among the myrtle trees, the Angel of the LORD, answered Zechariah about the other angel, "These are they [*spirits*] whom the Lord hath sent to walk to and fro through the earth." "And they answered the Angel [*Man*] of the Lord... and said, We have walked to and fro through the earth.... The Angel... said unto me,... Thus saith the Lord of Sabaoth; I am jealous for Jerusalem and for Zion with a great jealousy," etc. The following verses are even more convincing regarding the divine nature of the Angel, the direct Messenger of the Lord of Sabaoth:

> For thus saith the Lord of Sabaoth: After the glory hath he sent Me [*Angel*] unto the nations which spoiled you: for he that toucheth you toucheth the apple of His eye. For, behold, I will shake Mine hand upon them, and they shall be a spoil to their servants: and *ye shall know that the Lord of Sabaoth hath sent Me*. (Zech 1:8–17; 2:8–9)

The Angel of Jehovah appears again in the fourth, highly symbolic, vision of the future Messiah, i.e., again of the Son of Man, the Logos, and the Lamb—Jesus:

> And He shewed me Joshua the high priest standing before the Angel of the Lord, and Satan standing at His right hand to resist Him. Now Joshua [*The Son of Man*] was clothed with filthy garments, and stood before the Angel. [*God*]... spake... saying, Take away the filthy garments from Him. And unto Him he said, Behold, I have caused Thine iniquity [*of your people*] to pass from Thee, and I will

> clothe Thee with change of raiment.... they set a fair mitre upon His head, and clothed Him with garments.... And the Angel of the Lord protested unto Joshua, saying, Thus saith the Lord of Sabaoth;... if Thou wilt keep My charge, then Thou shalt also judge My house, and shalt also keep My courts.... Hear now, O Joshua the high priest [*God-Man and the High Priest after the order of Melchizedek*], Thou, and Thy fellows... behold, *I will bring forth My servant the Branch*. For behold the [*corner-*] stone that I have laid before Joshua; upon one stone shall be seven eyes [*spirits*]: behold, I will engrave the graving [*engraving of the image*] thereof, saith the Lord of Sabaoth, and I will remove the iniquity of that land in one day. (Zech 3:1–9)

We can see a quite concrete prophecy of the Incarnation of the Son of God, who became Man. Jesus took upon himself the sin of the world as a "garment" (image of action—prosopon). This is the prophecy of the divine Angel of the Countenance of God—Agaposophia, and of the eternal spermatic and communed Logos Emmanuel named *The Branch*: "Behold the Man whose name is The Branch; and He shall grow up out of *His* place, and He shall build the Temple of the Lord [*the Church*]" (Zech 6:12). The Branch-Emmanuel is the Logos and the Son of Deification, and it is said that the human race will be cleared of the original sin for "one day" of the Crucifixion unto death and the Resurrection of the Firstborn from the dead. This manifests a brand-new New Testament principle of the victory of the Logos over evil, "Not by might, nor by power, but by My spirit, saith the Lord of Sabaoth" (Zech 4:6). Then you will know that "the Lord of Sabaoth hath sent Me unto you," says Jesus the Messiah, and those "seven uncreated spirits" (cf. Isaiah), according to the Church Fathers, are "the eyes of the Lord, which run to and fro through the whole earth," the seven stars, as the seven Churches in the right hand of God's incarnate Son and Logos. This is the meaning of the seven levels of the Church of Christ Victorious, Who sits on the throne next to the Lord of Sabaoth, and of the seven gifts in the right hand of the King of Glory that are given to those who overcome.

Manifestations of Jehovah in the Likeness of an Angel

The final evidence of the Angel of Jehovah, which is also correlated with the coming of the Messiah and His Angel, can be found in the Book of Malachi:

> Behold, I will send My Messenger [*the Angel of My Countenance*], and He shall prepare the way before Me [*the Logos*]: and the *Lord*, whom ye seek, shall suddenly come to His Temple, even the Messenger [*Agaposophia*] of the Covenant, Whom ye delight in. Behold: He shall come, saith the Lord of Sabaoth. (Mal 3:1)

Without violating the meaning, we can certainly combine "the Lord [*i.e., the Savior*], Whom ye seek" and "the Messenger [*with the mysterious 'My name is in Him'*] . . . Whom ye delight in" into one statement—"Obey My Messenger [*Angel*], for My name is in Him," and this will be iconographically correct.

Taking into consideration the New Testament theology of distinguishing essence and energy, "the Messenger of the Covenant" can also be interpreted as God's Shekinah in the Ark of Moses. From the perspective of the New Testament, according to St. Isaac of Syria, the Shekinah left the Jewish Tabernacle and began to dwell in the Cross of Christ as the agapean-sophian power and beauty, as the Angel of the Resurrection. In their testimonies about the events following the burial of Christ, the Four Evangelists describe the appearance of the Angel of Christ (Mt 28:2–3; Mk 16:5–6; Lk 24:4–7), mentioning one or two Angels (Men) in shining white garments. "Mary Magdalene stood . . . at the sepulcher weeping: and as she wept, she stooped down, and looked into the sepulcher, And seeth *two Angels* in white sitting, one at the *head*, and the other at the feet [*of the linen cloths*], where the Body of Jesus had lain" (Jn 20:12). The two Angels testifying about the Resurrection of the Logos can be identified with the Angels Sophia and Agape standing on either side of the river in the vision of Daniel. The same two Angels in white robes are depicted in the Icon of the Ascension showing to the Apostles and to us the future coming of the Logos.

The man-made Ark of the Covenant was lost, but the acheiropoetic Church of the Habitation of God—the Shekinah of the Kingdom,

Power, and Glory of the Lord of Sabaoth — was recreated by the risen Christ. And this is important to those who offer prayers through the Sign of the Cross, strengthening and improving their faith in the iconographic image of Theophanies. And the initial words of the prophecy, "and ye shall know that the Lord of Sabaoth hath sent Me" (Zech 2:1), in the symbolism of Divine Economy, refer to the Logos who is the inapproachable Light of the Resurrection to Eternal Life.

In our overview of the appearances of the Old Testament Angel of Jehovah, it is necessary to see a continuous line of *images* depicting an iconographic establishment of the covenant between God and Man. The "Covenant" understood as the Shekinah (the energy of Presence, Incarnation, and Habitation in a real ontological sense), rather than as a set of laws, is a living communication and communion of humankind with the Logos who once planted the Tree of Life in the middle of Paradise and at present has reopened the gates to Paradise. We come to know the triad of God's image of action: the Logos — the essential Light of God, and the Tree of Life — His Wisdom and Love. These three pillars serve as the foundation of the Church of Salvation and Deification. The examples of God's appearance in the likeness of an Angel are so numerous and irrefutable that they give us every reason to consider the Angel of the Countenance of God to be an uncreated Angel, and the Logos Who has become incarnate, and in the real body of the Son of Man. Proceeding from these biblical facts, icon painters and theologians should pay special attention to the possibility of depicting the Angel of the Countenance of God in the following iconography: at the top of the icon — the incarnate hypostatic Son of God, Christ; then — the Angel of the Prosopon, the power and glory of Christ; the Logos Emmanuel on the breastplate of the Angel — Christ's prosoponic Name and the spermatic Logos of communion.

ICONOLOGICAL IMAGES OF THEOPHANIES

5
Iconological Images of Theophanies

MEMRAH-LOGOS-WORD-SPEECH

"In the beginning was the Memrah."[1]

In connection with our above discussion about the appearances of the biblical Angel of Jehovah, it is necessary to unfold the idea of the Logos in the religious and philosophical meaning that began to develop among the Jews in the biblical period, was later picked up by the Hellenistic tradition, and was finally adopted "bodily" by the theology of the Christian Church, and enshrined by the first seven Ecumenical Councils.

Logos (λόγος) is a term in Greek philosophy. It has many meanings and can be translated as "word," "meaning," "definition," while in the mystical sense it means "meaningful word," "ineffable beginning," and "seed of formed consciousness." The word "logos" can also be understood as "conceptual logical-numerical formedness," i.e., as a presence of "full consciousness" or "pure consciousness." "Logos is both the objectively given content, of which the mind must 'render an account,' and the 'accounting' activity of the mind itself, and, finally, the all-encompassing, meaningful order of being and consciousness. Logos is the antithesis of everything that is unaccountable and non-verbal, unresponsive and irresponsible, and senseless and formless in the world and in man."[2] As we can see, the meaning of the term "logos" is much deeper and broader than its modern interpretation used in many translations of the Scripture as "word." Archimandrite Cyprian (Kern) says,

> The fact that *logos* extends beyond the term "word" to also mean "reason" and "meaning" is evidenced by extracts from the Holy Fathers who discuss the "seminal *logoi*" of the creation. New Testament expert Mitrofan

---

1 *Targum* to John 1:1.
2 Sergei Averintsev, *The Encyclopedic Dictionary*.

Muretov, a professor at the Moscow Theological Academy, in his article "On the Suggested Preparation of the Slavonic-Russian Version of the New Testament," suggests that the Slavonic-Russian "Word" be replaced by the original *Logos* and accompanied by the word-for-word translation "Reason-Word" in the translation of the Prologue to the Gospel according to St. John. According to the professor, this replacement is necessitated by the fact that by *Logos* the Evangelist means both "reason" and "word." In addition, the Slavonic-Russian version in verse 2 retains the masculine pronoun *sey* for "this" rather than the gender-neutral pronoun *sye* or *siye* for "this"; whereas the Russian "Word" is gender-neutral while the Greek *Logos* is masculine. Even left untranslated, the Greek *logos* expresses much more fully its hidden meaning than the limited "word" or, as in the quoted academic translations of the Holy Fathers, "law."[3]

Taking into account the increasing impoverishment of the sense and meaning of words caused by the huge flow of modern information, the simplicity of this translation becomes especially obvious.

The Word of God is always Speech (in action), because God does not utter empty or inactive "words." For Philo of Alexandria, Logos is the "image of God." St. John of Damascus adds: "God, although invisible by nature, becomes visible through His *operations*, ... for there never was a time when God the Word (*Logos*) was not."[4] "The concept of Logos became part of the teachings of Judaism and (*via Greece*) Christianity, where it was reinterpreted as the *Word* of the personal and 'living' God who with this Word summoned (*spoke through the prophets*) things and called them forth out of nonbeing."[5]

But let us go back to more ancient times. The Jewish synonym for "Logos," Memrah (Aramaic: מימרא; Hebrew: מאמר, "Maamar"), is often used in the Targums (Chaldean paraphrases), Aramaic translations of the Bible that are part of the traditional Jewish literature

---

3 Archimandrite Cyprian (Kern), *The Anthropology of St. Gregory Palamas.*
4 *An Exact Exposition of the Orthodox Faith.*
5 *The Philosophical Encyclopedic Dictionary.*

Iconological Images of Theophanies

dating back to the time of the Second Temple. Ancient translations of the Holy Scripture into Aramaic (fourth century BC to the first three centuries AD) arose in connection with the general spread of this colloquial language related to Hebrew. The Jews returning from the Babylonian Captivity found it difficult to understand the holy Old Testament books written in Hebrew. This necessitated rendering the Scripture into forms more comprehensible to common believers, which helped the Targums to become more authoritative. According to researchers, Christ himself often spoke Aramaic understandable to common people. "The principal objective was to have the Targum to conform as closely as possible to the original text, and the grammatical structure of the Hebrew was thus followed closely. Yet there are numerous exceptions where the Targum does not adhere to the original."[6] The main idea guiding the Targumists was not only to exactly preserve the sacred text, but also to achieve the highest possible readability. "The parts whose literal translation, in the opinion of the translator, is not acceptable (especially the parts containing anthropomorphic images of God), are described allegorically or paraphrased,"[7] yet strictly adhere to the biblical canon. Therefore, the Targums contain a special concept focusing on Theophanies in Their connection with the doctrine of the Logos-Memrah.

The meaning attributed to the concept of "Memrah" in these interpretations is somewhat different from the interpretation of "Logos" as "World Reason" in Ancient Greek philosophy. In the Targums, "Memrah" also meant "speech," i.e., a manifested active word as a dynamic and always acting basis of the creative *"beginning"* ("In the *beginning* was the Word"), and even at that time, in its latest religious interpretation, referred not to the Cosmos, but to the Divinity — the "image of action" of God. "In addition, Memrah is introduced instead of God only when the Divinity is directly manifested in the world."[8] The Word of God was an acting speech when God spoke to the patriarchs and prophets. Sometimes Memrah becomes a revelation

---

6   *The Jewish Encyclopedia.*
7   Ibid.
8   Archpriest Dmitry Leskin, *Metaphysics of the Word and Name in Russian Religious and Philosophical Thought.*

of a visible "image," for example, in the appearances of one or three Angels to Abraham or Jacob. In this regard, an interesting question may arise: "Does God really have three Logoi?" No. God has one essential Logos, but the Logos itself, being the inapproachable and purest Light, is revealed in two intelligible images — Sophia and Agape, or as one Angel — the general image of Agaposophia. This is the trinitarian symbolism of all "beginnings" of the origin of life.

God is personified through His Memrah in the power of Revelation. For example, the Targum Neofiti (first–second centuries AD) to Genesis 1:1 says, "In the beginning, with Wisdom, the Memrah of the Lord created and perfected the heavens and the earth." Or, "Thy almighty Memrah leapt down from heaven out of *Thy royal throne*" (Wis 18:15).

> As an ancient interpretation of the Scripture, the Targum has a quite definite place in the study of the Bible, and the public reading of the text along with the Targum during the divine service is an ancient institution, dating back to the Second Temple, established by Ezra. This tradition has survived to the present day among Yemenite Jews.[9]

According to Professor Santala, there is the Rabbis' way of grading the old writings according to their source value:

> "The Old Testament leads to the Targums, the Targums lead to the Mishnah, the Mishnah to the Talmud, and so on" (*Sifrei Shoftim, piska* 160a). Proceeding in this way the Targums give earlier information on the Rabbis' exegesis than even the Mishnah, the oldest part of the Talmud. Therefore, from the point of view of our subject, it is worthwhile familiarizing ourselves with these roots of our Christian faith which are concealed in the Targums.[10]

The most authoritative Targums are the Targum Onkelos to the Pentateuch, Targum Jonathan to the Prophets, and the Targum of Joseph the Blind. They usually used two main Targums to the Pentateuch:

---

9 *The Jewish Encyclopedia.*
10 Santala, *Messiah in the Old Testament.*

Iconological Images of Theophanies

the Targum Onkelos (used in the Babylonian rabbinical schools) and the Targum Yerushalmi (the Palestinian Targum). There are also less authoritative translations. Generally accepted in the third Christian century, the Targum to the Prophets was read in synagogues after the Pentateuch. Showing Syriac characteristics, the Targum to Proverbs was adopted by Syrian Christians: for example, St. Isaac of Syria used this Targum's term "Shekinah" in his writings, speaking of the glory and power of God.

The Aramaic word "Memrah" (or "Mimrah") comes from the Semitic root in the verb "to speak" and means "word." In the texts where the Name of God, Elohim, occurs with the verb in the plural as "God's actions" in His manifestations, the translators used the word Memrah. In the Targum Yerushalmi, for instance, the Angel of Jehovah who appears to Abraham is called "the Memrah of the Lord" (Gen 22:8). The Targum Onkelos paraphrases Jacob's words (Gen 28:20) as follows: "If the Memrah of the Lord will be my help... the Memrah of the Lord shall be my God," with some difference from the King James version: "If God will be with me... then shall the Lord be my God." Or, while the Masoretic text reads, "And Moses brought forth the people out of the camp to meet God" (Ex 19:17), the Targum reads that "Moses brought the people out of the camp to meet the Memrah of the Lord."

Quite often "Lord" is substituted by "Memrah" in the translations of Psalm 118: "the Memrah of the Lord will help me," etc. According to Targum researchers, this word is very often used in the Scripture. The Mimra concept associated with God and His manifestations appears 596 times in the Targums, but not once in the Talmud. The Targum Onkelos uses this word 179 times, the Targum Yerushalmi 99 times, and the Targum Jonathan 321 times. Over half of these references to the Mimra approach it as if it were "personified." Taking into consideration that Christianity was born in a Jewish environment, there is a genetic link between the Old Testament Memrah and the New Testament Logos, the only difference being that the Revelations in the New Testament are no longer noetic appearances of the Logos; but those of the incarnate Logos Who already "conversed with men." This boundary separating the "old" and the "new" was drawn in the

THE ANGEL OF THE COUNTENANCE OF GOD

Prologue to the Gospel according to St. John: "In the beginning was the Logos, and the Logos was to God, and the Logos was God" (in the Church Slavonic version and other ancient translations). So, if the Logos was *to* God in the *beginning*, in the oeconomy of the Revelation the Logos is already addressed *to* the chosen people.

In the Targum, the Memrah figures constantly as the manifestation of the divine power, or as God's messenger in place of God Himself, wherever the predicate is not in conformity with the dignity, or the spirituality, of the Deity. For example, "the Memrah," instead of "the Lord," is "the consuming fire";[11] therefore, the Targum attributes "flame" to God's Prosopon rather than God Himself. "And also Deuteronomy 33:27, 'The eternal God is your refuge, and underneath are the everlasting arms,' is interpreted by the Targum as, 'these arms are the Mimra, through whom the world was created' (*Targum Onkelos*)."[12]

"Like the Shekinah, the Memrah is accordingly the manifestation of God. 'The Memrah brings Israel nigh unto God and sits on His throne receiving the prayers of Israel.'"[13] In this connection, it is interesting to compare the description of the Shekinah with the Orthodox iconography of Sophia sitting on a throne in the likeness of a royal Angel. This brings to mind again: "Obey My Messenger [*Angel*], for My name is in Him"; "My Shekinah [*Angel*] I shall put among you, My Memrah [*the Logos, God's Name*] shall be unto you for a redeeming *Deity*, and you shall be unto My Name a holy people."[14] As we can see from this text, the Shekinah and the Memrah are not completely identical: the Shekinah refers to the general essential Image in God's actions, while the Memrah refers to the named Speech, to God's Name. Yet the divine synergy of both terms is mystically expressed holistically as an "image-kind" and a "word-speech" of Theophanies, which, in the unity of them both, Christians profess in the physical appearance of Jesus Christ, and, according to Paul the Apostle, He "is the Image [and the Logos] of the invisible God." Peter the Apostle

---

11　*Targum to Deuteronomy* 9:3.
12　Santala, *Messiah in the Old Testament*.
13　*The Jewish Encyclopedia*.
14　*Targum Yerushalmi to Leviticus* 22:12.

Iconological Images of Theophanies

reminds us, "ye are... a royal priesthood" (1 Pet 2:9), because you sacramentally commune with the Logos, i.e., God's divine Speech (command) and the Son's Divinity.

Philo of Alexandria developed, as it is said, a "semi-Jewish" logos philosophy, which he did on the basis of ancient Greek philosophy and using Jewish word-for-word traditions, especially translations of the Targums. "Philo's 'divine thought,' 'the image' and 'first-born son' of God, 'the archpriest,' 'intercessor,' and 'paraclete' of humanity, the 'archetype of man'... paved the way for the Christian conceptions of the Incarnation."[15] While the Neoplatonic Logos is a created "mediator" between God and the world, the biblical Memrah represents an inseparable yet discrete unity of the logos Speech and God Himself. Therefore, all God's appearances to people, including the appearances of the logos Angel and God's Memrah, look like real Revelation images rather than figurative or metaphorical mythological images. The biblical Memrah is not a representative of the noetic or cosmic world, but a special ontological symbol of God's presence in these worlds. Eternally destined for the Incarnation, the Logos repeatedly appeared in an angelic form in a flame of fire or in a cloud, but then appeared in the real image of the Son of Man as had been prophetically foretold by Daniel: "Behold, one like the Son of Man came with the [*Light*] clouds of heaven, and came to the Ancient of Days, and they brought him near before Him" (Dan 7:13). Only God's energy triad—Logos, Sophia, and Agape—are God's uncreated and direct messengers, and this idea immediately returns our mind to the notion "the Angel of the Countenance of God." The thought of the existence of some intermediate beings, demigods-demihumans, as was the case in the Greek and other mythologies, is incompatible with the general spirit of the Scripture, which is confirmed by some Jewish scholars, "because as soon as this idea arises, the line between God and his creation becomes obliterated and God loses His transcendence."[16]

God's "stepping out" of His inapproachability through His essential Light gains a new significance, because, according to Isaiah, God *creates* darkness (*matter, pigments*), but forms the light (cf. Is 45:7),

---

15 *The Jewish Encyclopedia.*
16 Yosef Ben Shlomo, *The Jewish Encyclopedia.*

THE ANGEL OF THE COUNTENANCE OF GOD

creating conditions for our iconographic seeing of God. Visible as icons of the Theophany, *various images of the unapproachable Light* are the actions of the supreme Speech, which "going over land and sea" burns "human hearts"[17] in the prophets. Therefore, the term "Memrah" should be understood not only as a "word-in-itself," but also as the Word that mystically forms God's *action* in His Revelation. This can be exemplified by the *diversely* recurring biblical formula: "And God *said*," "and *it was so*." "Said" is the form of emergence of "light," while "*it was so*" is the form of the emergence of "life." The Gospel of John expresses the connecting fullness of Christ's existence in the direct combination "*Light*—Logos, Life—Image": "In Him was *life*; and the life was the *light* of men" (Jn 1:4–5).

As the Memrah concept, after Philo of Alexandria, virtually merged together with the Logos in New Testament theology, Jewish interpreters consciously stopped using it; identifying it first with Michael the Archangel and then with the Archangel Metatron—the Prince of the World, who assumed leadership after Moses on Israel's path to salvation. Alternatively, they used more general terms such as "glory" and "will." As is known, the Talmud was written around the second to the fifth centuries AD, that is, when Christianity already existed as a separate religion. And as a reaction to Christianity's claim to replace Judaism, Talmudists began to avoid anything that could somehow associate them with the new faith: therefore, the term "Memrah" was avoided, although it was not deleted from the Targums. "The absence of 'Mimrah' from the Talmud may be a reaction to the first Christians' interpretation of it as indicating Jesus."[18] So, the much later (fourth century AD) Midrash (from the Hebrew verb "to study," an in-depth exposition of the Holy Scripture) Tanchuma, talking about the death of Moses, reads, "And God addressed the ministering angels, and He called Metatron and said to him, I give you My name instead of your name." Here, we can surely notice an obvious diminishment of the Memrah, having a divine origin, to the position of the greatest, yet created, Angel who is given a Name consistent with the Divine. By contrast, the Targums show a full

---

17 Alexander Pushkin, *The Prophet*.
18 Santala, *Messiah in the Old Testament*.

Iconological Images of Theophanies

correspondence between the Memrah and the uncreated Angel, the significance of which is complemented by the identity with the Christian Theophanic Logos. The Midrash Abkir comments on God's words about the Angel, but this commentary absolutely misinterprets God's Name (Ex 23:20). Avoiding identifying the Memrah with the Lord, it interprets the texts in an entirely different sense than that intended in the Scripture: "If you were worthy, I would have led you Myself, but because of your sin I will send you My messenger, the angel Metatron, who bears My name. Beware of opposing him, because he is only a messenger and *is not empowered* (?) to forgive sins as I am." This quotation from the Talmud clearly misrepresents the essence of the original biblical texts, because the Angel here is, firstly, created and, secondly, lacks the ability to forgive sins. The Talmud describes the angel Metatron as a special and exalted personality, a high Messenger, but the text is ubiquitously filled with the Neoplatonic idea of this angel being *created*, even though "before all ages." This idea provided the basis for the Arian heresy and harassed the Christian Church for many decades until it was condemned by the Ecumenical Council. Another late Jewish mystical book, the Book of Enoch (not earlier than the second to the fifth centuries AD), gives a detailed description of Enoch's transformation into Metatron. In the haggadic literature, Metatron is moved further away from the essence of the biblical worldview, and the topic of the uncreated Logos becomes increasingly vague and cosmological, acquiring an imprint of the late Gnostic influence. The Midrash commentaries also run counter to the Christian interpretation of the Trinity, considering the vision of Abraham to be one of created beings: "the main of the three angels was Michael, and was called the Lord, and the angels Gabriel and Raphael were on each side of him." With this explanation, the vision to Abraham is not a Theophany at all, which means that it is of no saving importance. And here is another commentary—from the Targum Yerushalmi by Rabbi Yonatan ben Uziel—on Abraham's words, "My Lord, if now I have found favor in Thy sight, pass not away, I pray Thee, from Thy servant" (Gen 18:3): "The Lord mentioned in this verse is the Word of the Lord, and it was He Who rained fire and brimstone upon Sodom and Gomorrah."

Unfortunately, some Christians are still under the influence of "logical" Judaism and endorse false views, without understanding the entire mystical depth of the biblical personification of the Trinity. Proceeding from this point of view, the direct icon of the Most Holy Trinity does not exist — it is possible only indirectly as an "allegorical" depiction of created Angels. This rectilinear thinking is certainly at variance with the iconology of "symbolic realism," the biblical truth, and the entire structure of liturgical theology of the Christian Church, and will lead to a revival of iconoclasm. However, the Christian liturgical texts precisely determine the nature of the Theophany to Abraham: "Blessed Abraham, you saw Them, and received the Godhead, both *one* and *three*."

To theologically understand God's Logos, contemplated and communed in the identity with the name of Jesus Christ, is to mystically perceive the formula: "For THINE is the *Kingdom*, and the *Power*, and the *Glory*." The essential names of the Deity belong to the whole Trinity. In biblical history, these names are gradually and liturgically revealed in the *figurative Energies* of the creative Logos:

In the Shekinah, as the Presence and the Place of Habitation of God's Logos; the Father's volitional, creative, and dispensational power (a temple, a church, Man, an angel);

In Sophia, as the Wisdom of God's Logos; the providential sense; the doctrinal and evangelical power of the Son, Christ (laws, covenants, canons);

In Agape, as the Love of God's Logos — the sacrificial, all-fulfilling, and life-giving power of the Holy Spirit (sacramental actions, sacraments, theological contemplations [Theoria], and deification).

Belonging to the Logos and the whole Trinity, these uncreated energies are the thrice-radiant gracious Gifts and Fruits of the Tree of Life that are bestowed again to Man by Christ the Savior.

THE SON OF MAN

> Since in sacred Scripture we find many things said symbolically of God as if He had a body, one should know that since we are men clothed in this gross flesh, we are unable to think or speak of the divine, lofty, and

Iconological Images of Theophanies

immaterial [noetic] operations of the Godhead unless we have recourse to images, types, and symbols that correspond to our own nature.[19]

The biblical mystery of the Shekinah, Sophia, and Agape is holistically revealed to us in the name of some special person, whom the Prophet Daniel, in his noetic vision, refers to as "the Son of Man." The identity of this "Son of Man" is a profound anthropological mystery lifting our minds to vertiginous theological heights. The Logos was always addressed *to* God, and God was the Logos. In addition, God repeatedly sent His Logos to the physical world, and the Logos was God's multiform voice addressed to the world until He became God-Man. In the Gospel, Jesus repeatedly says that He was sent by His Father to *fulfill* His will.

Daniel saw the Son of Man, "clothed with a cloud of the Shekinah," who was given the kingdom, the power, and the glory even before His Incarnation on earth. The Son of God descended upon earth in the Logos and the luminous Shekinah and was born of the Virgin Mary, and *became man*, visibly fulfilling this prophecy about Him as the Son of Man. Jesus Christ called Himself so because the prophecy about the coming of the Messiah was fulfilled: "And no man hath ascended up to heaven, but he that came down from heaven, even the Son of Man which is in heaven" (Jn 3:13), "When the Son of Man shall sit in the throne of his glory [*Shekhina*]" (Mt 19:28), and "the high priest asked Him, and said unto Him, Art thou the Christ? And Jesus said, I am: and ye shall see the Son of Man sitting on the right hand of power, and coming in the [*mystical*] clouds of heaven" (Mk 14:62). Hearing the name "the Son of Man," the Pharisees were afraid. They knew that this name, according to Daniel's prophecies, belonged to the King, clothed in God's Shekinah, who would restore the kingdom of Israel, but they did not recognize the Son of Man in the form of a servant who came to suffer and then save mankind. Many Jews considered Jesus to be a powerful prophet, but they did not associate Him with Daniel's vision, because otherwise they would have to admit that the Logos of God became the Messiah in the

---

19 St. John of Damascus, *An Exact Exposition of the Orthodox Faith*.

person of Jesus. The first person who, with the power of the new age, confirmed Daniel's vision in his own vision was St. Stephen, the First Martyr: "Behold, I see the heavens opened, and the Son of Man standing on the right hand of God" (Acts 7:56). With regard to Daniel's vision, John the Apostle says, "And behold a *white cloud*, and upon the cloud one sat like unto the Son of Man" (Rev 14:14). From the times of Abraham and Moses to the Transfiguration and the Ascension of Christ, the Scripture mentions the mysterious "Shekinah cloud" — the mystical throne of the Logos who physically became the Son of Man.

The iconology of Theophanies leads to the idea that man was created after the image of the Son of Man seen by the prophets with their spiritual eyes, and after the *image* and *likeness* of the Logos. Both these concepts coincide in Jesus Christ as the God-Man. The firstborn who entered the kingdom of God with the body of a perfect man — this is the purpose of the chosen people who profess the religion of Deification in Christ. As the above-mentioned pertains to iconology, we should also focus on the iconography of the Theophanies under discussion, because They should be conveyed visually through the icon approved by the fathers as "theology in color." Over the history of icon painting, hundreds of iconographies of Sophia and the creative Wisdom of Christ have been created. However, there are still no icons of the Shekinah or Agape, which would mystically connect the Son of Man, after the images of Theophanies, with the Father and the Holy Spirit. In addition, no general iconography of the Angel of the Countenance of God has been developed either.

NAMES OF GOD

6
Names of God

Only through its name does the reality reveal itself to any reasonable eye and makes it possible to understand itself as compared with everything else. Only when the reality starts talking does there emerge a fundamental possibility for its own objective formation and for making it understood and learnt by whomever and whatever.... To start talking means not only to exist in reality and have some certain image, but also to send its image outward, actively using its expression for one or another external purpose.[1]

TO NOT ONLY UNDERSTAND THE MEANING of Theophanies in the biblical history and virtually feel Their vital force, but also to discover the continuous biblical evolution of iconological images of Revelation, it is necessary to practice distinguishing between "where," "when," and "who" acts in Them. Although Theophanies can be observed in special historical periods in the "heyday" of religion, after which they somehow "discontinue," the beneficial power of their images remains for centuries and holds its mystical vitality for both angels and the human race. The Son of God was born of the Virgin Mary once in the history of mankind, but mystically His "logos spermatikos" Emmanuel *is* constantly *born* in the "veils" of Man's inner faith. This is exactly how Christians greet each other at Christmas: "Christ is born." They do not say "was born," because that would only sound like a memory of two thousand years ago. They say "is born," because Christ *is* eternally *born* and grows in every Christian soul, in the same way as He *is* hypostatically *born* in the bosom of His Father. The biblical events are lost in the mists of time, but their essence is of unfading significance for religious life, forming the basis for the perception of future Theophanies. The

---

1   Aleksei Losev, *Thing and Name.*

beneficial power of Theophany, in Its various forms, can be revived by activating faith, because the knowledge of Theophanies is embedded in the mind of every person. In this connection, all people who pray and meditate upon the enlightenment and transfiguration of their souls should focus on God's names.

The names of God are indeed diverse, but they differ in the nature rather than the essence of Revelation images. Through its dogmas and iconology, mystical theology reveals to us the ability to see and discern in God:

1. *essence elements*, as a "mode of existence" of the Trihypostatic God;

2. *energy elements*, the Divinity, as an "image of action" in the energies of the Trinity's Prosopon.

"God's life-giving actions in the world are God Himself, which excludes *separation*, but does not eliminate *distinction*."[2] Accordingly, God's diverse names fall into two categories:

a. essential, logos-related, and hypostatized names (such as "the Father, the Son, and the Holy Spirit");

b. prosoponic, "homoiousian," figurative, and symbolic names (such as "the Logos Emmanuel"),

For example, the biblical name "Yahweh (Jehovah)" — "I am the Existing One" — is the name affirming the essential principle of faith in the Living and Hypostatic God, because "the Existing One" is higher and precedes the notion of "essence." The names that help reveal perfect faith and approach the Divinity of God — such as "Adonai," "Elohim," "Sophia," etc. — are prosoponic names, because they perform acts and *form a mystical sphere* of faith with their energies, rather than "designating" something. These names are essential for prayers, which is why it is equally important to understand them and distinguish between the *existing* God and the cosmic "god" of created elements.

A name is a formula, the essence of one or another action that fixes and stabilizes faith. A correct name acting, like life, cannot have any gap between the *actor* and the *action*. The Existing One is mystically imprinted in the image of action, and this iconographic imprint can really be experienced and known in physical space and time. In the

---

2   Georges Florovsky, *Dogma and History*.

fourteenth century, the Church's previous mystical experience resulted in the establishment of a hesychastic tradition of distinction: God is indescribable, while the Deity (by energy types) is iconographically depictable.

The Divinity of God, in which all conceivable names pour out from the essential, unique, and enhypostatic Name—the Trinity's Logos—has an "iconological" nature of revelation, and God becomes visible in them. For example, we can, without any distortion, paraphrase Exodus 23:20–23 as follows: "Obey the Angel of My *Divinity*, in whom my Name, My hidden Logos, is." This verse reveals not even two, but four possible meanings of Theophany:

1. "Angel"—God's revealed *Eidos*; *energy*, which acts and forms the symbolic hieroglyph of life;

2. "Person," Divinity, Prosopon—God's revealed power (*dynamis*), Idea, which opens the conceptual direction of faith;

3. "Name"—the profound *Logos*, "atomic seed," "spermatikos," which is bestowed in the Eucharist for communion and clothed in the Light of Life;

4. "Speaker Himself"—"I" and "My"—so speaks the Lord, the speaking God of Revelation.

We recognize and believe that various forms of Theophany are manifestations of God Himself, but we see and know Him through the ICON of Revelations rather than by essence.

The practice of strong and deep faith is about prayerfully invoking the Name of God. Faith itself is not disciplined, because it is the result of devotional "burning," i.e., a *reasonable movement* of the discursive mind toward God, and in this process faith becomes a flame, "liquid gold," in the same way as water turns into the fiery substance of wine. In this "spirit-to-spirit" flame, God's Revelation is iconographically depicted and, like a visible icon, contemplated and understood by believers. Critics who prohibit the iconographic depiction of the Lord of Sabaoth should, finally, realize that the icon, as a method of symbolic realism, makes it possible to depict not only "persons," but also the theological ideas of Theophany. Icons cannot be deprived of their legitimate rights to reveal the trinitarian meaning of salvation through images. This is the true *educational* meaning of icons, about which the Church Fathers said, "If they ask you about the meaning of Christianity, show them an icon."[3] Icons should serve not only as an illustrative example of depiction of some or other Christian persons, but also as a dogmatic confession and liturgical action of God's dispensation.

The examples of icons that may find their future iconographic development are as follows:

- An icon of the *Logos* in accordance with the iconography of Jesus Christ after the Incarnation, and an icon of the Logos, Lamb, and Youth Emmanuel in accordance with the eucharistic canon — the Bridegroom of the Church;
- An icon of the *Shekinah*, the radiant and animate Tabernacle, the Temple and Place-Throne, the Presence of God, which is symbolized by the order of eight-winged ophanim of the Celestial Hierarchy;
- An icon of *Sophia*, the regal Virgin and the Angel of Christ's Wisdom, which symbolically expresses its mystical actions and *gifts* through the order of many-eyed six-winged cherubim;
- An icon of *Agape*, the Divine Love, iconographically depicted in a fiery form as the regal Virgin and the Angel of Love in the actions and *fruits* of the life-giving Holy Spirit, which is symbolized by the order of fiery seraphim of the Celestial Hierarchy.

To summarize, we can assume that all these are the names of the Miraculous Angel that represent luminous personifications of the creative energies of the essential and only Name — the Trinity's Logos, symbolically reflecting the idea: "Holy" — three, but one Lord of Sabaoth, the iconographic Image of the Trinity.

The essential and hypostatic names of God express the Jewish concept of God's nature, or God's existence, as well as His attitude toward his chosen people, in the context of which they may change. Faith is a dynamic concept pertaining to the life forms of relations with God. Therefore, for example, a "name" discovered in ancient times acquires over time, in the process of the transformation of mythology into

---

3   John of Damascus.

religion, a new meaning for believers. A Divine Name is used as an equivalent to such concepts as God's Presence, Power, Kingdom, or Glory. According to the Talmud, Abraham was the first to recognize God's power over the world and, therefore, called Him the *Lord*, as distinguished from the prior generalized name "God." We should see the ontological difference between these names, because "God" is a generally valid name, while "the Lord" is a personal name that is directly related to a believer's improvement of life. Almost all people are believers to a greater or lesser extent, but not every believer can call God "the Lord," but only those who are willing "in the Spirit" to recognize His authority over them and do His will. It is said that "the devils also believe, and tremble" (Jas 2:19), but they do not do His Will at all and, although they listen to God, they are afraid to call Him "the Lord."

According to Midrash Shemot Rabbah 3:6, the variety of God's names is interpreted as follows:

> God said to Moses: You wish to know My name. Well, I am called *according to My work*: sometimes I am called El Shaddai, El Tsevaot, Elohim, Adonai. When I am judging created beings, I am called Elohim, and when I am waging war against the wicked, I am called El Tsevaot. When I suspend judgment for a man's sins, I am called El Shaddai, and when I act mercifully towards My world, I am called Adonai (*the Lord*).

Therefore, the prayer "Lord, have mercy" features this, as it were, intimate Name of God, rather than any other name. Considering the theme of "names" in terms of iconology, we realize that God iconographically depicts Himself through prosoponic energies, which "conceal" His spermatic life-giving Name, and it is also important that God's Image is not exhausted in any of His Names. This gives reasons to assert that the iconography of God's names may significantly extend beyond the limits set by the fanaticism of onomatoclasts (therefore, secret iconoclasts) and by the straightforward logic of some art critics.

The development of religious consciousness results in a more extensive differentiation of God's names, because gods in pagan mythology were given numerous names in accordance with their attributes. To some extent, this situation persisted in the Jewish tradition too, in terms of verbal "utterance" rather than "depiction" of God's name. Christianity gave a new understanding of God's Name, characterizing not only His properties, but also His existence as a special plane of existence of the Trinity. Theology reveals to us proper names that determine hypostatic differences: the Father, the Son, and the Holy Spirit, which is consistent with monotheism, because they are the names of the three Hypostases as the "mode of existence" of one God. At the end of the age, however, according to the Book of Revelation, *one* Name of God and the new name of Christ will be revealed to victorious believers.

Born in the heart of Israel, religious thought continued to develop, and God's Names, already cleared of any pagan impurities and gross anthropomorphisms by the Talmudic period, became exceptionally universal and monotheistic. So, "seventy names of God are manifest, while all the other ones are secret."[4] The Christian tradition gives evidence that it is possible to "see God," but the important thing about this "mental gymnastics" of the Talmud is that God's Names are *manifest*, i.e., *depictable*, because, like some kind of "seed," they can *form* all sorts of iconographic Theophanies *in the Light*. An example of one of these biblical "*manifest*" prosoponic names is "the Lord of Sabaoth" — the Lord of creative powers that form the oeconomy of salvation and deification of created beings. However, as a "consubstantial Mode of Existence of the Trinity," His name will be among hypostatic names.

God's manifest Names (or *prosoponic Names*, as we call them) imply precise philosophical and dogmatic definitions. They are comprehended through both literary "words" and visual "images," corresponding to and following the same conceptual series of contemplative theology and practical iconology. All these names are specifically characterized by their "deverbal" origin as an "image in action" and, therefore, indicate the ontological properties and attributes of God's Life rather than the Theophanic essence itself.

On the other hand, there are *secret hypostatic* names of God — the Father, the Son, and the Holy Spirit, which are not depictable, because

---

4 *The Alphabet of Rabbi Akiba.*

Names of God

they only indicate the distinctions (relations) or origin of the Hypostases within the Trinity. The only exception is the name of the incarnate Son — the God-Man who became the Christ, because, according to Paul the Apostle, He is the "hypostatically visible *image* of the invisible God." The secret names are only of *intelligible*, contemplative, and purely theological nature. They are "spatially" unapproachable names that can be comprehended in a state of *ekstasis* directly through sublime prayer experience. This explains why the Church forbids the emergence of mental "images" during prayers to prevent worshipers' minds from descending to mundane feelings. The secret names "have no roots in any verb and denote precisely the essence of the eternal Creator Himself, the only independent entity."[5] However, both types of names are of equal importance for "dogmatic faith" and "existential faith." The God of Israel is the Living God, so neither the philosophical concept of "pure existence," nor the mythology of false pagan gods who are alive only by description yet dead by essence, is typical of developed Bible-based thought. The ancient Jews are characterized by a much more integral and symbolic perception of the world than modern people. Professor (at the Kiev Theological Academy) Mikhail N. Skaballanovich, in his largely remarkable commencement address of 1911, explains as follows:

> The language of the Jews and of classical antiquity was more lively and specific.... The Jews equally applied the word "spirit" to the wind, a person's breathing and soul, and the Spirit of God. Even though applied to such different phenomena, this word had the same meaning, not literal in some cases or figurative in other ones as compared with its modern usage, because the ancient Jews found in all these phenomena something so homogeneous that it should be denoted by the same word as essentially the same thing. They found no essential reason to use two different words for the breath of wind vivifying the environment and the source animating Man and the world.... Unlike modern people, ancient people did not distinguish between

---

5 *The Jewish Encyclopedia.*

corporeal and spiritual things, as if the biblical writers' concept of the spirit was not as abstract as it is nowadays.... Equally specific, for example, is the Book of Proverbs about the Wisdom of God: it does not significantly distinguish between the Wisdom with which God created the world and the one that can be heard in songs and in conversations on streets and squares (Prov 1:20), making it possible to feel this apparently so unattainable "wisdom" as vividly as every reality in the world. The analogy between visible and invisible things was so clear and essential that the present gap between them in our understanding would have been unthinkable in those days.[6]

M. Skaballanovich further explains that the Hebrew language had no general polysemantic words having such long-lost root meanings as "God," "Deus," "θεός," so God was always named in accordance with aspects revealed through certain actions: Elohim or El, or Yahweh, or Adonai, or Shaddai. At present, we make up for this poverty using such words as "sky," "Providence," etc. Therefore, "theology, which ought to go into the iconology of 'images,' should give up abstraction and turn to the figurativeness and concreteness of the ancient thought and language."[7]

HYPOSTATIC NAMES OF GOD

There is a separate category of God's Names that do not exist in accordance with internal nature as, for example, such *hypostatic* names as the FATHER, the SON, and the HOLY SPIRIT do. They are *enhypostatized* names in accordance with God's mode of existence in terms of dispensation of the world.

JEHOVAH-YAHWEH—the so-called Tetragrammaton (יהוה, YHWH), i.e., "four-letter word"—is a particularly characteristic name of the God of Israel. It occurs 6,823 times in the Bible. According to Exodus 6:2–3, this Name was not known to the patriarchs: "I am the Lord (*Jehovah*): And I appeared unto Abraham, unto Isaac, and unto

---

6 *On Symbolic Theology*, published in *The Works* by the Kiev Theological Academy, November 1911, pp. 538–40.
7 As quoted by Archimandrite Cyprian from *Anthropology of Palamas*.

Names of God

Jacob, by the name of God Almighty (*El-Shaddai*), but by My name Jehovah (*the Lord*) was I not known to them." This example shows the difference in the names: "the Almighty" and all similar names describing God's properties are prosoponic iconological names. To Moses, however, God revealed His hypostatic and essential name to show "some such mark of true Godhead as this, that we know nothing else of God but this one thing, that He is."[8] This Name, despite its apparent simplicity, has many meanings. According to Bishop Hilarion:

> The Hebrew expression 'אֶהְיֶה אֲשֶׁר אֶהְיֶה' (*ehyeh asher ehyeh*), translated into the Septuagint Greek as ἐγώ εἰμι ὁ ὤν (*ego eimi ho ohn*), literally means "I Am that I Am." This statement may be perceived as a formula indicating that the speaker is reluctant to answer the question directly. In other words, this can be understood not as God's revelation of His personal name, but as an indication that human language has no word that would serve as God's "name" in the Jewish understanding — i.e., as a comprehensive symbol fully characterizing its bearer. God's answer to Moses's question about the name of God has the same meaning as the refusal of the Miraculous Angel to give his name to Jacob. It is impossible to unequivocally establish the original meaning of the name "Jehovah," and all the scientific interpretations of its etymology are no more than hypotheses.[9]

This Name combines three forms of the verb "to be." This makes it possible to translate It as "The One Who Was, Is, and Will Be, or The One Who Gave, Gives, and Will Give Existence to the whole world, i.e., the Source of Existence."[10] This gives rise to the formula of monotheistic faith: we believe in God who Lives and manifests His Life in His Revelation.

Among all the names of God, the Tetragrammaton is distinguished by its special holiness and importance. "The life at Solomon's Temple is focused on honoring the name of God: the Temple is called after

---

8   Gregory of Nyssa, *Against Eunomius*.
9   Hilarion (Alfeyev), *Sacred Mystery of the Church*.
10 Dmitry Shchedrovitsky, *The Introduction to the Old Testament. The Book of Exodus*.

THE ANGEL OF THE COUNTENANCE OF GOD

the Lord's name; the Temple is where the Lord's name dwells; they come to the Temple having heard the Lord's name; and they profess the Lord's name in the Temple."[11] However, since the name was written only in consonants (YHWH), the exact literal pronunciation soon fell into disuse and the name became just an ideogram.

> Even the vowel marking for its four consonants is hypothetical. The fact is that after the Babylonian captivity, at least not later than the third century AD, the Jews out of reverence ceased to pronounce the sacred name Yahweh, which came to be perceived as God's proper name. This sacred name was pronounced only once a year, on the Day of Atonement (Yom Kippur), by the High Priest who entered the Holy of Holies. In all other cases, it was substituted by *Adonai* or other names, which, however, were not pronounced: even the combined name *Adonai Yahweh* (the Lord Yahweh) was read as *Adonai Elohim* (the Lord God). From the sixteenth century, in the West, they began to use the artificial vocalization *Yehowah* (Jehovah), based on putting the vowels from the name Adonai together with the consonants YHWH. Only as late as the middle of the nineteenth century, scientists showed that the tetragrammaton should be read as *Yahweh*.[12]

In addition, Christ, in the Book of Revelation, says that the literal pronunciation of the name of God of the Old Testament and the name of God the Son and the Logos will be given at His Second Coming before "those who overcome" and sit on the throne next to the Son of Man: "Him that overcometh will I make a pillar in the temple of my God, and . . . I will write upon him the *name of My God*, and the *name* of the city [*the New Paradise*] of My God, which is the new Jerusalem, which cometh down out of Heaven from My God: and I will write upon him *My new Name*" (Rev 3:12).

The Greek Septuagint and the Gospel invariably translate the name Jehovah as Κύριος. Interestingly, the word κύριος in the legal sense

---

11 Hilarion (Alfeyev), *Sacred Mystery of the Church*.
12 Ibid.

denotes a person who in court and other legal institutions represents someone having no rights or limited rights (for children that would be their father or guardian). So, this may be another reason why Christians seek intercession with the Name "Lord" in their prayers: "Lord, have mercy."

The hypostatic name not only is as sacred as God Himself, but also, in union with prosoponic names, has tremendous power and develops faith, making a person a victor over material darkness and a child of Light. According to the Talmud, the Ark of the Covenant was home to the Name of God, so the ancient Israelites carried the Ark into battle and, therefore, were confident of victory over their enemies. The relation between *hypostatic* and *prosoponic* names can be compared with that between "one" and "zero," but the depth and perfection of faith are perceived from a level where these numbers are combined ($1+0 = 10$), giving rise to fullness and a new height of mystically experienced faith. This involves a synergy of God's *mode of existence* and *image of action*, resulting in a possibility for Man to commune with the Divinity and come to be in the image and likeness of God. "Zero" is a state of *rest*, but it already gives life to "one": these are dynamics whose creative power elevates the inherently iconological human soul to the heights of hypostatic, theological, likeness. Adding zeroes to one, Man will have not ten initial states of faith, but a hundred, a thousand, and more opportunities that are similar to diverse dimensions of existence, with an increasing ability to see God and to know Him. This example may be too exaggerated, but it expresses the religious idea of compatibility of God's diverse Presence ("zero," because it is not hypostatic) and God Himself ("one" is hypostatic) in a single manifestation, which indicates the way of understanding the biblical uncreated and miraculous Angel of Jehovah.

EL is a name often translated as "God." Its exact origin, however, is not known. Probably, this word derives from the Hebrew root meaning "to be powerful," "to govern" and "to be ahead." As a common and general name for God, this word occurs in such languages as Hebrew, Assyrian, Phoenician, Aramaic, Arabic, and Ethiopian. In addition, El is part of such angelic names as Michael, Gabriel, etc. As the name of the God of Israel, El is used chiefly in poetry and

THE ANGEL OF THE COUNTENANCE OF GOD

prophetic discourse, and then usually with some epithet attached, as "a jealous yet merciful God." Other examples of its use with some attribute or epithet are: El-Bethel—the God of Bethel (Gen 31:13; 35:7), El-Olam—the Everlasting God (Gen 21:33), El-Roi—the God of Seeing (Gen 16:13), El-Elyon—the Most High God (Gen 14:18), El-Shaddai—the Almighty God (Gen 17:1), etc.

ELOHIM is the ancient name most often used in the Pentateuch for God as the Creator of and the Provider for the entire existing cosmos and its well-being.[13] In Hebrew, there are two related words for "God"—*El* (plural: *Elim*) and the comparatively rare *Eloah* (plural: *Elohim*). "However, the word 'Elohim' is always used with singular verb forms and with adjectives and pronouns in the singular, which, for monotheistic consciousness, brought plurality to logical unity."[14] According to some researchers, the plural form arose to express the high dignity and greatness of God, whose power by far exceeds that of any other gods which are also denoted as "el" in the Scripture. We can find the expression "the God of gods"—El-Elohim (Ps 50:1) or El-Elim (Dan 11:36) In the later Jewish literature, the name Elohim expresses the idea of God as "the universal and transcendent Lord."

ELYON ("the Most High God") occurs in combination with El, YHWH or Elohim, and also alone. It appears chiefly in poetic and later biblical passages.

SHADDAI ("Almighty") is derived from the Hebrew word meaning "Dominion" or from the Assyrian "shadu" meaning "mountain, hill." The Septuagint translates Shaddai as "Pantocrator." This name most often occurs in combination with "El," but in the Book of Job it is used independently. It is assumed that this is the name by which God was known to Abraham, Isaac, and Jacob.

ADONAI ("the Lord") occurs in the Bible as an independent name of God (in the appearance of the Trinity to Abraham). In addition, the Masoretes used it as a substitute for the word Jehovah while reading the Scripture aloud.

---

13 Archbishop Theophane (Vassily Bystrov), *The Tetragrammaton or the Divine Name of Yahweh in the Old Testament*.
14 Ibid.

Names of God

YAHWEH TSEVAOT—the Lord of Sabaoth, the Lord God of hosts, the angelic forces of Heaven. This name sometimes occurs in combination with "Adonai," which means "the Master Lord of Hosts." Most often, "the Lord of Sabaoth" is mentioned in the prophetic literature and in the Book of Revelation. Serving as a symbol of God's Presence in the midst of the armies of Israel, the Ark of the Covenant is called the Ark of the Lord of Sabaoth "that dwelleth between the cherubim" (2 Sam 6:2). The compound divine name "Lord of Sabaoth" has a special connection with the appearances of the Angel of the Countenance of God, as described in the Book of the Prophet Isaiah and in the Revelation of St. John the Divine. The angels glorify Him in the Trisagion Hymn: "Holy, Holy, Holy, is the Lord of Sabaoth: the whole heaven and earth are full of Thy glory." The liturgical meaning of this name occurring at the Eucharist service was particularly adopted by the New Testament, and some Christian Fathers (especially St. John of Damascus) interpret the name "Lord of Sabaoth" as the *uniform* Image of the Trinity in the revelations of the "militant" and "triumphant" Church. In iconography, especially popular is the image of the Lord of Sabaoth dressed in white "cloud-like" clothes of the Eternal Light, and His holiness is emphasized by the eight-pointed star on His halo as a symbol of the "Eighth Day" in the Coming of Christ. The Lord of Sabaoth is called "the Ancient of Days" of Alpha and Omega in the visions of the Prophets Daniel, Zechariah, and Malachi, and in the Revelation of St. John the Divine. This comparison makes it possible to identify Him with Christ Himself. The representation of the Lord of Sabaoth is especially iconologically and theologically correct in the iconography of "The Paternity" ("Fatherhood"). The name "Lord of Sabaoth" is also connected with the name of the incarnate Logos mentioned by Isaiah: "Behold, the Virgin shall conceive and bear a Son, and shall call His name Emmanuel" (Is 7:14; 8:8). The same name is mentioned in the Gospel according to St. Matthew (1:22), where the birth of Christ is described.

EMMANUEL ("God with us") is the New-Testament Logos-Lamb having the force and power to open the Book of Life held on the lap of the Lord of Sabaoth. It is said, "and His name shall be called the Angel of Great Counsel (*the Trinity*)" (Is 9:6).

PROSOPONIC NAMES OF GOD
(BY THE IMAGE OF ACTION OF GOD)

All names denoting perfection and creativeness of God's actions, especially in relation to Theophanies and His dispensation, are the names of God's *actions* rather than *existence*. From among numerous characteristic names, dogmatic theology distinguishes between names expressing *apophatic* (from Greek *apophatikos* — "negative") *properties* and names expressing *cataphatic* (from Greek *kataphatikos* — "affirmative") *properties*. The former names define what God is not and assert that He is absolutely transcendent and has nothing to do with definitions existing in the created world, while the latter names define what God is and His *properties* with respect to the created world. The apophatic properties of Theophanies are concealed in the mystery of the internal relations and existence of the Trihypostatic God. However, even saying that they are inexpressible in visible forms, we should remember the presence of apophatic definitions in Theophanic iconography. Apophatics forces us to always keep in mind that the names we use to refer to His Essence are approximate. For example, it is said that "God is Love (*Agape*)" (1 Jn 4:8), but, when correlated with the apophatics of names, we understand that God is above any names, while "Love" is the property and energy of His life-giving action. God is good, but He is the giver of goodness and, therefore, He is above goodness. We call Him "the Living One" or "the Wise One," "the All-Knowing" or "the All-Seeing," admitting that He is not knowable through any of His names, because His "names" are His Theophanies, Revelations, and Images that help creatures become closer to the Creator.

So, according to apophatic theology, God is not comprehensible, definable, or depictable. Giving names to God, however, we to some extent understand that our nature is connected with His Divinity. God's presence in the created world is the main reason for naming Him, because the strengthening of faith and the deification of Man depend on the extent of awareness of His characteristic names. God's Name invoked from the bottom of the heart immediately affects Man and forms his spiritual nature. "Thou shalt not take the name of the Lord thy God in vain" (Ex 20:7). Taking the name of God

Names of God

in vain is mortally dangerous, because God's Name is Energy, and calling upon God, we enter into the dynamics of His Revelation moving with love towards us, so Revelation would be devastating if the heart is not prepared for the meeting. Only in a heart where trust and faith are at work, "God is born and writes on it His laws, as on a clean tablet," imprinting "only those images through which it is appropriate [for God] to be manifested."[15] God's action in the world is a symbolic inscription of the "name" and "icon" of Light saturated with His Presence.

So, *apophatic* names denote properties attributed to the perfect MODE OF EXISTENCE of God and are uttered to assert the immortal Life of God, while *cataphatic* names denote properties relating to the perfect IMAGE OF ACTION of God and are uttered in the act of Divine dispensation and salvation of creatures.

APOPHATIC names of God's properties: *Uniqueness, Infinity, Independence, Immeasurability, Unchangeability, Omnipotence,* and so on. For characterizing God's unknowability, there are many other names based on associations from the life of our created world. Even though these names give only a very faint idea of the real power and meaning of the properties they denote, we need them to clear our outer mind of anthropomorphism and polytheism. Essentially, apophatic names are more relevant to theological methodology. For example, the name *Uniqueness* exalts God as having a real existence and denotes His complete independence from any other existence. Another name, *Omnipresence*, denotes His ubiquitous Presence, as the Prophet David exclaims: "Whither shall I go from Thy spirit? or whither shall I flee from Thy Presence?" (Ps 139:7).

CATAPHATIC names have positive meanings and correlate with iconology, revealing themselves to strengthen faith and bring God closer to believers for their higher exaltation. As dynamic energy, they are filled with the energy of grace and elevate the soul, directing it from Transfiguration "after the Image of God" to Resurrection "after the Likeness of God." In this sense, cataphatic names are as follows: Light, Will, Glory, Wisdom, Love, Counsel, Holiness, Providence,

---

15 St. Maximus the Confessor, *Two Hundred Texts on Theology and the Incarnate Dispensation of the Son of God.*

Truth, Goodness, Mercy, Immortality, etc. In the general order of symbolization, cataphatic names are formed according to the number of "spirits" of uncreated energies mentioned by the Prophet Isaiah (11:2): the Spirit of the Lord — the Shekinah, the spirit of Wisdom and Understanding and the spirit of Counsel — Sophia, and the spirit of Knowledge and of the Fear of the Lord and Might — Agape. Iconographically, they are depicted as "stars," or seven Angels who are in charge of the one apostolic Church. In the Scripture, they are mentioned as "seven lamps of fire, which are the seven Spirits of God" or "seven eyes, which are the seven Spirits of God" (Rev 4:5; 5:6).

Among God's numerous energy names, according to cataphatic theology, there are three main names that — being enhypostatized in the Trinity and, in this case, personified — become visible not only through spiritual and intelligent contemplation, but also in handmade Icons. These names are frequently mentioned in the Bible. According to sacred tradition, they are in particularly close relation to the unknowable essence of God. Being fundamental to the Christian faith, these names connect the human soul with the God-Man Christ:

"God is the LIGHT-PRESENCE" (Phos-Shekinah, Φώσ);

"God is WISDOM" (Sophia, Σοφία);

"God is LOVE" (Agape, Αγάπη).

Being closest to the essential Logos of the whole Trinity, they are the creative "beginnings" of any Revelation. In reality, these three divine elements constitute triune Life and interpenetrate each other. Without ever being separated, they are always distinguishable in their connection with the Divine Economy, in accordance with the times of the approaching Kingdom of God. Through Light, Wisdom, and Love, mortal life becomes filled with the Presence of the Holy Trinity. If we gain insight into these names by experiencing God's grace rather than by using our discursive minds, we can see the following "non-separating" distinction: the Presence of God in the Shekinah (the image of action of God the Father), in Sophia (the image of action of God the Son), and in Agape (the mode of action of God the Holy Spirit).

These are the main iconological points relating to the dispensational energies of the Trinity. However, let us emphasize again that we should always remember apophatic theology and understand that all properties, being essential, are inseparable and interpenetrable and belong equally to the Three Hypostases, but they differ in accordance with their creative use in various Revelations of God. The *"Three Hypostases"* of God's existence in the *"Three Energies"* of God's creative actions are the *Great Antinomy* of Life and the *miracle of Deification* of the entire created world.

LOGOS
MIRACULOUS ANGEL IN THE MANIFESTATION OF ENERGIES:
SHEKINAH, SOPHIA, AND AGAPE

7

Logos—Miraculous Angel in the Manifestation of Energies:
SHEKINAH, SOPHIA, AND AGAPE

She is the breath of the power of God, and a certain pure emanation of the glory of the almighty God.
Wisdom of Solomon 7:25

BEFORE PROCEEDING TO STUDY THE THEophanies described in the New Testament, we should focus on the development of theological thought by the later prophets in the Wisdom books. The Holy Scripture includes seven Wisdom books: the Book of Job, Ecclesiastes, the Proverbs, the Book of the All-Virtuous Wisdom of Joshua ben Sirach, the Book of the Wisdom of Solomon, the Book of Psalms, and the Song of Solomon. These books continue to reveal, to a considerably wider didactic extent, the mystical history of formation of faith in the one God. The basic idea of the Old Testament path is to prepare believers' minds for the perception of the future real Incarnation of the divine Logos and God the Son. So, an invisible line of Theophanies continues from Adam and leads through essential actions to the revelation of the idea of "coming to the logos" and then the fact of "Christianization": "he that believeth on me hath everlasting life" (Jn 6:47), i.e., it is "faith in God," rather than "knowledge of God," that leads to salvation.

Iconography always follows iconology, and the source of iconology is Tradition, especially in the form of liturgical theology of "hymns," "akathists," "canons," "prayers," and other liturgical texts. The concepts of "Logos," "Shekinah," "Sophia," and "Agape" are not new to iconography, but they have not yet found their full expression or comprehension in the history of icons, even though upon a closer view their personifications are implicitly present in many icons. The

THE ANGEL OF THE COUNTENANCE OF GOD

Logos, together with Sophia and Agape, appeared in the form of Three Angels not only to Abraham. According to Christian Tradition, Three Angels repeatedly visited St. Alexander of Svir, and this is reflected in iconography. And only God knows how many other hermits were visited by the Angel of Prosopon clothed in an "intelligent cloud." The image of the Shekinah, the glory of God, is depicted in "snow-white robes" in the icon of the Transfiguration of the Lord Jesus Christ. Often depicted as sitting on the Tomb in the icon of the Resurrection of the Lord, two *white-robed* angels can be interpreted as the Sophia of Christ and the Agape of the Holy Spirit; in the icon of the Ascension, the same two *white-robed* angels point at the ascending Lord and warn the apostles that His final coming will happen in the same way. Some icons and miniatures feature the Evangelists, with Angel Sophia standing behind them in *white robes* with an eight-pointed halo, as a representation from the Lord of Sabaoth. In the icon of the Apostle Luke, the latter's iconic work is blessed by a radiant Angel, as an example for painters and a reminder of the sacramental meaning of iconography. Although not widespread, there were attempts to depict the Angel Agape in ancient miniatures and embroideries. We are discussing the continuation of the tradition of iconographic subject matters, because neither theology nor, even more so, liturgical iconology, has exhausted the potential for a "detailed" profession of God.

Iconography is a cataphatic type of creative work. It translates verbal "names" into the pictorial basis of the symbolic realism of the icon. So, the question is: can icons fully express liturgical theology in symbolic forms? The only answer is affirmative, because the roots of iconography are within the symbolic possibility of depicting actions of the Divinity of God and, Christologically, the Divinity of Christ; for He is the visible "Image of the invisible God" and indicates the mystical actions of the whole Trinity. He *revealed* to the world the doctrine of the Most Holy consubstantial and undivided Trinity not only in terms of dogmatic and mystical theology, but also as a *tropos*, as a "figurative method," and as the iconography of the Divine Economy. This thesis may serve as a basis for drawing conclusions to define the objectives of iconography. Taking into account the prospects for further development of iconography, it is necessary to give a more detailed and careful consideration to God's main names that are mentioned in the Old and New Testaments, and whose iconography has not yet been created. For example, the iconography of Logos Emmanuel and Angel Sophia is relatively well developed, but there are basically no icons of the Shekinah, or Agape, or the Angel of the Countenance of God. In this century, however, Theophanies have not discontinued. Being associated with the modern state specializing in the development of engineering sciences and humanities, they become intrinsically necessary for more internal relations between any person and the Logos of Christ. That is why it is of primary importance to develop the iconology of the Angel of the Countenance of God, because "the miraculous name of God is in Him."

SHEKINAH—GOD'S DWELLING PLACE

> O house most lightsome and delightsome! I have loved
> Thy beauty, and the place of the habitation of the glory
> of my Lord.[1]

"Shekinah" is a Hebrew and Aramaic term that literally means "tabernacle," "tent," "cover," "residence," "presence," "settlement," "habitation" and everything that is connected with the concept of "place." The basic meaning of the term comes from the Hebrew "שכן" for "settle" or "dwell." In the Bible, this concept is associated with God's personified habitation in the world, and mystically means the divine "presence, settling in," from which the Greek paronym "skene" (tent) derives. It is constantly mentioned in the Targums alongside with the concept "Memrah." For example, instead of "They cried unto thee, and were delivered" (Ps 22:6), we read: "They cried unto Thy Shekinah." Another example can be found in the following famous psalm: "Hide not Thy Shekinah [*Your Spirit*, according to the Synodal Version] far from me" (Ps 27:9). The Shekinah is the mysterious and uniform "beginning," the mystical "place," "bosom," the Holy of Holies, and the mystical Kingdom of God, where the Logos of Revelation remains inapproachable: "In the *beginning* was [*reclined*]

---

[1] St. Augustine, *Confessions*, Book XII; cf. Psalm 25:8.

THE ANGEL OF THE COUNTENANCE OF GOD

the Logos." "The beginning" does not mean "time." It means the sacred *place* of God's presence. In the Revelation at Sinai, the Shekinah (Heavenly Tabernacle of Light) was revealed to Moses, and that is why God demanded that Moses put off his shoes from his feet, saying "for the *place* whereon thou standest is holy ground."

The Shekinah is the "energy of a place," which makes it possible to feel God in a temple, in oneself, or in any other special space. The concept that is the most applicable to the word "Shekinah" is "God's Presence." The Shekinah, Divinity, is a term that was used to denote God's name describing His attitude to the world (again, the world as a place) or to the chosen people, because a "people" is a special "place" of God's Presence.

"While the Jewish-Alexandrian religious philosophy understood God as a being standing outside and above the world and manifesting Himself in the world only indirectly through special created and independent beings (angels) or hypostases, religious teachers in Palestine and Babylonia strictly followed the biblical Divinity concept,"[2] according to which God manifests Himself through His Name-Logos and His *Glory*, and *His Spirit*—the Shekinah. Incidentally, the Targums prefer using the word "Shekinah," as God's *essential* Light, to the word "Glory" (כבוד, kaVOD) of the Lord, which is His *outpoured* energy. Given the increased religious consciousness, this substitution was necessary to avoid confusion about the understanding of God's "essence" and "energy." In the Orthodox tradition, the energy manifested by the Lord in the Transfiguration is the Light of God's Glory. This Light is poured out, taken as Communion, and, therefore, knowable. But He Himself, white as snow, was clothed in the Light of the Shekinah. Energy means "action," which makes it possible to know God's actions and, through them, the Actor.

According to the strict monotheistic concept, the idea of God's translocation or presence in a specific place is not permissible. God is in everything! (cf. 1 Cor 15:28) It is the Shekinah of God's will, rather than the omnipresent God, that can stay in a certain *place*. Therefore, the Shekinah is God's name or "image of action." The Targum Onkelos translates the words of Moses as follows: "Unless your Shekinah

---

2   *The Jewish Encyclopedia.*

goes with us, we will not move from this place" (Ex 33:15), or "Let the Shekinah of God go among us" (Ex 34:9). From the day the tabernacle, and later, Solomon's Temple was built, "the Shekinah settled there." The Shekinah is a generalized notion of the uncreated, light-bearing, and life-asserting Glory of God, but its particular importance lies in its close relation to the concept of God's *place* (Bethel): the Holy Land, the tabernacle (tent), the temple, the Church of God's people, and, in general, Man. That is why it is said, "Ye are the Temple of the Spirit of God." In the time to come, the Shekinah will come as the Kingdom of Light and as an uncreated city in the likeness of Jerusalem chosen for the Jews. The New Paradise, "of urban type," will be built after the fashion of the Holy Cross. According to the Syrian tradition represented by St. Isaac of Syria, the Shekinah once dwelt in the Ark of Moses and after the crucifixion of Christ removed to the Holy Cross, manifesting Its life-giving power whenever the sign of the cross is made. In the later midrashic literature and the Talmud, the Shekinah was identified with the Memrah-Logos and given some personality, but the idea was misrepresented and the Shekinah's nature was belittled down to the created level. According to Mosheh ben Maimon, "It is a free *creation* of God and a (naturally created) intermediary." In addition, the Western Church recognizes the Shekinah (and Sophia) as some "light" essence *created* before all ages, which caused dogmatic controversies with the Eastern Church. In the fourteenth century, the dogmatic controversies between the Eastern and Western Churches resulted in the so-called "Palamite" disputes about the nature of "the Light of Tabor" and in a final break in dogmatic positions between the churches. However, as we can see from the perspective of orthodox theology and the doctrine of St. Gregory Palamas, the Shekinah is God's creative energy and the uncreated yet essential *beginning*, where the eternal Logos of Light is directed to both God and the world. In the Shekinah, which is identical to the Kingdom of God, Man is in the process of becoming closer to deification, and this is an irrefutable argument in favor of Its divine nature.

The Shekinah is associated with a sanctuary, God's house (temple) or a *place* where the Lord will record His name (Ex 20:24), a *place* which the Lord God will choose in order to put His Name *there* (Deut 12:5). Let us recall again that the Shekinah dwelt on the cover of the Ark of the Covenant, flanked by the two Cherubim (more precisely, a Seraph, as a symbol of Agape, and a Cherub, as a symbol of Sophia) also depicted on the cover. On the Ark itself, the name of the Lord of Sabaoth was written. "Temple" is a polysemantic notion, which is inextricably linked with the notion of the Church of faithful people. All Christians form a living Church—the body of Christ, the place and the temple of habitation of God's Shekinah, where the Lord is present. The Temple, the Shekinah, is "the place of the name of the Lord" (Is 18:7), a repository of grace, the bosom of the Lord's Name, while the Name is the Logos of the Trinity. In Leviticus 24:11–16, we can see how mystically God's Name and all its energy and power attributes were perceived in ancient times: "And the Israelitish woman's son blasphemed the *Name* of the Lord.... And the Lord spake unto Moses, saying, 'Whosoever curseth his *God* shall bear his sin. And he that blasphemeth the Name of the Lord, he shall surely be put to death.'" These verses show how closely God and His Name are connected. Deuteronomy 28:58 says, "If thou wilt not ... fear this *glorious* and *fearful Name*, The Lord Thy God; Then the Lord will make thy plagues wonderful, and the plagues of thy seed," which is followed by an enumeration of diseases and perditions for those who are disobedient.

Having the meaning of a place, a tent, and a tabernacle in Hebrew, the Shekinah definitely refers to some "space" where God's mystical name "Memrah-Logos" is always present and connected with it, in the same way as God is discretely connected with His Divinity. Therefore, the Angel of the Countenance of God, in whom the Name of the Lord is, can have all the characteristics of the Shekinah too. We have already said that, firstly, God permeates all His names and, secondly, all His names permeate each other. And yet, it is necessary to distinguish between them. The world is filled with the divine action through the Shekinah, because it surrounds and extends over the whole world like a heavenly radiant Tabernacle, *making it possible* to communicate with God. The famous verse from Psalm 104, "who stretchest out the heavens like a curtain," can also be interpreted as "[You] extend the heavens like a tent (*Shekinah*)." It is the Shekinah that determines that God is present specifically "here" and may not be present "there," regardless of a person's faith.

The Logos is God's name, and, according to Philo of Alexandria, "The Logos surrounds everything (*with the Shekinah*), without being surrounded with anything (of created things); It is the shelter of everything and a place of Its own (*in the Shekinah*); It contains everything, but nothing fully contains It."[3] If we understand that the *Logos* is the Son in His hypostatic logos Name, rather than some independent created intermediary between God and Man, it becomes clear to us that God fills the whole universal space with the Shekinah and that there is no place where It is not present. This fundamental idea can be repeatedly found in the Bible, and, if this idea is specified, it becomes clear that the Shekinah fills, moves, and forms mystical places in the world, while the meaning of the birth and *formation* of spiritual life in these places is the Seed-Logos put into these formations. Therefore, the Targums mention God's Shekinah where it is necessary to speak about the divine action. Jewish tradition compares the Shekinah with the soul: "Just as the Holy One, blessed be He, *fills* the whole world, so the soul fills the body. Just as the Holy One, blessed be He, sees, but is not seen, so the soul sees but is not itself seen" (Babylonian Talmud: Tractate Berakoth, Folio 10a). On the basis of these ideas, Judaism adopted the mystical definition of "space" of the Shekinah. However, we should again remember the Orthodox position stating that God's "space" is not something created before all ages, but the eternal *outpouring* of Energy (Glory) from God's spiritually uplifting essence, His throne over the whole created world (hence, the name: the *Most High God*). As God's "space," it is the heavenly Tabernacle that was shown to Moses on Mount Zion. It is not uninteresting that the name "the Most High God" occurs mainly in the verses mentioning the Temple, i.e., a specially prepared place. "The Scripture and the Church Tradition speak of the existence of special places where God is (*entirely*) present in some special way."[4]

The Shekinah, as a light *place* and as God's *heavenly Tabernacle*, also organizes space for Man called by God to deification: "Behold,

---

3 *De somniis,* Mangey 630.
4 Priest A. Davydenkov, *Dogmatic Theology.*

the Tabernacle of God is with men, and He will dwell with them" (Rev 21:3). In the New Testament, the Shekinah idea comes alive mainly in the verses mentioning the "holy place"—the Mother of God. In addition, all persons having the spermatic Logos in their hearts are surrounded by the Shekinah Light, as by the "maternal womb."

> With regard to the theme of the Incarnation of God, it should be noted that it presupposes a feasible explanation of such religious phenomena as the existence of intuition of the divine Motherhood and everlasting virginity from ancient times to the actual appearance of the Mother of God in this world and the Ever-Virgin Mary.[5]

The earthly, heavenly, and divine *presence* are fully reunited in the Mother of God. This also brings to mind the feast of the *Intercession* of the Mother of God, whose establishment is associated with the appearance of the Theotokos in the Glory of the Lord to Saints Andrew and Epiphanius during an all-night vigil in the Blachernae Church (AD 910), when Constantinople was threatened with seizure by the Saracens.

> Having finished her prayer, (the Mother of God) took off the great and awe-inspiring lightning-like veil, which She wore on Her most pure head, and, holding it with great solemnity with Her most pure hands, extended it over all the people standing in the church. For quite a long time, these wonderful men saw the veil spread above the people and God's glory shining like a lightning; and the veil was visible as long as the Most Holy Mother of God was visible. After Her departure, the veil became invisible too. Taking it with Her, however, she left the grace to those who were there.[6]

Based on the fact that the Shekinah is the *energy of a place, and God's temple*, we can see that this general concept finds its reflection and forms in different worlds, and on different life planes, which iconology should distinguish as follows:

---

5 Eykalovich, *Genealogy of Sophia*.
6 St. Dmitry of Rostov, *The Hagiography*, October 1.

Logos—Miraculous Angel in the Manifestation of Energies

- the Kingdom of God;
- the Kingdom of Heaven;
- the Temple (a building) of God's Presence in the Old Testament service;
- The Church (a people) in the Eucharistic service;
- Anthropos (Man) — the temple of the Spirit of God;
- Theocosmos (an angel) — the temple of God's Light;
- Cosmos — the material (minerals, plants, animals) kingdom.

SOPHIA—GOD'S WISDOM

> The Lord possessed me in the beginning of His way, before His works of old. (Prov 8:22)

"Wisdom" (Greek: Σοφία; Hebrew: Chokhmah) has various interpretations: a) practical wisdom, expert skills, proficiency, and survival experience; b) in an ontological sense — the ability to penetrate deeply into the essence of things and their interrelations. As late as the sixth century BC, the word "Chokhmah" acquired a religious connotation. Sophia, having features of some independent entity, is mentioned in the Wisdom books, which, after the prophetic books, became part of the Judeo-Alexandrian literature. "As early as the Book of Proverbs, Wisdom is mentioned as a character, a person or even a personification, and as a subject of some action; moreover, we can hear not only about it in the third person, but also its own voice."[7] In the Book of the Wisdom of Solomon, Sophia reveals itself as a "representative" — a Person (Prosopon) of God.

Not coincidentally, the Slavonic "Premudrost," the Greek "Sophia," and the Hebrew "Chokhmah" are feminine nouns. Sophia is a personified "live" (enhypostatized) *conceptual energy* perceiving God's creative impulse, "a breath of the power of God (*Logos*), and a certain pure emanation of the glory of the almighty God" (Wis 7:25). It is a nursling (Prov 8:27–31) who forms divine ideas and submits them to the created world for consideration, making it possible to comprehend the *virginal Beginning which generates Life in the Divinity*. It mysteriously reveals the meaning and content of that which is hidden

---

7 Sergei Averintsev, *Wisdom in the Old Testament*.

in the inapproachable Light of the Shekinah, the Logos. Sophia is the creative, all-permeating, and cognitive energy of God's "consciousness." It is the inspirer of prophets and sages. Often used in the Bible, the concept "beginning" consists of God's equally creative energies: Logos — Idea — Eidos. The *Logos* — the only unchangeable seed of God — permeates and fertilizes the whole creation; *Ideas* are conceptual and diverse energies of the generative power of Wisdom; Eide are ecstatic energies that form the breath of Love's beauty and form.

The term "wisdom," whose rudiments are found in the ancient books of the Bible, was particularly developed in the Judeo-Hellenic period. Unlike the Greeks, whose approach to wisdom was purely philosophical, the Jews professed adherence to the Divine Wisdom based on the belief in one God. The Wisdom books are characterized by the absence of national characteristics and by the affirmation of the idea of forgiveness of sins, which is associated with God's mercy and obedience to Him rather than with sacrifice. Through Wisdom, the subject of God's justice in the life of all the people (an ancient point of view) was transferred to and focused on the individual. So, the sophianic books can be considered to be an introduction to the New Testament, which reveals the God-Man Christ who earlier was "hidden" in the Old Testament Wisdom.

Chronologically, the Wisdom texts are found in the Book of Job, the Book of Psalms, the Proverbs, Ecclesiastes (Kohelet), the Book of Psalms (8, 20, 30, 38, 50, 74, 91, 93, 104, 105, 108, 140, 147, 148), the Song of Solomon, the Book of the Wisdom of Solomon, and the Book of the All-Virtuous Wisdom of Joshua ben Sirach.

"Who would deny that the Church apologists and fathers used some *appropriate* concepts of pre-Christian philosophy while developing the Christian doctrine?"[8] "Evidently, the biblical Wisdom and various pagan versions that Carl Gustav Jung would call a feminine Archetype, evidently have some common features; it would be very difficult, perhaps impossible, to imagine a complete lack of similarity."[9] According to the description, Sophia's birth is quite mythological, which is also applicable to her mythological Greek "counterpart" — the

---

8   Eykalovich, *Genealogy of Sophia*.
9   Averintsev, *Wisdom in the Old Testament*.

goddess Athena, who was born from the head of Zeus. The biblical Wisdom says about Herself: "I came forth *from the mouth of the Most High*, and I covered the earth like *mist*" (Sir 24:3). "The mouth of the Most High" is the Logos, while Sophia is His *spoken* word. Many of Athena's properties are characteristic of the Sophia of God. Already at this point, however, we can see the initial difference in the mythology of these images: the goddess represents herself in her properties of wisdom, craft, and justice, which relate to the existence of the Cosmos, because she was born from the cosmic god of space; Sophia, in the same properties, represents the Logos of God—to be more exact, the Son of God—rather than herself. Sophia is the uncreated Wisdom of God rather than a "package" of virtues. However, Athena too was called Zeus's virgin thought implemented in action and the implementer of his will and ideas. According to the myth, she was born from the head of Zeus after he had devoured his pregnant wife Metis, whose name can be translated as "thought," "reflection," and perhaps even "wisdom."

In many religions, the symbol of wisdom is a snake, and Athena is the patroness of snakes. Athena's sacred tree is the "olive tree" as the "tree of destiny." Athena is always considered in the context of artistic crafts, urban development, arts, and craftsmanship. According to the myth, she invented the flute and taught Apollo to play this instrument. In late Antiquity, this goddess served as an image of the cosmic Mind, a symbol of Wisdom, and an evidence of the organizing and directing power of Reason. But the mythopoetry also shows such features of the virgin goddess Athena as motherhood, virginity, and purity. "We must still admit that paganism revealed sacred and reverent mysteries through the worship of the female deity."[10] In *The Dispute about Sophia*, Gennady Eykalovich says that

> the phenomenon of the cult of female deities can be regarded not only as anthropomorphism or *anticipation*, but also as a personification of the feminine-existential element of every reality, with this personification being observed in the immanent plane, which is different from logos-ness in the transcendent plane.

---

10 Archpriest Sergei Bulgakov.

Consideration of this aspect ("Logos" and "Energy") starts to slightly unveil the distinction between "masculine" and "feminine" services, applying, in some way, the analogy of "God" and "Divinity."

"But where shall wisdom be found?" and "Whence then cometh wisdom?" (Job 28:12, 20) In contrast to the many gods who knew Athena and even argued with her, only God knows Sophia. "God understandeth the way thereof, and He knoweth the place thereof" (Job 28:23). In the Jewish tradition, Chokhmah surely incorporated some Hellenic features, but monotheism added a special supracosmic aspect to them, personifying the Sophia-Virgin as an energy outpouring and an uncreated *beginning-arche* of "the ways of God" ("The Lord possessed Me in the BEGINNING") and, therefore, bringing Her closer to the essential Logos of God" ("In the BEGINNING was the Logos"). The essential Logos, being the *name* of God, is enhypostatized and inseparably reunited with the Son of God, Christ, while Sophia, as the *image of action* of the Hypostasis, is connected and enhypostatized with Christ's Logos in the Prosopon.

The development of Wisdom "ideas" is intricately intertwined with the concept of the Logos (Idea is the Bride of the Logos) and sometimes, i.e., in the Stoic school, with the concept of Pneuma. But the difference between Sophia and the Logos is in the ways of relating to the world: the Logos (Youth-Bridegroom) is the essential Light and the life-giving power, the seed of all living things; Sophia (the Virgin-Bride) is "the *brightness* of eternal Light, and the unspotted [*virginal*] mirror of God's majesty [*itself*] and the image of His Goodness [*Love*]" (Wis 7:26).

She "is a breathing out of the power of God," while the Logos is the *power* of God (1 Cor 1:24). Sophia is the Paradigm (example), the everlasting Idea, and the logos breath of God (wasn't it Her Light that was breathed by God into the mouth of the cosmic man, making him rational?) and, in this sense, is inseparable from the Logos, just as light rays are inseparable from the Sun. In liturgical theology, the Logos-Bridegroom calls on the human soul to mystically reunite in marriage, while Sophia's task is to fascinate the soul, kindle its love, and direct it, dressed in wedding wisdom garments, to the gate of the Marital Chamber, because only the "wise" can recognize the Bridegroom of the Church of God. At first glance, Sophia only decodes the symbolism of Theophanies. In the experience of mystical contemplation, however, She helps "straighten the path" to the Kingdom. Like cherubs, Sophia *forms* people spiritually, giving Her royal robes to the Soul. At this point, it should be noted that Sophia does not operate without her "sister" Agape, because both of them are in front of the Bridegroom on both sides of Him. Like uncreated "banks," they form the path of the fertilizing stream of the mystic power of the Logos. They are consubstantial to each other, yet differ in the "image of action," and in the Song of Solomon the Bridegroom calls the Shulamite now "bride," now "sister."

From Judaism, Christianity adopts the personal understanding of Sophia. Origen describes Wisdom as "the incorporeal existence of diverse thoughts that envelop the logoi of the whole world" which is, however, "animate and, as it were, alive." It should be specified that God's energy is implicitly alive and conscious. Indeed, given that God is alive according to the tradition, how can the energy flowing from God's essence not be alive? And anyway, how could God create anything that is dead? To understand that dead things do not exist, you should be not only logical, but also iconologically-minded.

The regal Virgin Sophia, a living Artist before God, iconographically depicts His Theophanies creatively and vividly. She is "the Daughter of the Father," "the Maiden-Bride of the Son," and "the Sister of the Spirit of God." Sophia is happy and joyful with Her creative (rather than reproductive) answer to the Voice of God. In the freedom of emptiness, God "has poured Her forth upon all His works" (Sir 1:9) as a wise Light. Man has this radiant freedom too, because God "in Wisdom . . . made them all" (Ps 104:24). Owing to Her artistic talent, Sophia turns (changes) Theophanies into the visible images of Wine and Bread when She extends an invitation to the Eucharist of the Lord, identifying Herself with Him, like the Angel of Jehovah, "Come to Me, you who desire Me, and from My produce be filled" (Sir 24:19). Perhaps it was Her artistic freedom, which is inherent to all kinds of creativity, that enabled the Jewish and Christian traditions to personalize Sophia, giving Her independent existence in *words* and *icons*, while surely being aware of the extent of Her enhypostatized relations with the Hypostasis of Christ. Sophia is the Prosopon of Christ; and God engenders a *new seed* in Her, as it is written, "Behold, I make all things new," and, therefore, She "was daily His delight, rejoicing always before Him" (Prov 8:30). In this characteristic context, we can also consider the Song of Solomon, where the relations between the Bridegroom and the Bride and their images are presented mythopoetically and understood by the ancients as "God and Israel," or "the Spirit and the Soul," and, in the Christian tradition, as "Christ and the Church." The Song of Solomon can be read in a literal sense as an expression of personal creative relations between Christ and His Sophia — His direct Bride by nature and His uncreated Icon.

Oftentimes, mainly based on Paul the Apostle's words that the Son of God is Wisdom, St. John of Damascus, in *An Exact Exposition of the Orthodox Faith*, clarifies that the *hypostatic* Wisdom, which is also according to his *Dialectic* (see below), can be understood in terms of its "hypostaticity," and, therefore, *inseparability*. The identification of the Logos with Sophia cannot be understood literally either, which also applies to the expression "God is Love." The Logos Christ is a Hypostasis, while Sophia is a Prosopon, the creative image of Christ. The terms "hypostasis" and "prosopon" give grounds to fully distinguish between *God* (Christ) and the *Divinity* (Sophia). There are no grounds for identification, and this assertion is indicative of a mystical lack of distinction between the concepts of "essence" and "energy." We will not go into further theological reflections on the subject, because for our study it is important to identify Sophia's place in the appearances of the Angel of the Countenance of God. Once again, we should note that the Orthodox speculation is that Sophia is Christ's uncreated Image (rather than His Hypostasis), His Idea of Ideas (Idea Idearum) — the conceptual Pronoia (of the providence and care, wisdom and power) of God. "By the word (*Logos*) of the Lord were the heavens made; and all the host of them by the Breath (*Sophia*) of his mouth" (Ps 33:6). All the angels were created in the image of the Divine Wisdom. Traditionally they are called "bodiless minds."

There are distinctions between Sophia and the Logos, and the essence of these distinctions lies in the terminology of "origins" established by the Orthodox dogmatics:

1. *birth-procession* is a theological "type" of hypostatic origin of the Son and the Holy Spirit from the Father;

2. *outpouring* is an iconological type of prosoponic origin of uncreated energies: the Shekinah, Sophia, and Agape of God;

3. *creation* is a cosmological type of origin of the created noetic (intellectually perceptible) and esthetic (sensually perceptible) worlds.

Considering the outwardly similar paradigms of mythology and religion, it should be remembered that the problem of the lack of a spiritual viewpoint regarding them does not lie in mythology itself or Hellenism, Platonism, or Neo-Platonism as such. Instead, it lies in the fact that they attributed the origin of all spiritual "things" and their ideas to the third type of origin and, therefore, "multiplied" cosmic gods. Attributing Sophia by genealogy to created entities of various kinds, modern occult teachings consistently find themselves among the disciples of Philo, Plato, Plotinus, and other philosophers who, with all their religiosity, did not distinguish between the cosmos and God outside His Creation "withdrawn" from and not determined by the cosmos. The Catholic Church also holds that Sophia is created, adding to the "*Filioque*" another departure from the teachings of the Eastern Fathers. This is not surprising, because these two false positions are directly interconnected. According to Metropolitan Amfilohije (Radović),

> he who does not accept the two modes of origin of the Spirit on the basis of the distinction between essence and energy inevitably agrees, according to St. Gregory Palamas, to the *Filioque*, because he is automatically forced to identify God's uncaused existence and His caused manifestation. This results in an identification of the *mode* of existence (*being*) of the Holy Trinity with the *image of its manifestation*.[11]

But if God's Wisdom is created, the essential Logos, in terms of its direct relation with and likeness to Sophia, would also look "created before all ages," and, in this case, They are only "intermediaries,"

---

11 As quoted by Hieromonk Hilarion from *The Confession of the Orthodox Faith of St. Gregory Palamas.*

THE ANGEL OF THE COUNTENANCE OF GOD

"messengers," and, at best, "carriers" equivalent to created angels, rather than direct actors of Theophanies.

SOPHIA IN THE SPECULATIONS OF THE CHURCH FATHERS

> Now the Only-begotten and very Wisdom of God is Creator and Framer of all things; for "in Wisdom have You made them all," he says, and "the earth is full of Your creation." But in order that what came into being might not only be, but be good, it pleased God that His own Wisdom should condescend to the creatures, so as to introduce an impress and semblance of Its Image on all in common and on each.... And therefore has this impress of Wisdom in the works been brought into being, that, as I said before, the world might recognize in it its own Creator the Word, and through Him the Father.[12]

The philanthropic Spirit—Wisdom—"can do all things: and remaining in herself the same, she reneweth all things, and through nations conveyeth herself into holy souls, she *maketh* them friends of God and prophets" (Wis 7:27, Slavonic version), awakening the action of the spermatic Logos in them to meet the hypostatic Son and Christ. The uncreated spark and seed of God ("the particle of the Divinity," according to Gregory the Theologian) is given by God from birth, but in Holy Baptism it is awakened and renovated by the action of St. Sophia, growing in the soul and becoming the human *spirit* proper. Then, using its energies, the Wisdom of God acts in a variety of forms of the created world, enlightening and guiding it toward conscious faith. According to Theodoret of Cyrus (fifth century), "There are three Sophias. One through whom we are gifted with understanding, reason, and knowledge of what is to be done, through whom we practice art, pursue science, and know God; another who is seen in creation; and a third who appeared in our Redeemer which unbelievers call foolishness."[13] At this point, it is appropriate to mention and clarify the popular word "philo*sophy*"

---

12 St. Athanasius, *Against the Arians*, Discourse 2.
13 *PG* 3:171.

having a great mystic potency to reunite Love and Wisdom. This connection, at the highest levels of faith through the transformation of "philia" into "agape," becomes agapo*sophy*, which is directly close to God. St. Clement of Alexandria (second to third centuries AD) writes: "Philosophy is a form and the practice of wisdom; wisdom is the scientific understanding of things divine, things human, and causes."[14] In the biblical tradition, as noted above, divine things should not be understood abstractly; this is also applicable to the image of God, because Sophia is the *conceptual* personification of God's *actions*, forming *theophanic images* in diverse descents to people. St. Gregory the Theologian (fourth century) writes: "Wisdom is knowing oneself,"[15] asserting that only the uncreated energy of God's Wisdom enables the inert human nature to open up for intelligent contemplation of Divine Revelations. The Prophet Isaiah teaches about the seven Spirits, including the Spirit of Wisdom; the Fathers of the Church consider them to be the uncreated foundations of God's actions (energies).

It took some time for the terminology of "origins" to take shape, and it is difficult to find these distinctions in the works of the Fathers of the first centuries. For instance, St. Justin (second century), without going into the refinements to be established as Christian dogmas in the following centuries, wrote about "a certain rational Power [proceeding] from Himself, who is called by the Holy Spirit now the Glory of the Lord, now the Son, again Wisdom, again an Angel, then God, and then Lord and Logos."[16] St. Theophilus of Antioch (second century) distinguishes as follows: "God the Father, who brings forth from Himself before everything else His inner (*endiatheton*) Logos with His own Sophia."[17] St. Irenaeus (second to third centuries) marks the difference in the actions of God: "God made (*the third type of origin*) everything through His Logos and made everything beautiful (*the second type of origin*) through His Sophia."[18]

---

14 *PG* 8:721B.
15 *PG* 36:200.
16 *Dialogue with Trypho*, Chapter 61.
17 *PG* 6:1064C.
18 *PL* 7:1932B.

THE ANGEL OF THE COUNTENANCE OF GOD

The Logos, the male principle, creates and structures creaturely life, while Sophia, the female and "spherical" principle creates and structures the multiplicity of life, which is decorated and harmonized. St. Maximus the Confessor holds that Adam is the male logos principle, which is *contemplative* and oriented toward God, while Eve is the female sophian principle, which is *active* and oriented toward making Life forms. It is worth considering, for example, the following: "The Logos and Creator of all . . . brought [into being] *natural logoi* of all manifested and intelligible [things] together with the *incomprehensible* (*sophian*) *thoughts* of His Divinity," which "from time immemorial were mysteriously prepared by Wisdom by means of a chalice and sacrifices, [as is evidenced by] the Book of Proverbs."[19]

As has been noted above, the prosoponic Logos by its creative nature is always oriented TOWARD God (in contrast to the inaccurate synodical translation: "The Logos was WITH God"), and God recognizes the religious state of the created world by His uncreated logoi "brought" into the world. In the Prologue, it is written: "In the *beginning was the Logos*," and Sophia says, "I am the *beginning* of the Lord's ways," i.e., "the beginning" is identical to God's Wisdom and is God's Wisdom. The "*Beginning*" has a *contemplative* tension (dynamis) of the Logos toward God; while the Logos in Sophia has an *active life-giving* tension toward the Universe. Understanding Sophia as a created being and identifying it with the Logos, Arius concluded that the Logos was a being created "before time and eons." Not realizing that God has the second Hypostasis of the Son and Christ named the Logos, he destroyed the consubstantiality of the Holy Trinity. Even though Paul the Apostle wrote that Christ is "the power of God, and the wisdom of God" and John the Apostle added that "God is Love," this "generalization" by no means ran counter to the idea of the unity of God and His Divinity. As theology developed, however, the Church Fathers by the fifteenth century, due to the urgent need to clarify terminological differences, finally approved the following dogmatic definition: God is the *Hypostasis* that freely disposes of Its *Prosoponic* energies rather than being determined by them, because energy is poured from the *Essence* rather than some

---

19 St. Maximus the Confessor, *Questions to Thalassius*, 35.

Hypostasis or other. Therefore, Christ, in the first place the hypostatic Son of God, has both Wisdom and Love in creative relations with both the other two Hypostases and the world of human hypostases. In this case, we also avoid going to the extremes of (1) subordination in the Trinity and (2) the merger of the Shekinah, Sophia, and Agape with the Hypostatic Trinity. Everything should be placed in its own place: in GOD—the hypostatic mode of existence, *tranquility, and simplicity of the Logos*; in the DIVINITY—the prosoponic image of actions, *movement, and complexity of Sophia and Agape*. The distinction is already clearly seen in the meaning of the terms: "logos" is the only "seed" containing the mystery of God's Revelations, while "sophia" is the energy of "growth" and development of diverse types (*eide*) of Life that contains the life-giving seeds (λόγοί) of the Logos and gives them (as grace) for growth to the created world to the extent of the perception of each hypostasis. The Logos is the male word-acting principle (a noun), while Sophia is the female implementing principal (an adjective) producing the fruit of Life.

By fully identifying Christ with Sophia, we would confuse without distinction the masculine name Logos and the feminine name Sophia; i.e., we would confuse the notions of "noun" and "adjective," which was contrary to the whole world outlook of the ancient Jews. This confusion occurred when Philo of Alexandria (13 BC–AD 45) transferred the functions and attributes of the Old Testament Sophia to the Greek cosmic "logos." Following Philo, many later accepted this theologoumenon about the Logos being identical with Sophia and, therefore, prepared a sort of "uniate" without distinction, a mixture of theology and iconology. Even at present, many onomatoclasts (Sophia can be understood as the Name of the Logos) make absolutely no distinction between Them or, for example, adherents of esotericism completely separate Sophia from God and are even convinced of Her fall. Simplifying the liturgics of the *Mysteries* of the Logos and of the *Sacraments* of Sophia, one may take a negative stand toward so-called "sophiology," but the resulting confusion does not make it possible to *distinguish* among the inseparable concepts of "hypostasis," "essence," and "prosopon," which was urgently advocated by the later fathers of the Orthodox Church.

THE ANGEL OF THE COUNTENANCE OF GOD

Continuing our reflections on Sophia, we should again focus on the word "beginning," as the *method* of reasoning depends on its understanding as well. Many Western exegetes, commenting on Sophia's words "The Lord *possessed* [in other translations, *made*, or, even completely wrong, *created*] Me in the *beginning* of His way," identify the word "beginning" with the first "step" of Creation, which is contrary to the subsequent verse—"before his works of old; I was set up from everlasting, from the beginning, or ever the earth was" (Prov 8:22, 23). For the discursive mind, the *beginning* of the way is already the first "step." For the spiritual mind, however, the *beginning* is hesychia, the state of silence, spiritual "poverty" and void before the first "step" of movement. On the basis of reason, some writers consider Sophia to be part of the creation process and, therefore, separate Her "by nature" from God. But the Holy Fathers provide evidence to the contrary. In addition, in the history of Christianity, the victory over Arianism explicitly solved this issue.

> For the Old Testament era, this issue is an anachronism. Meanwhile, if the Christology of the Church Fathers had been entirely guided by the *evolution of ideas* law without the miracle of Revelation, the evolution of ideas from both the Wisdom literature and the Greek Platonic sources could have inevitably led only to Arianism. Therefore, the victory over Arianism was about overcoming the imaginary autonomy of the *evolution of ideas*.[20]

St. Athanasius the Great, opponent of Arius, identifying Wisdom with the Son and even with the essence of God (in his time, corresponding dogmas were not established yet), completely denies Her being created: "By Solomon Wisdom says of Itself with cautious exactness, not 'I am a creature,' but only 'The Lord created Me at the *beginning of His ways* for His works,' yet not 'created Me that I might have being,' nor 'because I have a creature's beginning and origin.'"[21] He says that God "created" Sophia not as Her "being,"

---

20 Averintsev, *Wisdom in the Old Testament*.
21 *Against the Arians*, Discourse 2.

Logos—Miraculous Angel in the Manifestation of Energies

but as "a beginning of the uncreated ways" of making and creating the world.

If the first verse of Genesis ("In the *beginning* God created the heaven and the earth") is understood as an action in time, there again arise the following questions: And then what? Did God create something after that?; and Why is "in the *beginning*" used here? Wouldn't it be better to understand "in the beginning" as follows: God created the heavens and the earth "in the state of Hesychia" rather than "in space"? According to the Hasidic interpretation, this verse in the Tanakh is not intended to indicate the order of creation or that the heavens and the earth preceded everything else, because in this case a different Hebrew word would have been used in the original. This opinion is shared by outstanding biblical scholar S. Averintsev:

> The opening expression of the Torah and, in fact, the Bible is "*bereshit*," which is translated as "in the beginning," but its meaning cannot be reduced to a purely temporal "starting point," something like the "Big Bang." Etymologically, the noun *reshit* stems from the word *rosh*, which means "head," and, therefore, means the "main thing" that is "at the head"; Aquila, an ancient translator of the Bible into Greek, who prepared his work as an alternative to the Septuagint, focusing on etymological accuracy, translated *bereshit* as Ἐν κεφαλαίῳ ("in principal"); and in modern times André Chouraqui, also an adherent of etymological accuracy, translates the same expression into French as *Entête*. Generally, "beginning" can be easily understood as "principle" as an ontological basis, but also as some instrumental first Creation, "*in which*" the Creator created the heavens and the earth. It is noteworthy that the same noun *reshit* refers to Wisdom in the Book of Proverbs 4:7 (in the meaning of "the principal, most important thing"). It is not surprising that the Targum Yerushalmi, an ancient Aramaic explanatory translation of the Torah, replaces the opening words of Genesis, "In the *beginning* God created the heaven and

the earth," with the following explanatory version: "In *Wisdom* [*be chokhmah*], God created the heavens and the earth." When famous medieval Jewish exegete Rashi interpreted "beginning" as a synonym for the Torah, he specifically referred to the Book of Proverbs 8:22, identifying God's law and God's Wisdom as the essence, measure, and purpose of Creation that preceded Creation.[22]

We will only clarify that, *Beginning* (or *Wisdom*) is surely named *first Creation* just tentatively here, because the world of divine Ideas, existing eternally with God, is as eternal as God Himself.

One of the stages of painting man-made icons is called "the thin red line around the halo," which symbolizes Alpha, the *beginning* of the "color" way, but it is the next stage — "the primary stage of painting" — that is the first step toward *revealing* the image in color. In this sense, the Beginning of the way is the Divinity — the "place" (Shekinah) of the Logos, and the state of tension of His silence (Hesychia) between the essential *quietude* and the energetical *movement* to the creation of the world. In this stable Beginning of God's actions, all paradigms, uncreated exemplars (*archetypes*), of all ideas and things of the future creation are formed and preserved "until a certain time" in the unapproachable and essential Light. From this Beginning, just as from an "epicenter," beginnings-logoi of God's actions are sown into the world to fertilize the existence of all of the dimensions of the existing Universe. In *The Triads*, St. Gregory Palamas writes: "Certainly, all such 'beginnings' are nothing else but the meanings (logoi) of beings and the prototypes (paradigms) with whom beings (creatures) commune, yet as a gift, for they dwell and preexist in the mind of the Creator; *by them* all things were made." So, considering the above-mentioned, the biblical verse "in the beginning was the Word" can also be interpreted as follows: "In the Shekinah of silence was the Word." The Logos always reclined in the "Hesychia" of the Divinity's own divine Sabbath, and after the creation of the world the Logos (like in the icon of *The Unsleeping Eye*) "rested on the seventh day (*Sabbath*) from all his work.... And

---

22 Averintsev, *Wisdom in the Old Testament*.

God blessed the seventh day, and sanctified it" (Gen 2:2, 3). The Book of Genesis shows us the great importance of the sanctified "beginning," which is not included in the actions of the six days of Creation of the world, but left as an already existing "beginning" of the following Eighth Day, on which Christ the Lord is risen.

In a more biblical general sense, "Beginning" should be understood as Light, the sphere of all "beginnings," rather than an already existing action (because there was no "thereafter"). Both the Book of Genesis and John the Evangelist, after mentioning the Logos in the Prologue, immediately proceed to the topic of Light. The exclamation "Let there be Light" already outlines all possible providential plans of the Logos, the Ideas of Sophia, and the Eide of Agape for the future creation; "And the Light shineth in darkness; and the darkness comprehended it not" and the Logos "came... to bear witness of the Light" (Jn 1:5, 7). The formation of Light is not the first Day of Creation. It is the *zero, beginning*, included in all of the subsequent six Days of Creation. There is a folk tradition of sitting down for a moment before going on a trip to get ready by concentrating and praying. In this state, a person is not "here," yet still not "there" either. This concentration is very important, because it clears the mind of the past to get a clearer idea of the future and prevent the past from affecting a new stage of the journey. This association indicates one more aspect of the participation of Christ's Sophia in the dispensation of our salvation: She is the *beginning (alpha)* of the ways of salvation — "The Lord by wisdom hath founded the earth; by understanding hath he established the heavens" (Prov 3:19) — and the one who prepares the Communion Chalice, while the *end (omega)* of the Lord's ways is Agape — the sacrificial Love of Deification.

This word has another biblical sense: "Beginnings" is the Church Slavonic name for the third order of the heavenly hierarchy (Principalities). Iconologically, this angelic order can be compared with the notion of "Symbols," because the level of symbolic meanings reveals the theology of faith, and life through religious symbols is already contemplated as the Icon of God's Revelations.

Therefore, the angelic Beginnings make it symbolically possible to accumulate "silence" before making a mystical ascent. The angelic order of Beginnings does not go into the subsequent Virtues, Powers, or Dominions, always remaining the "beginnings"—the gate through which it is possible to enter into a different dimension of Existence. As part of our nature is made of the noetic (intelligible) plane, the issue of *beginnings*, principals, and *symbols* is an issue relating to the transition of our faith from the discursive state of empiricism to the mystical state of noetic energies.

In Christianity, God the Trinity has one essential *Image* (Icon) and one *Will*, yet three iconographical Light energies: the Light of the Shekinah—from the eternal Father, the Light of Sophia—from the Son *being born*, and the Light of Agape—from the *proceeding* Holy Spirit. In these Three Ones we find the original enhypostatic completeness and, therefore, perfection of God's works. "For it was fitting, whereas God is One, that His Image should be One also, and His Word One and One His Wisdom."[23] St. John of Damascus writes that God creates with His idea (Sophia), and the idea becomes an operation (energema). God contemplates His Divinity so that in His Creation "each one (*thing*) comes to pass at the foreordained time in accordance with the *predetermination* and *image* and *exemplar* contained in His timeless will and design."[24] The paradigms of the Divinity constitute "the eternal and immutable Counsel of God, in which everything is foreordained. And this is the IMAGE of God. The second type is the Image oriented toward the creature—the image by *imitation* [*mirror*]."[25] Based on St. Dionysius the Areopagite, St. Maximus the Confessor writes about the same thing: "Everything preexists in the cause (arche-*beginning*) of all things as in the *idea and the prototype*";[26] and "created beings are the *images and likenesses* of Divine ideas."[27] In contrast to Plato, who distinguishes ideas from God, the Church Fathers speak about *images and logoi* in God. In other words, *images or eide* are the energies of diverse types (forms) of Revelation, while *logoi or ideas* are the powers (δυνάμις) of Revelation that strengthen the consciousness of believers. In addition,

---

23 St. Athanasius, *Against the Arians*, Discourse 2.
24 *An Exact Exposition of the Orthodox Faith.*
25 St. John of Damascus, *On Holy Images*, III, 19, PG 94.
26 *Schol. in lib. de divin. nomin.*, V, 7, PG 4.
27 *Schol. in lib. de divin. nomin.*, VII, 3, PG 4.

St. Augustine, somewhat confusing concepts, says: "The word *ideas* can be translated into Latin as 'forms' or 'types'.... Indeed, there are primordial ideas—some forms or logoi of things that are stable, unchanging, and always *self-identical*, because they are contained in the Divine Mind."[28] "We say that we know our God *from His operations*, but do not undertake to approach near to His essence. His operations [*energies*] come down to us, but His essence remains beyond our reach."[29] God's actions are knowable and describable, and personified ones are perceived as "live" Icons of Theophany, as the angels of the Logos, Sophia, and Agape.

Having said "I am Alpha and Omega, the Beginning and the End, the First and the Last" (Rev 22:13), Christ actually speaks about a certain "space" between "the beginning and the end" where Alpha-Sophia washes and polishes the old man like a diamond, preparing him for intelligent, conscious, and multifaceted faith so his new Soul could perceive the Omega-Agape of Christ's Light refracted as through a prism; for the Logos is the seed, the center of the human *person*, while His Sophia acts and develops the creative *individuality* of Man, transforming his natural abilities into the spiritual talent of staying in communion with God. Individuality not only represents characteristic *traits* of a personality, but is the personality itself. Using iconological categories, we call personality a person's "image," prosopon. Christ is called Sophia after the Image of His *Existence*, as a Hypostasis, while Sophia exists enhypostatically rather than independently and, therefore, is depicted after the Image of *Actions*. God's Hypostasis and Prosopon differ in IMAGE rather than nature: the former is the mode of existence (an unchangeable state), while the latter is the image of action (a changeable state). "Hypostasis is about existing by oneself and being different, while person (*prosopon*) is about operating separately and by oneself."[30] So, if Christ is the Son of God, Sophia may be said to be the Virgin of God. Having her appearance, the Angel of the Countenance of God has the virginal features of the Virgin. The canon of depictability of personified Theophany

---

28   *De divers. quaest.*, 46, n. 2.
29   St. Basil the Great, *Epist.* 234, *ad Amphil.*, PG 32.
30   St. John of Damascus, *On the Faith, Against the Nestorians.*

energies, as everything in the religious consciousness is specific and personal, should really reflect God's "personality" in accordance with the method of symbolic Icon realism.

St. Augustine writes: "The Spirit of Wisdom is called 'manifold' because it contains many things in it; but what it contains it also is, and it being one is all these things," for there is one Logos and one logos Image (Icon). We can draw the following analogy: as Christ the Son is the Icon of God the Father by the nature of *hypostatic* distinction, so Sophia is the Icon of the Son by the nature of *prosoponic* distinction. Surely, no sane person would confuse a "portrait" with its "original," making Sophia an independent being in the Trinity; but in the field of creativity we should distinguish between the Logos and Sophia and between the icon of Sophia and, for example, the icon of Agape.

There is another puzzling issue related to the topic of Sophia. Some believe that Sophia is embodied in the Virgin Mary and, therefore, the Mother of God is Sophia. This cannot be found in any works of the Church Fathers, because, according to St. John of Damascus, it is personality, Hypostasis, that can be embodied, not the Divinity; energy *pours out* into the world rather than is embodied.

> The Holy Spirit and the power of the Highest were announced to the Theotokos and the Apostles, but hypostasis of the Spirit did not descend upon or embody itself within the Theotokos; therefore, it was not the hypostasis of the Spirit that descended upon the Apostles either, but it was the grace and energy that filled them, having appeared and divided in the form of tongues of fire; and it is not said that the Spirit came down [here] as essence, so it was not some part of the energy that poured out as before, but it was the entire energy — in conjunction with essence, inseparable from it, and common to the three [Hypostases] as essence.[31]

It is appropriate to recall once again the theological distinction between the terms related to hypostatic origin (the *birth* of the Son

---

31   St. Mark of Ephesus, *On the Spiritual Gifts of Grace.*

Logos—Miraculous Angel in the Manifestation of Energies

and the *procession* of the Holy Spirit) and prosoponic origin (the *outpouring* of Energy [as seed] of the Divinity, the life-giving Spirit of God). The Bible contains many verses determining the Spirit as the Energy of God: "I will *pour out* my spirit upon all flesh" (Joel 2:28), or "I will *pour* my spirit upon thy seed, and my blessing upon thine offspring" (Is 44:3), and "Grace is *poured* into thy lips" (Ps 45:3). However, it is not all that simple in the iconology of Revelations.

In the Icon of "Sophia-Wisdom" (see the Icon), we can see rows of figures arranged crosswise: Angel Sophia and Christ the Logos (vertically); six angel-spirits of Wisdom (horizontally); the "Prepared Throne" (in the middle). On both sides of Sophia, symbolizing yet not replacing her, there are two figures: the Mother of God with the eternal Emmanuel — "*after the image*" of Sophia, and John — "*after the likeness*" of Christ.[32] This icon expresses the fullness of the Divine oeconomy. Therefore, the objective of diverse iconographies is not simply to depict one or a number of "persons." As a didactic art, iconography, using its figurative language, can express theological *ideas* to the same extent as theology or even to a greater extent, and at least far more extensively than is required by the advocates of iconographic "simplicity." Icon images are liturgical and always *sophianic*. Summarizing the Fathers' teaching of God's essence and actions, Georges Florovsky writes: "The properties of God are not only mentally conceivable or thinkable attributes. They are not abstractions or inventions. They are *powers and actions* — actual, essential, and *life-giving* revelations of the Divine Life."[33] These "life-giving revelations" can be accurately depicted only in icons painted in the style of *symbolic realism* — in fact, only they are icons in the true sense of the word.

The Church Fathers constantly talk about God essentially revealing Himself and operating in a prayerful person, and this certainly proves the possibility of depicting His image in man-made icons too, because Man is an icon created after the Image of God, while the man-made icon is created after the "image" of just such a person. In the icon, "His Divinity becomes visible in the true sense, actually and really, not deceptively existing in invisible divine things or existing

---

32 Based on the prophecy of Malachi 3:1.
33 Florovsky, *Dogma and History*.

only in the human mind."³⁴ Indeed, how can what is depictable in Man—the figurative presence of the Father, the Son, and the Holy Spirit—not be depictable in the icon? The answer is obvious and the task of iconography is solely to find the correct symbolic form and method for representing this Presence. Perceiving Man as a mentally conceivable Icon, we obtain the man-made icon as an instruction book and a practical guide for a liturgical prayer of "face-to-Face" contemplation of God. "God's powers (*haris*) are the [*sophian*] Face of God's living life-giving glance at the creature."³⁵ God's Sophian Face, which can be depicted by means of acheiropoesis, is revealed by the power of Incarnation of the Logos in Man, and the instruction to live—in the depiction of *properties and actions* of the Logos—is revealed through paint in icons.

ICONOGRAPHY OF SOPHIA

> God created man to the Image of His own likeness.
> (Wis 2:23, Slavonic version)

In the history of iconography of Sophia-Wisdom, there are distinctions between two close yet independent images:

a) Christ Emmanuel, the Logos as the hypostatic Wisdom of the Father (for example, in the icon of the "*Angel of Great Counsel*"), and

b) Personified Wisdom proper, according to the books of the Bible, in the iconography of the royal Virgin Sophia, the creative image of Christ in the creation of the conciliar Church.

The oldest known image of Sophia is found in the Codex Rossanus—the "purple" sixth-century biblical manuscript from Calabria (southern Italy). In this miniature, Sophia blesses Mark the Evangelist. In the Laurentian Library, there is a Latin biblical codex of the sixth century featuring a picture of Emmanuel in golden robes against the background of a red circle. Another ancient miniature (sixth or seventh century), contained in the Codex Syriacus in the National Library of Paris, depicts the Virgin Mary with Emmanuel in a mandorla on her breast; on her right side is Sophia in royal

---

34 Bishop Sylvester, *Experience of Orthodox Dogmatic Theology*.
35 Florovsky, *Dogma and History*.

robes with a cross in her hand, and on her left side is King Solomon holding a book. A similar miniature depicting King David between two virgins — Sophia and Prophetia (Prophecy) — can be found in the tenth-century Paris Psalter. The Hildesheim Service Book of the twelfth century features a miniature having an original composition: Sophia supports a sphere showing Christ and the inscription reading "With Him I created the world." The Lyon Prudentius manuscript has an image of regal Sophia surrounded by seven virgins — the seven spirits of liberal arts. Later, miniatures become increasingly iconic in their style: the images most often found in the Gospels are those of Sophia, with an eight-pointed halo symbolizing her Divinity, who stands behind the Evangelists and dictates a text to them. Sophia's images of the same style can be seen in miniatures of the thirteenth–fifteenth centuries and also in the icons created by evangelist and first icon-painter Luke, where She blesses the Virgin and Child icon painted by the Apostle.

A mosaic in the fifth- to sixth-century Church of Hosios David in Thessaloniki features an image of the Youth Logos Emmanuel holding a scroll in a mandorla in glory, with the Apostles Peter and Paul worshiping Him. The apse of the Basilica of San Vitale (sixth century) has a mosaic image of the Youth Logos Emmanuel sitting against the background of a sphere and holding a scroll of the Book of Wisdom in His left hand and a crown in His right hand; He is flanked by two angels who can be interpreted as the Angels of the Countenance of God: Sophia and Agape. A similar composition, known in Georgia from the seventh to the ninth century, is located in the Church of Venerable Dodo. One of the earliest murals in Gaza (sixth century) is an image of Sophia, which is known from its contemporary description by John of Gaza: Atlas carries a flaming ball, the rising sun, supported by two virgins: Sophia and Arete (Virtue), whose name can be interpreted as Agape (Love). The catacombs near Alexandria (fourth century) featured an early image of winged Sophia in the likeness of Emmanuel, having the inscription: "The Sophia of Jesus Christ" (the painting has not survived). A mosaic in a chapel (seventh century) in Durrës, Albania, depicts the Virgin Orans, with the figures of Eirene and Sophia on both sides of Her. So, we can

THE ANGEL OF THE COUNTENANCE OF GOD

see, even in the earliest versions of Christian theological thinking, a never-ending series of sophian ideas personified in iconographic images.

The first church dedicated to the Sophia of God was built in Constantinople by Emperor Constantine in the fourth century. Later, the topic of God's Wisdom gains a special mystical significance in connection with the construction by Emperor Justinian of the majestic cathedral of Hagia Sophia (in Constantinople in the sixth century), which eclipsed the glory of Solomon's legendary creation. The church's ceramics (Greek: *keramos*—tiles) had the inscription: "God is in her midst, she will not be shaken." Probably, this edifice gave an additional impetus to the development of the iconography of "*Wisdom hath builded her house*." The church was named after Sophia on the basis of a legend about the appearance of a mysterious Angel of the Lord who swore by the name of St. Sophia and said, "I am the guardian put in charge of this church." It is believed that the huge fresco depicting an angel on the wall of the cathedral is also associated with the legend of the miraculous appearance of the church Guardian. Some art historians assert (for simplicity and out of habit) that this painting, located in the great sanctuary of the church, depicts Archangel Michael, providing no arguments for their supposition. But most likely, it was the Angel of the Countenance of God—Sophia, because the later tradition was to portray Sophia in the sanctuary, all the more so as Archbishop Anthonius, who saw the painting in the twelfth century, mentioned that the "Guardian" Angel was surrounded by three more Angels.

From the time of Justinian, the image of Emmanuel, "the Only-begotten Son and Word of God," came to be firmly associated with the veneration of Sophia. After the construction of Hagia Sophia in Constantinople, they began to build churches dedicated to Sophia in other Byzantine cities, and then in the Balkans and Rus. The images of the Virgin Sophia and the Logos Emmanuel, sometimes with a sophian scroll, or in the likeness of the Virgin Mother of God having God's "name"—the Child Emmanuel—in Her womb, become the main types of iconography of God's Wisdom incarnate. The idea of Sophia was not approved dogmatically, but had various interpretations as a theologoumenon and, being a living and active symbol of the Church, spread throughout the Christian regions. In Rus, the hagiography of St. Cyril the Philosopher served as a folk and iconographic interpretation of Wisdom as a regal Virgin. Having found fertile ground in Rus, the idea instantly caught fire and was revealed in the construction of numerous churches and in the painted icons of St. Sophia.

The first cathedral churches in Russia's major cities were dedicated to Sophia the Wisdom of God. In the first year of the conversion to Christianity (988), a *thirteen-domed* oak-timbered Sophia church was erected in Novgorod, which was followed by a six-domed stone Sophian cathedral in 1045–1050. A grand cathedral dedicated to Sophia was built in Kiev in 1017–1037. The same years were marked with the construction of St. Sophia Cathedral in Polotsk. "The fact that the concept of Sophia, the Wisdom of God, was fully conscious and quite definite in Russia in the eleventh century is evidenced by the similarities and differences of its interpretations prevailing in Kiev and Novgorod."[36] Frescoes and icons for sophian churches were created in accordance with how the idea of the Sophia of Christ was understood. Russian paintings were characterized by the fact that frescoes were painted over entire wall surfaces rather than fragmentarily. The mosaic image of the Virgin Orans, "The Unbreakable Wall," created in the sanctuary of the St. Sophia Cathedral in Kiev has the sophiological meaning of the Virgin Bride, the Mother, and the Church; the name of the iconological triad "Sophia — Maria — Church" inherits, so to speak, the tradition of mythological interpretations of the goddess of Wisdom in various pre-Christian Eastern and Greek cults, personifying both virginity and motherhood. In Christianity, the same name began to be used in its superlative degree — the Wisdom of Christ, which had a theological rather than mythological meaning. The ancient church icon has not survived in the St. Sophia Cathedral in Kiev. Its copy, apparently modified, and painted not in the ancient iconographic style, dates back to the seventeenth century.

The Novgorod Cathedral of St. Sophia, right after its construction, was decorated (eleventh–twelfth centuries) with frescoes of biblical

---

36 Vera Bryusova, *Sophia the Wisdom of God in the Ancient Russian Literature and Art*.

scenes, of which little has survived. The prophets' tier in the drum of the dome starts with images of David and Solomon who hold sophianic scrolls. The bottom tier featured an image of the Only-Begotten Son, Emmanuel in Majesty — probably, it was similar to the surviving copies of the icon having the same name — in the personifications of the Law and Grace. The image of the Logos Emmanuel in the sanctuary painting of the Novgorod Cathedral of St. Sophia is not evangelical: it is based on the prophecy of Isaiah. The ancient church icon of God's Sophia has not survived. However, the Cathedral had its fifteenth-century copy, which was often copied later for other churches. Many fourteenth-century churches in Rus, Bulgaria, Serbia, and Macedonia have frescoes depicting Sophia. Of particular interest is a fresco in the dome of the fourteenth-century Rila Monastery in Bulgaria. In the center of the dome, Sophia is seated. She has a triangular halo and invites everyone to the Meal, with a Communion Chalice in front of her. Surrounded by "seven spirits" in the form of reclining infants having wings and haloes, Sophia is flanked by two angels, each holding a Chalice and inviting apostles, saints, prophets, and martyrs.

It is interesting to note the ancient trend of a constant iconography of a "triad" of mysterious figures. The Rila fresco depicts Sophia in front of a Chalice and two Angels with Chalices on each side of her. The Gračanica Monastery in Serbia is home to a fresco featuring three figures: winged Sophia, seated before a throne with scrolls, and two allegorical females figures at her sides, one of whom holds a Chalice while the other holds Bread. Later, canonical iconography was established: enthroned Sophia flanked by the Virgin Mary and John the Forerunner. It can be assumed that those were attempts to express an as yet unformed early *trinitarian iconological* idea of trying to depict the oeconomic theme: Logos Emmanuel with Sophia and Agape standing in front of Him.

A huge number of paintings and hundreds of icons dedicated to Sophia in churches (and now also in museums) show that in ancient times there was a deep tradition of worshiping the Virgin Sophia as a virginal Image of the enhypostatized and dispensational energy of Christ the Logos. However, the "dispute about Sophia" still continues, which means that God's Wisdom is of great importance not as an abstract power; and that It has innermost yet personal features in the iconological teaching of the Church, which encourages us to liturgical attention: "In Wisdom let us attend!" This means "God's Sophia *is coming in*, stand straight!"

THE DOCTRINAL MEANING OF SOPHIA

> We speak the Wisdom of God in a mystery, even the hidden wisdom, which God ordained before the world unto our glory. (1 Cor 2:7)

> How long, ye simple ones, will ye love simplicity? and the scorners delight in their scorning, and fools hate knowledge? (Prov 1:22)

"The concept of the Divine Wisdom is inherent in the human consciousness. It was not alien to the pagan worldview and it permeated the ancient Judaic religion, the highly developed thought of antiquity, Hellenism, and Eastern religions."[37] The subject of God's Sophia, despite all kinds of resistance among Christians themselves, increasingly took root throughout the history of icon-painting and developed both in a narrow field of its iconography, and in a broader sense, determining the basic principles of iconology. The practice of faith was always searched, in order to find the connection between God's Wisdom and the human mind. In fact, the Divinity is called "God's Mind" by the Church Fathers. The Sophia of Theophanies was revealed under various images in the ancient and the new world, and found a special expression in Christian iconology. Disputes about Sophia prove even more that it is necessary to have an accurate and completely formulated dogma for a better liturgical and iconological understanding of the images of faith. Strange attempts on the part of some writers to try to fully eliminate the difference between Sophia and Christ (following to the letter the expression: "Christ is Wisdom") in dogmatic and Christological theology are indicative of religious ignorance and the inability to distinguish between the

---

37 Ibid.

Actor and the *action* itself, which, therefore, means ignorance about the theological differences between "God" and "His Divinity." This situation may result in a destruction of the Christian liturgical culture, which means that faith may be deprived of its dispensational and church-creative aspect, and the idea of sacrifice and instructive guidance.

"All Wisdom cometh from the Lord, and is with Him for ever. Wisdom hath been created before all things, and the understanding of prudence from everlasting. The word of God most high is the fountain of wisdom; and her ways are everlasting commandments" (Sir 1:1–7). In the West and the East theological opinions (theologoumena) about Sophia have different starting points, but God's Sophia continues Its sermon in *words and icons*. This is the sermon of the Christian dispensation, and there cannot be any Church without Wisdom acting in the world. In the same way as history inexorably moves towards the eighth Day of the Coming of Christ, Sophia untiringly "facets" souls with Its double-edged sword, preparing a *diamond* where the Light is refracted in souls and where Man will be "sophianically" recognized by Christ.

Interest in the sophiological theme, which runs through the entire mythological and religious history of humankind, has long engrossed the minds of theologians, philosophers, and, of course, icon-painters. Wisdom, however, is still one of the most mysterious "persons" in the tradition of monotheism and polytheism. A lot of works, ranging from mythological, esoteric, and occult to etymological and humanitarian ones, have been dedicated to this subject. In fact, this is not about a common interest on the part of researchers. Instead, this is about trying to answer the eternal question about "the meaning of human existence," the practical answer to which can only be given by the God-Knowing Sophia.

> Wisdom — an unquenchable thirst for knowing the world — has attracted human minds throughout history. The structure and organization of the Creation, Existence, can comprehensively be divided into several levels: natural (from the cosmic macrocosm to the microcosm of

elementary particles), geopolitical (throughout human society), and social (from a state, a people, and a nation to a self-organized individual).[38]

The cosmos is not just a conglomeration of "dead" (material) bodies. In fact, it is a living organism animated by good Theophanic powers, which connect, organize, and vivify the entire Universe. Sophia is "in the beginning" of any (cosmic, human, noetic, and divine) beginning, because "She reacheth therefore from end to end mightily, and sweetly doth she order all things" (Wis 8:1). Sophia is an unceasing quiet "breath of God" — "And the Spirit of God moved upon the face of the waters" (Gen 1:2), "a still small voice" (1 Kgs 19:12) — and the whole universe is filled with this breath of God. However, Man is the essential actor who unites in himself God and the Universe and is destined to transform and improve the Universe. Man is a rational being — a *microtheos* and a *microcosm*. So, it is natural that, owing to the ontological affinity of souls, a chosen person taking Sophia's breath into his heart and mind (nous) becomes a carrier of Theophanic iconography and a prophet-king of the Universe. Jesus Christ became the first Man who called upon His Sophia for the salvation of all.

At the First and Second Ecumenical Councils, the Church Fathers determined that God's Wisdom is the second Hypostasis of the Trinity, which was important for settling the dogmatic dispute over the *hypostatic* Jesus Christ. But Sophia, considered in terms of the hesychastic tradition as the *prosopon* of the Logos and the Son of God in the dispensation (oeconomy) of the Trinity, can also be considered personally as a life-giving Energy of the Divinity and an iconological Angel who follows Christ's will to create the Church detached from the old world. Through the names of properties of the hypostatic God, Wisdom — named the *stewardess of salvation* and the *church creator* — is iconographically established on the seven pillars of the rainbow of the New Testament and is understood as the Sophia of preparation of liturgical Sacraments, and, therefore, "the gates of hell shall not prevail against" the Church.

---

38 Ibid.

THE ANGEL OF THE COUNTENANCE OF GOD

Liturgical theology mentions uncreated Sophia who was not created before all ages or afterwards. This vital Church issue was raised in the fourteenth century and settled in the course of a dispute between Archbishop Gregory Palamas and the Calabrian monk Barlaam, which finally clarified the previously arisen confessional division between the Eastern and the Western churches. Being vital, the dispute continues to this day, because many non-Orthodox confessions adhere to the thesis about created Energy rather than Energy poured out from the essence of God. The Orthodox hesychastic and liturgical prayer practice argue the opposite. Recognizing that the nature of the Light of Tabor is sophian and uncreated, it also establishes specific features of Sophia's iconological image. This issue is neither idle nor far-fetched, and requires a final decision, because Christ's Sophia, being the *"stewardess of the church,"* was left to us by the risen Jesus Christ to strengthen and comprehend faith until His Second Coming. It is Sophia who calls upon us to enter into the Holy Communion liturgy: "Come and partake of the Gifts of Salvation." A discussion based on an accurate understanding of the term "wisdom" and of the ontological relation between Divine Revelations and the world should prove that Sophia, in terms of Christology and liturgical iconology, is a creative and constructive Idea of the Logos. Being a church-iconological and prosoponic name of God rather than an abstract philosophical idea, Sophia bears one of the three images of the Divine Revelation. In symbolic icon realism, iconography depicts Sophia as a regal Angel, a Virgin, because by nature She is Christ's Bride bearing His seed — Emmanuel — in Her bosom.

Icon-painters, as artists committed to iconology, had no doubts about that. According to icon history and theology, if God is indepictable, His "thought" should be indepictable, so as not to fall into "Judaic temptation." In the light of the New Testament Revelation, cataphatic Theophanic theology already operates through symbols, allegories, metaphors, and parables. These are usually verbally described in liturgical texts, but may also be personifications in the iconography of church Icons.

The subject of Sophia was developed quite intensively in Russia: in literature, iconography, and mural painting. According to the conservator, artist, and academician A. Grabar, no other subject is so closely associated with Russia's religious history as the Sophia of God: from antiquity to modern times, this subject has been considered with astuteness by commentators who conclude that "a close connection between literary texts and iconography can be traced in visual art works."[39] Verbal and iconographic interpretations of *"logos"* and *"image"* permeate and complement each other. They are based on church "assumptions" as theologoumena and express not only theological thought, but also the culture of folk life, serving as a complement to the liturgy, and a formulation of faith. As long as such opinions are possible, faith will be a festive state of joy and exhilaration, like Sophia who "was daily His delight, rejoicing always before Him" (Prov 8:30). Furthermore, the Apostle Paul says that different opinions are acceptable "to evince the truth." It is noteworthy that iconography draws its pictorial evidence mostly from the liturgical heritage of hymnography, Tradition (including the Apocrypha), and hagiography rather than from Church dogmata. The icon itself is already *a symbol* and requires the development of its own symbolic and metaphoric confirmations, which are vital not for God, but for the world living on different planes of faith and comprehension, yet searching after one truth "to see God as He is." The Icon is the Song of Songs flowing from ontological sources of faith; as spiritual poetry, it cannot be forced to fit into the framework of strictly logical and dogmatic accounts concerning God; it needs "legends," because it arranges and sets them to the theological sounds of living, conscious, and pragmatically applicable faith!

One such legend was the vision of the Virgin Sophia described in the hagiography of St. Cyril the Philosopher (827–869), the enlightener and the first teacher of the Slavs. When Constantine (in Holy Baptism Cyril) was *seven*, he saw a clear symbolic dream: the procurator of the city gathered all the virgins from the city before him and told the youth to choose one for a wife. Constantine chose Sophia, a radiant-faced maiden who was the most beautiful of them all. When he told his parents about his dream, they blessed him for the service and dedication to the Wisdom of God. St. Cyril, called the Philosopher, was notable for his exceptional talent and his penchant

---

39 Ibid.

for knowledge. When he was a schoolboy, he read the works of St. Gregory the Theologian. He was appointed as a curator of the library at the church of Hagia Sophia, but then he left it and settled with his brother at the Olympus monastery. In Chersonesus (where one of the churches was dedicated to St. Sophia), St. Cyril, already a bishop, and his brother Methodius worked on the translation of the Scripture from Greek into Slavonic. For the Slavs, they devised the *Glagolitic and Cyrillic alphabets.* In the new alphabet, the order of letters, their pronunciation, and the way of their writing was almost the same as the Greek alphabet. There was a total of 36 letters. Just like Greek letters, they were also used to write numbers. The students of Cyril and Methodius spread this writing system to Rus as well, along with the philosophical idea of Christian Sophia, the everlasting Bride of God's Logos even before the Incarnation. In addition, Rus was quite deeply attuned to the verbal and graphic preaching concerning the wisdom of Christ.

The first cathedral churches built in major cities in Rus were dedicated to Sophia and, as early as the mid-eleventh century, the Wisdom theme gained an extraordinary development in paintings and church icons in various iconographic versions and interpretations. To understand the relationship between Man and God through Sophia, they created literary commentaries on the Holy Scripture. "Copies of thirteenth-century liturgical texts containing interpretations of Sophia have survived to this day."[40] In turn, those interpretations strengthened and extended iconographic interpretations, resulting in the creation of icon versions determining an exact relationship between the Word and Wisdom; in Rus, people deeply felt the relationship "Logos — Sophia" in the likeness of a regal Virgin Angel, and the image of believers' sophianic Soul — the Virgin holding Emmanuel — firmly became part of the tradition of religious art. The Russian soil was the most prolific in producing thousands of Marian icons having various names.

The deepening understanding of the relationship between Sophia and the Logos was accompanied by further development of the idea of Sophia as the creator of the church; later, this idea was transformed

---

40 Ibid.

into a personification of Sophia through the Theotokos Mary, on the basis of the fact that St. John Chrysostom called the Virgin Mary "the mother of Emmanuel." The canon of St. Cosmas of Maiuma for Holy Thursday already glorifies Mary as a personification of Sophia:

> Cause of all and Bestower of life, the infinite Wisdom of God has built His house, from a pure Mother who has not known man. For, clothing Himself in a bodily temple, Christ our God is greatly glorified... You faithful, let us give ear to the exalted preaching of the *uncreated* and consubstantial Sophia of God.

In hymns, the Virgin Sophia is already liturgically established as "uncreated." At the same time, we can hear about Her own creative preaching and about Her preparing the Eucharistic Chalice of the spermatic Lamb in the mystical "Pascha of blessing of all the faithful." At the Divine Liturgy, we hear the exclamation: "Wisdom, stand aright" — stand straight, "straighten the way of the Lord," Sophia is coming!; close "the doors, the doors! In Wisdom let us attend," because through the state of Christ's Sophia, believers not only receive Communion, but also perceive the Sacrament of Communion!

In the fourteenth century, Rus saw a convergence of the Wisdom and Trinity themes, and an expansion of believers' consciousness through an analogy between the Trihypostatic God and the Thrice-Holy Deity. In his comments on Sophia, Hippolytus wrote: "We profess the *trinity* mind. We acknowledge the exalted preaching of the *trinity deity* of the Father and of the Son and of the Holy Spirit." Theology says that Sophia belongs to the whole Trinity, but in icons She is depicted in conformity with Christ who in Wisdom did the will of the Father in heaven. The image of the eucharistic Logos Emmanuel — the Child often depicted within the Communion Chalice — also has a sophian meaning. Indeed, Sophia together with the Cherubim mysteriously forms the Eucharist, and She also invites everyone to the Meal. For example, the Moscow Kremlin is home to an embroidered chalice veil featuring a hagiographic image of St. Basil the Great holding the Child Emmanuel in the eucharistic Chalice. Greek frescoes also depict the eucharistic Child in the Chalice.

THE ANGEL OF THE COUNTENANCE OF GOD

The Sophia theme permeated the religious space in many cultural and liturgical areas. In the second quarter of the seventeenth century, the spiritual writer Semyon Shakhovski wrote for the Novgorod Cathedral a liturgical service dedicated to God's Sophia; later, it became widespread, far beyond Novgorod. The service glorified not only Sophia, but also the Theotokos — the miraculous uncreated temple of Christ's incarnation and presence. In addition, the icons of Sophia and the Theotokos were mentioned on equal terms in the text. In the subsequent versions of this canon, the interpretation of Sophia as a prototype of the Theotokos was strengthened, but iconographic copies continued to develop the idea of Sophia as a *regal* and *fire-like Angel*. In Rus, the veneration of St. Virgin Sophia manifested in many ways in the sensitive perception of the Russian soul strenuously seeking a holistically vital faith, because She came to be perceived ontologically as a way to Christ. (Cf. below: the perception of Agape by St. Symeon the New Theologian.) On this path to God, two characteristics of the Russian Soul were naturally combined: the *word* of interpretations and the *image* of manifestations, which in the unity of their perception imprinted themselves as orthodoxy in unsurpassed masterpieces of ancient icons.

Icons of fiery-eyed Sophia in the likeness of an Angel with wings of flame (in Deisis versions, Sophia was accompanied by the Theotokos and John the Forerunner, who is also often depicted with wings in the likeness of the angelic Sophia), with Christ the Savior at the top and a prepared Throne in a scroll of the Heavens, appeared around the fifteenth century and gained predominance in iconography. It is noteworthy that the image of the *Virgin Sophia*, whose revelations through icon-painting continued the tradition of revelations of the Old Testament patriarchs and prophets in the likeness of the Angel of the Countenance of God and the Angel of the Covenant (Mal 3:1), found some resistance before entering the New Testament as a result of theological interpretations. All other personifications of Wisdom — already known in Byzantium as Emmanuel, the Virgin Orans, Archangel Michael, Christ the Angel of Great Counsel, and the Great Hierarch — were adopted in Rus without significant changes.

Logos—Miraculous Angel in the Manifestation of Energies

Man is an acheiropoetos Temple of the uncreated sophian Spirit: "Know ye not that ye are the Temple of God, and that the Spirit of God dwelleth in you?" (1 Cor 3:16). Sophia is the Artist of God, but in Man too She prepares the spiritual beauty of pure focused consciousness, in which a believer can learn God's names and discern God's creative powers working for salvation.

> I must say that the entire system of the Christian doctrine encourages us to make the distinctions that we make. In essence, they were already given in the ancient and primordial distinction between "theology" and "oeconomy." The Church Fathers sought to clearly and accurately distinguish between these areas and between God-related definitions and names in terms of theology and oeconomy. This is founded on the distinction between "nature" and "will." This is associated with the distinction between God's "essence" and "what is around His essence," which is only related to it. This is about distinction, not separation.[41]

Based on this "postulate," we can conclude that everything that does not fall within the scope of dogmatics in terms of theology can be depicted in icons in terms of oeconomy, because icons follow their own direct source of Revelation — the iconology of seeing God. In fact, oeconomy is a synonym for "iconology," i.e., dispensation in "images of action." If we iconologically approach Florovsky's statement, which is based on the patristic Tradition, the iconographic substantiation of depictability of Sophia becomes quite clear. Sophia not only is enhypostatic to Christ, but also correlates and is in close creative association with the Logos. Without drawing away from Christ, Sophia, having diverse forms of life-giving energy, is the image of implementation of the Church Oeconomy. She is a creator of the Church, an Architect, and an example of the Church that is being built on Earth yet already triumphant in Heaven. Distinguishing Sophia and iconographically singling Her out as a separate "persona" of an angel-like and crown-bearing Virgin is an iconological technique. Accordingly, Sophia does not have to do with hypostatic

---

41   Florovsky, *Dogma and History*.

distinctions in God. Rather, She has to do with the Prosopon, with what is around God, and with the World into which Man will enter some day for his complete deification; and the Sophia of Christ is contributing to this even now. Given that Sophia is an energy IMAGE and an uncreated Icon of Christ's consciousness and that "Christ is God's" (according to Paul the Apostle), the depiction of Her in icons, without any pretense at substitution, affects the deepest foundations of theology.

Iconography is not photography. It deals with depicting invisible things that have a secret and hidden meaning, as Paul the Apostle said. In iconography, everything commanded by the Church Logos can be depicted with a mysterious movement of lines and colors. The world is created in accordance with God's Wisdom, and the Prototype's *conformity* with the establishment of the incarnate Christ in the Universe and especially in Man is the establishment of Man after the *image* of Sophia and after the *likeness* of the Logos. As Gregory Palamas says, "God's action (energia) *pours out* from the *essence*, yet without separating from it while pouring out. Outpouring (because it is energy) means an unspoken difference that does not violate the transcendental unity."[42] How can we talk about a complete substitution of Christ by personified Sophia if She is the "image of action"? Christ is a Hypostasis, while Sophia is His Prosopon and the *feminine*, or, more precisely, *everlastingly virginal* beginning of the Divinity, because Man in his completeness was created on the model of the divine antinomy: Adam was created after the image of the Logos, while Eve was created after the image of Sophia. According to Tradition, the Theotokos Mary is the "second Eve." Being of created nature, she is identified, in terms of *conformity to*, rather than having a nature in common with, Sophia. The Church has magnified the Virgin Mary to heaven in the highest "Most Holy," but no sane person would think that she is equal to the Son and to Christ. Mary is Christ's Mother and Bride — an everlasting virginal aspect of the "image of action" of religion, while Jesus Christ is the hypostatic Son and Bridegroom of any human soul — a masculine creative aspect of the "mode of existence" of religion; there can be

---

42 Theophanes, *PG* 150:940.

no theological or iconological confusion in this respect. Even Christ's human body is called His mystical Bride by the Church Fathers.

Through this method of distinction, manifested especially in iconography, we come to understand many aspects of the differentiated existence of created being by analogy: "God *is* Life" and "*has* life"; "God *is* Wisdom" and "*has* Wisdom"; "God *is* light" and "*has* Light"; and so on. In this consideration, the first — the noun "I am" (is) — is an incommunicable property (*name*), while the second — "has" — is communicable and iconographically depictable. None of these "properties" is self-hypostatic, but through enhypostatization they become personified, and this should be shown visually in the spirit of symbolic Icon realism rather than metaphorically. If Christ is a visible Image of the invisible God, the invisible Sophia will be a visible Image of Christ in an icon. Hence, as in the interpretation of the Song of Solomon, Her name is "Christ's Bride." Being enhypostatized into the hypostasis of Christ, She directly indicates that Christ is the Bridegroom of both the Church and the Soul. Given that Paul the Apostle said that "the woman is the glory of the man" (1 Cor 11:7), i.e., his prosopon, Sophia is surely the active beginning and the image and glory of Christ. It is Sophia who manifests the mystical Christ and His divine Hypostasis, standing as His "prosopon" "in front of" (or "around") Him. The Church Fathers say that every creature is contained in the Divine Image (Icon) and His Counsel (Word). Even from the beginning of the world, Man was put to the task of becoming similar to God, and Sophia together with the Cherubs mystically prepares the Communion Chalice to deify Man "after the likeness the Logos."

AGAPE—GOD'S LOVE

> Love alone harmoniously joins all created things with God and with each other.[43]

The third uncreated element, energy, and power of God, alongside with the logos Light and Wisdom, is Love (Greek: Ἀγάπη). While Wisdom is the living Water of new spiritual birth and "baptism into

---

43 Thalassios the Libyan, *On Love, Self-control and Life in Accordance with the Intellect* (written for Paul the Presbyter), First Century, 5.

eternal life and putting on Christ," Love — Agape — is the Fire of mysterious penetration of the Holy Spirit into the essence of a baptized soul, the element of a fiery initiation of Man into the beginning of Deification. Agape determines the fullness of the breath of life with God, and Life in its true, timeless, and immortal meaning is revealed to the world through the image of action of the Holy hypostatic Spirit. All energies equally belong to the Trinity, but the characteristic "color" of action of each divine element corresponds to the Hypostases' relations with one another and with the created world. The living Temple, the beloved and consecrated Church created by Christ with His wonderful Sophia sitting in it "on the seven spiritual pillars," became an altar on which the Holy Fire descended at Pentecost. From then on, in the Church beside Sophia there arose a *different beginning* of God's ways — the New Testament Agape, God's sacrificial Love, who sits along with Sophia on either side of Christ the Savior. From that moment in the history of humankind, the Church of the Son and the Holy Spirit appeared, making it possible for the Divinity to mystically enter into Man, which determined the nature and method of the Orthodox faith in God.

The "truth" of any Christian denomination should be measured not by the general nominal membership in the Church, but by the true saints who have attained fiery enlightenment in God's Love through the "tropos of existence" of the Holy Spirit in them. Throughout human history, no religion other than Orthodox Christianity has had so many elect permeated with Agape. Through the preaching and Calvary of Jesus Christ, Agape was revealed to the world in all its fullness and highest sacrifice; so, since then, Love itself ceased being a religious completion of "philia," fraternal love, or cosmic love determining only the anthropological importance of religion, and became a great power creating Man to be an enhypostatic and gracious Son of God. Paul the Apostle in his well-known dictum, which essentially means "if you have no love, you have nothing" (1 Cor 13:3), talks about Christ's divine Love acting in the flame of faith of the Holy Spirit. In the New Testament, where sacrificial Agape restored Man's senses to feel a new Life, a mysterious verse in the Psalms (104:24) sounds in a new way: "In *Love* hast thou made them all" [Slavonic text]. Here, in the revelation of the sacrificial Love of sincere relations between God and Man, there begins to shine a mystery as ancient as the time of Adam: "The kingdom of God is within you" (Lk 17:21). Agape awakens all the cooled-down strata of the ancient religious faith of humanity. Cleansed by Christ's sacrifice and inflamed by the Holy Spirit, they flare up with a new faith in one God acting in Three Hypostases, so people baptized in the name of the Trinity begin to understand in a new way that the Father's Will calls to them to return to the *Kingdom* (Holy God), the Son's *Wisdom* for that purpose graciously gives birth to them with Power (Holy Mighty), and the *Love* of the Holy Spirit directs them to an ecstatic participation in the *Glory of God* (Holy Immortal).

The concept of "love" has always been diversely revealed in everyday life, mythology, philosophy, and religion, which can be observed in all aspects of life. Love acts in irrational and rational nature — in the mineral, vegetable, and animal kingdoms — through *eros*; It penetrates us and lifts us to the heights of human creativity through *philia*; but Love finds its mystical perfection and completeness in holy people and angels through direct contemplation of God's *Agape*.

In ancient Greek and in the biblical language, the concept of "love" can be expressed by different terms: *Eros, Philia,* and *Agape*; and each term has its own aspect and level where God's essential energy acts to a greater or lesser extent.

Eros is a love that is closely associated with the movement of the discursive *mind* (Greek: *gnosis*) with its emotional and corporeal system of heart "passions." The Eros love moves and develops rectilinearly, increasing through a reunification of the thought and the heart. Despite the usual worldly definition of the sensual relation between eros and flesh, this Love energy can also be lifted to "the divine Eros" acting in the early stages of inner prayers.

Philia is a "brotherly" love associated with the intuitive or spiral motion of the *mind* (Greek: *episteme*); it calms down all aggressive movements and brings things together in terms of their essence, rather than concepts and opinions in relation to the general state of existence of the whole Universe. Philia is governed by the commandment "Thou shalt love thy neighbor as thyself." It organizes feelings related to an impartial attitude to things, helping the mind penetrate all living things without violence and recognize the meaning of Life. When there are no personal attachments or complaints, all things, according to the law of reverse perspective, while converging, come into a creative contact and achieve harmony, revealing the Presence of God in the Universal Life. Philia is the gate to knowing God.

Agape is a love that, once revealed in Philia, begins to turn to the divine Logos, attracting Its favor and attention. While Eros and Philia are equally natural to Man, Agape is a divine and selfless Gift, and its actions are primarily associated with Man who is *intelligent* in faith. Agape is governed by the commandment "Thou shalt love thy God above all things." Filled with Agape, the Soul kindles like a Virgin who comes of age and, starting to feel like a Bride, inevitably soars to her heavenly Bridegroom originally intended for her from the creation of the world. Through the action of Agape, the earthly and heavenly natures are reunited in Man. Agape is characterized by sacrificial love, because it predestines Man for a complete abandonment of oneself and even life for the sake of communion with the divine Life, as Christ says, "He that loseth his life for my sake shall find it." Agape takes the soul out of the scope of material and cosmic interest into the mysticism of the noetic *mind* capable of knowing God. In Agape, the human heart always revolves "around God" in constant contemplation of His Divinity. Being in Agape, Man becomes "an angel in the flesh."

Despite the difference in spiritual strength and the areas of life where the energy of love operates in different combinations and proportions, these three levels are the basis of life of all forms of consciousness, and true faith cannot be perfect if only one of these energies operates in Man. In addition, making a distinction among the positions of Agape's operations, we can say that God's Love for Man proceeds and develops depending on the extent of awareness of the meaning and breadth of faith: Love for the *Creator* (Eros), the *Father* (Philia), and the *Lord* (Agape).

The agapean *ekstasis* endlessly reveals the human spiritual essence, completely changing Man's view of the liturgical service of God, the Church, and the world. Speaking about the philosophical idea of "all-encompassing unity," we can say that such unity is only possible on the basis of the Divine Agape. This re-unification must be achieved by God's eucharistic Love rather than by Man, because what is differentiated by Christ's Wisdom is immediately reunified by the Love of the Holy Spirit without leaving any space among the material, noetic, and uncreated worlds. A symbolic example of this kind of faith is Christ's Sophia—a *double-edged sword glowing in the fire* of Agape of the Holy Spirit. As promised by God, this mystical sensitivity will be given to Man in the coming future: "And I will give them *one heart*, and I will put a new *spirit* within you; and I will take the stony heart out of their flesh, and will give them an heart of flesh" (Ezek 11:19).

LOVE IMAGES IN MYTHOLOGY

> O unfathomable power of love! O infinite power of love! Nothing is more precious than love, neither in heaven nor on earth.[44]

From olden times, the myths of many peoples featured personified love which was mainly understood in the forms of "erotic eidos." In Greek mythology, personified wisdom, Athena, coexisted with the equally important image of Aphrodite, the goddess of love and beauty. The understanding of ancient myths occurs simultaneously with an increase in religious consciousness, following from the philosophy of polytheism to the theology of Archetypes. In myths, we can also see a creative rise of the human genius evidenced by the formation of artistic and poetic images and expressive personifications based on the characteristic features, images, and qualities observed by archaic Man in his individuality. Then, moving from the contemplation of "ideas-gods" to the comprehension of real world images in symbolizations of one most high God, myths, growing to a certain extent in "wisdom," return to their true source and enter into a religion of "love" and the knowledge of God. An elementary example of personification and an absolutely essential stage in the development of children, especially girls, are games, toys, and dolls, in which children truly believe and find a real materialization of their sometimes most fantastic ideas.

---

44 St. Ephrem the Syrian, *On Love*.

THE ANGEL OF THE COUNTENANCE OF GOD

It is undeniable that ancient mythology found realization of its ideals in the New Testament, but Christian saints still contemplated not personification of gods, but God in the form of Light, Wisdom, and Love. Mythological gods and goddesses — who essentially were bearers and implementers of various philosophical or religious *ideas* understood in accordance with the spiritual level of peoples in those days — were not completely struck from subsequent religious life. Instead, they changed their "image" and, after the Incarnation of Christ, transformed their relations towards people, coming into contact with the emotional and intellectual aspects of their everyday lives. In modern history too, there have remained characters many of whom, while calling themselves Christians, are possessed with outspokenly demonic ideas of worldwide domination or occultism — all those conspiracies among states, intrigues, wars, and other events are caused by Man's relations with the universe of gods, just like in ancient myths. This proves that ancient myths have stayed within the religious consciousness of modern people, remaining active and continuing to have a very important role.

It is equally unsurprising that national mythologies also contained images of spiritual harmony that, even though intertwined with elemental pagan stylizations, essentially foretold the beauty and power of the future revelations of monotheism. Starting with the most primitive forms, mythology gradually transformed into religious philosophy, with its best works and most sublime images going back to the idea of the existence of "the unknown God." While mythology featured acts of love mainly at the "erotic" level, religious philosophy began to understand love, without any emotional intensity inherent at this level, as cosmic love — Philia. With the gradual recognition of monotheism and the idea of human salvation, the concept of "love" was undergoing an even greater transformation, and, by the time of the Incarnation of the Son of God, there arose a concept of God's sacrificial Agape.

The idea of pure and unearthly love found its expression and personification in the Greek myth of Aphrodite (derived from the Greek word "Αφρός" for "foam") Urania. Risen from the sea foam, she is a perfect image of birth given by the unity of the *water* element and the *air* of the heavens. The myth of Aphrodite reflects the ancient origin of the goddess of Love. She is the image of primary chthonic powers. Arisen even before the Olympian gods, Aphrodite contains the power of the cosmos, filling the whole world with ecstatic energies of fertility, eternal spring, youth, and healthy physical beauty, stimulating the body to love yet simultaneously elevating the human mind to heavenly elements. Land, seas, and mountains are embraced and permeated with the power of Aphrodite.

In terms of its Oriental origin, this goddess is close to and often identified with the Phoenician Astarte, the Babylonian-Assyrian Ishtar, and the Egyptian Isis. Emphasizing her independent creative power in the Olympic mythology, Parmenides writes about the birth of Aphrodite's first son, the god Eros (known as Amor), the winged infant with "arrows" rays (*energemas*) of amorous feelings. At different times, worshippers of Aphrodite associated her with "holy gardens" and "meadows," calling her "purifying," "merciful," "golden," "splendidly-crowned," "fair-eyed," etc. These epithets are quite applicable to the Theotokos, and some of them are even used in liturgical hymns. Owing to their figurativeness, they can serve to translate "words" into "images," which is important for the creation of icons of Agape of the Living God. However, we should remember that iconology, as distinguished from mythopoetry, speaks directly about the essential and embodied Love of the true God, who "Himself is Love."

Sometimes myths, almost prophetically, gave rise to images of a goddess who was both a "virgin" and a "mother," and sometimes a mother-goddess served simultaneously as a wife, a sister, and a bride in relation to a father-god or a son-god. This kind of myth was really fulfilled in Christianity and embodied in the Virgin Mary who was both the Mother of God and the "Unwedded Bride" of the Son. In addition, the Egyptian myth of Osiris and Isis—where a god suffered, died, and was resurrected—reminds us of the Son of Man! Isis, originally a goddess of the sky, was depicted with horns on either side of a sun disk, which is very close to the New Testament image of the Woman of the Apocalypse, Virgin, and Bride of the Lamb-Logos. Christ is the Sun, while the Woman clothed with the "sun of righteousness," with a two-horned moon beneath her feet, already expresses the mystical Light of the theology of the incarnate Logos rather than reflected light as in the myth. "A woman... and upon her head a crown of twelve stars" (Rev 12:1): does that not remind us of the zodiacal circle? Another similarity between Isis and the Virgin Mary is in her motherhood. For example, it is known that Egyptian figurines depicting Isis holding and breastfeeding her baby son Horus were for a long time kept as images of the Theotokos by Christians in the early centuries AD. In Sumer, the virgin "mother of all children" goddess Ninhursag was depicted inside an *eight-pointed* star representing all cardinal directions, which can also be seen in Christian iconography (for example, in the Icon of the Burning Bush, or in the halo of the Virgin Sophia). There are icons in which the image of the Theotokos is also depicted against the background of an eight-pointed star, reflecting the idea of the Eighth Day and the time of meeting the coming Christ the Savior. Sumerian Ninhursag was often identified with the brightest star in the southern hemisphere, Sirius. She often appears holding a bow resembling a moon horn. The brightest star in the northern hemisphere, Vega, was depicted with a bow-like lyre, which, according to Heraclitus, had the same symbolic meaning. So, we can see that these female images are accompanied by symbols that are similar in shape: a horn, a crescent, a bow, and a lyre. A "horn of plenty" is a metaphor and allegory of wealth and fertility; a "crescent" is a symbol of development, "inhalation and exhalation" of life (the lunar cycle begins and ends with a crescent); a "bow" signifies concentration of energy and its transition to a dynamic movement of an arrow rushing to its target. It is a symbol of war, but it does not always imply aggression: a bow in the hands of the god Eros means love; a "lyre," designed similarly to a bow, symbolizes harmony, concord, and achievement of love. According to Heraclitus, the bow is the father of all things, and the lyre is the mother of all things.

The brightest star in the zodiac is Alpha Virginis in the constellation of Virgo. This star was worshiped by the Sumerians and Egyptians as the central divine maternal revelation of the Virgin Mother. In the zodiac, Virgo is portrayed holding a sheaf of wheat, which reminds us of Christ's words, "I am the living bread which came

Logos—Miraculous Angel in the Manifestation of Energies

down from heaven" (Jn 6:51). This gives rise to a symbolic association: a Virgin, "the woman clothed with the sun," gives birth to the Bread of Life. Another association is as follows: when the constellation of Virgo rises to the zenith on the eastern horizon on a winter's night, the day starts to increase, giving birth to the Light for the world. In September, during the solstice in the constellation of Virgo, the Greeks celebrated the Eleusinian Mysteries dedicated to Demeter, the Earth Mother. The Christian feasts of the Assumption and Nativity of the Theotokos are celebrated on August 15 and September 8, when the Sun passes under the constellation of Virgo. Previously celebrated on the day of Epiphany (January 6), the Nativity of Christ was transferred to December 25, the day of winter solstice, when the pagans celebrated the birth of the sun god.[45] We can say that

> pagans reverently opened their eyes to see not only Christ's coming to the world, but also His immaculate Mother, and revered her, as best they could, under different images. While modern seekers for "religious and historical parallels" find a tempting similarity between Isis weeping over Osiris and the Theotokos bent over the body of the Savior, we are filled with astonishment bordering on reverence for that pagan anticipation of the Theotokos.[46]

The cult of female deities, goddesses of fertility, and the creative powers of the Universe can be regarded as the personification of the feminine and ontological element of any reality. The whole variety of goddesses, who had their own names with every people, was often reduced to one person and identified in one name. In Thrace, for example, the goddess Cybele—the Mother of the earth and gods—was universally worshiped and known under the names of other goddesses, including Aphrodite. In Carthage, Cybele was identified with the Heavenly Virgin and associated with the planet Venus; she was also identified with the constellation Virgo. By the time of Christ's birth, many peoples called Cybele "the mistress of

---

45 Rev. Gennady Eykalovich, *The Dispute about Sophia*.
46 Sergei Bulgakov, *The Icon and Its Veneration*.

all the elements" and "the life-giver," which fully coincides with the hymnography of the Virgin Mary. Earlier, Plato reconsidered the image and character of the ancient Aphrodite, attributing the features of sublime love, the heavenly Urania, to her. Herodotus wrote that Aphrodite Urania was worshipped by Syrians, Persians, Arabs, and even Scythians. Temples dedicated to her were erected in Athens and other areas of Greece. Aphrodite was especially worshiped in Asia Minor and Rome under the name of Venus (the goddess of gardens) as the progenitress and patroness of the Romans; she was regarded as the bearer of fertility and the personification of the abstract concept of "the gods' mercy."

The planet Venus played a major role in astrology. It was defined as "a merciful orb of night: a man or a woman." Interestingly, according to the hypothesis advanced by scientist E. Velichkovsky, Venus was included in the solar system only as late as about 1500 BC, during the exodus of the Jews from Egypt. Earlier, Venus was considered to be a comet, so ancient astronomical maps did not feature it. For example, Venus is not indicated in the Hindu map drawn in 3102 BC. Babylonian astronomy knew only four planets — Saturn, Jupiter, Mars, and Mercury — and did not mention Venus either. However, this bright star could not be unnoticed by ancient astronomers. At that time, Venus had a "tail" or "trace" consisting of hot gases and solid particles, and, according to an ancient Mexican legend, it "emitted smoke." The Chaldeans said that Venus had a "beard," while the Jewish Midrash Rabbah reads: "Venus's shining light illuminates the Universe from one end to the other." In Greek, the word "comet" means "long-haired." Egyptians described Venus as a rotating star emanating fire and flames. At present, this star is a little brighter than others, but the ancient descriptions of Venus were so impressive that they resulted in its mythologization. Just as the Moon, Venus passed through certain development phases, but the horns of its crescent were elongated trails whose outline resembled a bull's head with steep horns, so it was called the Horned Astarte. The cults of the bull Apis in Egypt, the golden calf of the Hebrews, and the sacred cow in India date back to that period.[47]

---

47 Eykalovich, *Dispute about Sophia*.

Logos—Miraculous Angel in the Manifestation of Energies

Venus was known as the "morning star," a name associated with Lucifer (Slavic: *dennitsa*, morning star). In the Bible and in the Christian tradition, the name Lucifer was used to denote Satan, a fallen Angel—the proud imitator of the uncreated Light of Glory and Deity. "How art thou fallen from heaven, O Lucifer, son of the morning! Thou hast said in thine heart, I will ascend above the heights of the clouds. Yet thou shalt be brought down to hell, to the sides of the pit" (Is 14:12–15). Venus is the brightest and most conspicuous planet in our solar system, but mythology regards it in an interesting dualistic aspect: Venus is given both evening and morning attributes; it is a goddess of both the sky and the earth; it is both virginal and androgynous. Shining on the horizon after sunset, it is known as the Evening Star. During a certain period of time, Venus is eclipsed by the Sun and cannot be seen owing to its bright radiance. Then it appears before the Sun and is called the Morning Star. The horns, with which Astarte and Isis were sometimes depicted, serve as a "figurative metaphor" of the crescent of Venus in its first and last phases.

There is no doubt that some of the figurative elements of ancient religions became part of Christian iconography: a crescent depicted beneath the Virgin's feet, stars on the robe of the Theotokos, an eight-pointed star in the halo of Sophia, etc. The ancient personifications of the ancient goddesses Astarte, Isis, Aphrodite, etc., in whose person they revered maternity and virginity—a combination of the female aspects of the Mother and the virginal mystical aspects of the heavenly Virgin—are specific manifestations of the later cult of the principal goddess Cybele. Therefore, mythology marked a transition from certain "embodiments" of the idea to the religious concepts of Shekinah, Sophia, and Agape in monotheism. The concept of the virginal Mother is wonderfully intertwined with the concept of the "spoken Logos" born into the world and the "pneuma-spirit" poured out into the world in accordance with the names of the Single Image of Theophanies.

Lucifer-Venus, however, has a negative meaning as the image of cosmic love acting at the level of discursive Eros. In this sense, love is based on an irresistible law—it is a "darkened" star and an adversary of Christ. The New Star of the true morning, the never-setting Light is Christ Who calls Himself "the bright and morning star... Alpha and Omega, the beginning and the end" (Rev 22:13, 16). Clothed with the Love of the Holy Spirit, Christ-Sophia gives the peoples Love itself, God's Agape, rather than the names of imaginary allegories of love. In the Byzantine tradition, the Virgin Mary, the Mother of God, is likened to a morning star; She stands on a crescent of the orb of night and represents the sun of righteousness — Christ, the God-Man (sixth-seventh century akathistos hymn). Origen applies the name "morning star" even to John the Forerunner, because John foretells the coming of Christ just like the "morning star" Venus heralds the sunrise. Probably, this is the reason why the Deisis iconography depicts the Virgin Mary and John the Forerunner on both sides of Christ seated on a throne (the same image can be seen in the iconography of the heavenly Sophia).

Numerous ancient Greek images of Aphrodite in sculpture, bas-reliefs, and vases rank among masterpieces of world art. Later, many Renaissance artists dedicated their works to Aphrodite. As early as the fourteenth and fifteenth centuries, mythological scenes depicting Aphrodite can be found in manuscript miniatures. Shown in images of Love, the experience of mythological art and pre-Christian literature suggests that, in addition to the divine Sophia of Christ, it is necessary to iconographically depict the divine Agape — the creative energy of the Paraclete-Spirit. "With fear, faith, and love draw near," priests say when they bring out the Communion Chalice. "The fear of the Lord is the beginning of Wisdom"; Wisdom reveals the Light of Enlightenment, while Love helps creatures commune with the Deity interpreted by the Universal Catholic Church as a Gift from above.

God's Agape penetrates the heart of the soul, and the soul becomes silent while contemplating the revelation of Beauty; this is how love gives birth to true, active, and therefore perfect faith. The gift of Agape is, as Plato said in the *Phaedrus*, "eternal, uncreated, and unperishing beauty, which does not increase or become depleted, remaining unchanged in all its parts, at all times, in all respects, in all places, and for all people." Beauty is not the third reality between created and uncreated things; it is a state of complete consubstantial harmony of

Light, Wisdom, and Love — the Exemplar revealed to Man in Theophanies. In matters of art, there is constant argument about the "relativity" of beauty. In religion, there cannot be any relative beauty (in accordance with Christ's words: "But let your communication be, Yea, yea; Nay, nay"). Holy souls contemplate the only accurate exemplar of Beauty, which is passed on through tradition and embodied in iconography as the Color of Revelations of Light. Revelations of God's Agape can only be relatively known from myths, philosophy, and ritual religion, while the mystical fullness of personal Knowledge of God is promised to Man in the future to come.

Myths, if they still exist in Man as a special language elevating us to a real Symbol, dictate temporary "fear" and "faith" to us, urging us to complete the search for God in everlasting Love. As part of the religious state of life, myths naturally participate in tradition and liturgy; therefore, mythological images reunited with dogmatic theology, just like chanted words of church hymns, should be depicted in icons as a poetry of iconological intuitions. God's Agape dwelling in the paradigm of the New Jerusalem "prepared as a bride adorned for her husband" is the Tabernacle where "God will dwell" with us (Rev 21:2, 3). While Church fathers and teachers interpreted Sophia-Agape in different ways, all of them attributed this essential energy manifested in Theophanies either to the whole Holy Trinity without distinction or mainly to one of the Hypostases (mostly to the Son).

THE THEME OF LOVE IN THE SONG OF SOLOMON

> The expression "The Song of Songs" (Greek: άσμα ασμάτω)... cannot be understood as a series or a collection of Solomon's songs.... On the contrary, in accordance with the Hebrew grammar, a word in the singular used in combination with the same word in the plural usually expresses the superlative degree of the notion expressed by the given word.... "The Song of Songs" can only mean the best song of all other songs... and this title fully corresponds to the form and contents of this sacred book. "The

THE ANGEL OF THE COUNTENANCE OF GOD

Song of Songs" is an excellent work of sacred God-inspired wisdom and sacred poetry in terms of its exquisite poetic presentation, ideological content, and riches in thought in the development of its mysterious sublime subject.[48]

Indeed, the title "The Song of Songs" (eighth century BC), according to one of the earliest Christian commentators, Origen, means "the best song of all." This is the most mysterious book of the Bible, according to commentators, and the most difficult one in terms of logic, which is not surprising, because it is a poem about Love. The language of love is deeply intimate, extremely symbolic, and ecstatically mystical. The Book of the Wisdom of Solomon is a "full-blooded sister" of the Song of Songs and both of them are amazingly rich in symbolism, but the Song of Songs is gold refined in the crucible of Man's fiery aspiration to God, and the Love described in this book is understood both as the Eros of the human valleys and as the Agape of the heavenly Spirit. In addition, the Song of Songs is a lyrical poem whose dialogues and monologues are not only about love. Preeminently, they are about praise of Love, the essential Agape of God. Like an abundant rain, Love is poured out without measure by the Lord on the created world, and we know about love reuniting us with God only owing to our inherent seminal Logos, the Bridegroom of our souls, who, having found an "earthly bride," returns with her to His Father. Through the Logos's Sophia operating in humans with the revelation of intelligent perfection, we inherit the revelation of the life-giving Agape of the Logos, because things are deified only in Love. According to St. Gregory the Great,[49] the Song of Songs poem elevates the soul from earthly love to the heavenly divine one. In this sense, the love Song's theme should be considered in the three states of perception that people have, all three unified owing to their physical and noetic nature:

- *Eros* — the physical attraction of the *Bride*'s Virgin-Soul to the Bridegroom;

---

48 Alexander Lopukhin, *The Explanatory Bible: The Old Testament — The Song of Songs*.
49 *PL* 79:473.

Logos—Miraculous Angel in the Manifestation of Energies

- *Philia* — the "psychic" attraction of the *Sister-Bride*'s Soul to the Bridegroom in the search for common principles of creative Life which are revealed in brotherly love which, according to Church Fathers, includes the attitude toward Angels;
- *Agape* — the spiritual attraction of the *Mother-Bride*'s Soul to the Logos Bridegroom, with whom a true marriage is effected for co-creation in "created and uncreated" life through the reunion of Man's physical, noetic, and divine habitation in the Kingdom of God.

Considering the "types" of love as a whole, as an anagogic movement towards God the Logos, this poem can be interpreted in a spiritual light. In the Song of Songs, everything is obviously intertwined, and all the relations among different characters are interpenetrated with love at different levels. It is absolutely clear that the main role in the Song of Songs belongs not to Solomon and the Shulamite, but to the Angel of the Countenance of God in the last revelation of the Holy Spirit, which connects the images of the bridegroom and the bride in God's Love. The Song of Songs is the New Testament written in ancient times, and that is why this book is prophetic. It is written in a special figurative, antinomial, i.e., iconological, language, whose height of expression and special tone of symbolism surpasses that of all the biblical prophets. Researchers note that "it constantly features masculine nouns accompanied by feminine adjectives or feminine verb endings; and vice versa — feminine nouns accompanied by masculine adjectives; or singular nouns accompanied by plural verbs and vice versa."[50]

The Song of Songs was included in the canon of the Scripture after some resistance on the part of those who understood it too straightforwardly and unambiguously. In the Jewish Mishnah it says that at one time the Jerusalem rabbinical school rejected the spiritual significance of the book while the Babylonian school supported it. The famous Rabbi Akiva (died in AD 135) supported the canonical books: "No man in Israel ever disputed the status of the Song of Songs.... The whole world is not worth the day on which the Song of Songs

---

50 Kerr Thomson, *The Interpreter's Bible*.

was given to Israel, for all the Writings are Holy, but the Song of Songs is the Holy of Holies." After that, the book was accepted by all Jews, but its strong symbolic eroticism prevented it from being sung at weddings. It was particularly customary to read it on Saturday, the day of domestic "peace and love." Christianity unequivocally accepted the Song, and the Church Fathers confirmed the authenticity of symbolic interpretation of the spiritual Love described in it.

There are also those who reject the spiritual significance of the Song of Songs in the new times of "scientific" interpretation of the Bible, because this book, like "a voice crying in the wilderness," calls to God, yet there is no mention of God in it. In addition, this book has no prayers or national features, unlike the other books of the Old Testament. All this shows that Love has an enduring value for all living things, because God Himself is Love, and He created the whole world with Wisdom and Love. In the Song of Songs, the beloved one is often called now "sister," now "spouse," and sometimes even both names are used: "Thou hast ravished my heart, my sister, my spouse" (Song 4:9–11). In the times of Solomon, a sister could not be a spouse, which means that the book symbolically refers to a mystical feeling of faith that connects God's Virgin Sophia and God's Agape into a single image of action. In his great wisdom, Solomon says, "Say unto wisdom, Thou art my sister; and call understanding thy kinswoman" (Prov 7:4) and "I loved her, and sought her out from my youth, I desired to make her my spouse, and I was a lover of her beauty" (Wis 8:2). Again, the Bridegroom takes a "sister" as a "spouse" for himself. So, the movement of God's Wisdom (Sophia) and Love (Agape) towards the Logos, who lives in the temple of the human soul, should be understood as inseparable. For the believer's Soul, Christ is a Brother, by the human nature, and a Hypostatic Bridegroom, by the divine nature. The soul is Christ's sister, by virtue of its created nature, and His Bride, by virtue of the gracious gift of conjugal deification.

Being a hymn to God's Agape, the Song of Songs is beyond time, history, space, or national differences, bearing the all-pervasiveness of a single holistic Agapean and Sophian feeling where the erotic love and the spiritual love are differentiated without being separated. Man is destined to be deified, including the body which should become holy in God's Love. That is why corporeal prayers are highly important for devotees of piety.

> Even though some scholars tried to create a pattern of development of the action or movement of the theme in the book of the Song of Songs, they could not achieve their purpose, which was impossible due to the fact that the book has no beginning, end, or middle. This is an excerpt or revelation from eternity about God's Love for Man and about the love expected from Man for his God as an essential response. Human language has no adequate words for Agape. It has to use imperfect human language and graciously descend to earthly images. The language of the book is special; it is absolutely above any language rules and, as it were, beyond human speech.[51]

It may be added that in the Song of Songs the Miraculous Angel of the Logos — God's Agape — inaudibly speaks and invisibly acts, revealing the secrets of marital union. The miracle of Agapean Love is unique due to the fact that it works not only between those who are equal by nature, but also, glorifying the Marital Chamber, reunites the uncreated Logos with the Bride of created beauty. The hidden Love urges them not to think about earthly pleasures and even to become free of "heavenly pleasures," but rather to look for each other in the Kingdom of God to jointly receive the eighth Sacrament — Deification.

IMAGES AND TYPES OF INTERPRETATION OF THE SONG OF SOLOMON

> Listen to the Song of Songs and try to understand it and, together with the bride, say what the bride says, so you can also hear what the bride has heard. If you cannot say, together with the bride, what she has said in order to hear what has been said to the bride, hasten at least to be with the Bridegroom's companions. But if you are lower than

---

51 Archimandrite Ambrose, *The Preface to the Song of Songs*.

they are too, be together with the maidens who abide in the bride's love, because in this book they are characters in the course of the described events and in the marriage song, based on which the Gentiles composed a wedding song for themselves, because the Song of Songs is a marriage song.[52]

Proceeding from on the foundations of theology, the Song of Songs was interpreted by many fathers and philosophers of the Eastern and Western churches. Usually, they single out three main types of interpretation, but some studies make it possible to conclude that there are seven levels of interpreting the book. The main motif featured with all the authors is surely the Christian idea, expressed by the Apostle Paul, that the Bridegroom is Christ and the Church is His Bride. Many commentaries, however, also contain ideas that are useful for the exaltation of faith, for instance, concerning the Logos–Bridegroom and the Human Soul destined be His Bride. After all, the Church is not a concept unrelated to the individual. It is made up of human hypostases, and the soul realizing itself in the heart is kindled with the flame of love for God from its birth. In this sense, the soul is a special image. It is a home to God's Agape, until an infant soul comes of age as the spiritual Bride. The ascetic practice of prayerful reunification of the mind with the heart gives the fullness of mystical reunification of God's Wisdom and Love, uniting an individual with Christ the Church's Logos and, through Him, with the whole Holy Trinity in the Kingdom of God. These conditions of relations between iconology and theology, and between contemplation and deification are glorified in the lyric poetry of the Song of Songs, which is called "God's revelation of Divine Love," "because the prophets have the ability to symbolically foretell what is to happen in the future."[53]

One can cite a long list of spiritual writers and Church Fathers who wrote Christian Orthodox explanations of the theme of Love and Wisdom in the Song of Songs. Among those who made the main and most profound interpretations of the image of action of Christ and the Holy Spirit in relation to the Church in general, and to the

---

52 Origen, *Homily* I *on the Song of Songs*.
53 *The Commentary on the Song of Songs* by the Most Pious Emperor Matthew Cantacuzenus.

Logos—Miraculous Angel in the Manifestation of Energies

Soul (called the Wedding Chamber) in particular, are the following:

St. Hippolytus of Rome — was the first who touched upon the theme of Christ and the Church in the Song of Songs.

Origen — interpreted the Song of Songs three times in his life: in his youth (the text is lost except for a small fragment), in two homilies on the Song of Songs, and in his greatest work — ten books dedicated to studying the text and interpreting the book in the sense of "Christ and the Church" and "Christ and the Soul as a Virgin and a Bride."

St. Jerome — interpreted the book in the sense of "Christ and the Church" in his translation of "Origen's homilies."

St. Athanasius the Great — a commentary in the sense of "Christ and the Church."

St. Gregory of Nyssa — dedicated fifteen homilies to interpretations in the sense of "Christ and the Church."

St. Cyril of Alexandria — interpretations in the sense of "Christ and the Church."

St. Nilus of Sinai (a disciple of St. John Chrysostom) — mainly interpretations in the sense of "Christ and the Soul."

St. Maximus the Confessor — his interpretations are lost and known only in general terms as rendered by the philosopher Michael Psellos.

Theodoret of Cyrus — extensive and fully preserved interpretations in the sense of "Christ and the Church" with some "Christ and the Soul" elements.

Michael Psellos — interpretations based on the works of Gregory of Nyssa, St. Nilus of Sinai, and Maximus the Confessor, entitled with the names of the three fathers.

Matthew Cantacuzenus — interpretations in the sense of "Christ and the Church" and "Christ and the Theotokos, the Bride Mary." The commentary on the book in the latter sense has not found any considerable development in the Orthodox tradition, although some commentaries in favor of this interpretation can be found in the works of some authors (Ephrem the Syrian, Ambrose, Epiphanius, Peter Chrysologus, Nicholas Cabasilas) and in liturgical texts. Being of iconological interest, and Orthodox, the theme "Christ and the Virgin Mary" does not disappear from liturgical theology, because in hymns the Virgin Mary is honored as the "Unwedded Bride."

THE ANGEL OF THE COUNTENANCE OF GOD

In the Western tradition, there have also been many remarkable interpretations of this book, especially since the twelfth century when they started to interpret the Love Song directly in an ascetic and chivalrous aspect as a quest of the Virgin Soul for the divine Bridegroom:

St. Ambrose, Archbishop of Milan — interpretations in the sense of "Christ and the Church."

St. Bernard of Clairvaux — wrote 86 sermons as commentaries on the Song of Songs, focusing on the ascetic value of the poem. Many other Western authors — for instance, St. John of the Cross and Jacques-Bénigne Bossuet — interpreted the book as an ascetic ascent to Christ in the Spirit of Love, while some theologians interpreted it as an expression of Love between Christ and the Virgin Mary.

Before the seventeenth century, commentators still adhered to the tradition of the ancient Fathers. The eighteenth century, however, saw a sudden change in view concerning biblical studies, and commentators began to identify the Song of Songs as folk erotic poetry rather than spiritual and sacred literature. This is understandable, because this was an era of triumphalist scientific thinking, with its discursive and material approach to everything, including Divine things. But even though the "philosophical" mind can somehow understand love at the Eros level, God's Agape is beyond it. Agape is moving further away from the children of men, and it seems that this process will continue until the end of the world. Instead of the virginal image of Agape, the substitute image of the apocalyptic harlot will be imposed upon humankind and prepared for the Beast's lair until the Parousia, the Second Coming of Christ.

For Orthodox Christians, if Orthodoxy is understood patristically as a reunification of earthly and divine aspects in Christ Jesus, who became the visible face of Sophia and Agape, there comes a time of heightened attention to rare "flashes" of Theophanies in the images of Agape. According to the Apostle Paul, God's Love is pure *gold* and everything else is "sounding brass," but we see more and more of "sounding brass" than "gold" in our loveless time. Against this background, it is pleasing to see the emergence of new translations of interpretations of the Song of Songs, including the in-depth study of Archpriest Gennady Fast, *The Commentary on the Song of Songs.*

Logos—Miraculous Angel in the Manifestation of Energies

According to many reviews, his book is a real encyclopedic guide to the Song of Songs. It is not our task to fully analyze Gennady Fast's book, so we will limit ourselves to comparing it with the previously described appearances of the Angel of the Countenance of God, referring, in this case, to the image of the "all-hymned" Virgin Agape, the Angel of the Holy Spirit.

Mysteriously running as a leitmotif throughout the Song of Songs, the love theme can be interpreted by seven methods, or seven deepenings of thoughts and feelings into the essence of paschal relations between the Bride and the Bridegroom given under the symbolic names of Solomon and the Shulamite.

SEVEN INTERPRETATIONS OF THE SONG OF SOLOMON

> Blessed is he who understands songs, and sings them, for no one does sing save on high festivals; but much more blessed is he who sings the Song of Songs. And as he who enters into the holy place, still needs much ere he is able to proceed into the Holy of Holies; and as he who keeps the Sabbath enjoined on the people by the Lord, yet wants many things that he may keep the Sabbath of Sabbaths, so, too, he who traverses all the songs of Holy Writ, finds it no easy thing to ascend to the Song of Songs.[54]

Origen compares the procedure for understanding the depths of the wisdom, and the spiritual heights, of the Song of Songs with a thorough spiritual, mental, and corporeal preparation of a High Priest for entering the Holy of Holies. For our part, we would like to focus on different levels of interpreting and understanding this book, keeping in mind that these levels have some conceptual analogies with the structure, or more precisely, the "courts," of Solomon's Temple.

1. According to a *literal* interpretation, which follows a straight-line movement of thought, the Song of Songs is a poetic story about an ordinary love between a young man and a young woman. The analogy with the Temple: *the Court of the Gentiles*. The literal interpretation should be differentiated from the literal "understanding" of the book,

---

54 Origen, *Homily* I *on the Song of Songs*.

THE ANGEL OF THE COUNTENANCE OF GOD

according to which it is classified as a folk erotic "marriage" song. This judgment is rejected by the Church. The literal interpretation, as an understanding on the sensual everyday plane of consciousness, represents a kind of general poetic "background" of the book. The Song of Songs "is a love song about two lovers' inner emotions, seeking, loss-related sorrows, and happiness experienced when they meet each other. Marriage customs and traditions always vary with times, nations, and places, but the love between a bridegroom and a bride is always equal to itself; it is eternal."[55] Therefore, the literal interpretation is necessary too. According to Ecclesiastes, however, one should duly remember that an overly naturalistic approach and coarse associations are "transient" and one should lift one's eyes to the next level of understanding love, which inconspicuously dwells at the same hour on another plane of consciousness. This lays a foundation, from which a discursive mind can climb through concrete images (a vineyard, fragrances, tents, spikenard, a cedar, a dove, etc.) to reach the heights of the noetic mind, and then the Divine mind. According to fathers of the Church, feelings should be guided by Wisdom, because the love for God is expressed by the *word* of a reasonable person, not exaltation.

2. A *historical and mystical* interpretation of the book reveals love as the relations between God and the chosen people of Israel. The analogy with the Temple: *the Court of Israel*. Not surprisingly, the purely historical interpretation, according to which "the young shepherd and lover identified with King Solomon and his beloved were considered to be the God of Israel and the community of Israel respectively," was characteristic of Jewish teachers of the law, the targumim, and the Talmud; "In this interpretation, the Song of Songs turns into a story about the deepest spiritual bonds between God and His people, a narrative having a mystical sense of consolation and hope."[56] In addition, there is a mystical sense of *anagogic* "love" as a basis for faith. Leaving the natural and wedded love, which is inherent in every believer or non-believer, in due time we will rise to the sphere of "chosen" Love, which can be attained not by

---

55 Priest Gennady Fast, *The Commentary on the Song of Songs*.
56 *The Jewish Encyclopedia*.

everyone "under the law of the flesh," but only by souls who are ready to embark on the path of ascent to the Exemplar of Love. This transition to "chosenness" is quite difficult for a soul continually looking back at the "Court of the Gentiles." This Court, however, was separated from the people of Israel by a *fence*—the Law, separating the pagan polytheistic faith from the faith in one God the Creator, who became the only Heavenly Father for the chosen ones. The first commandment for the chosen people, "Thou shalt love the Lord thy God," and the second one, which "is like unto it," "Thou shalt love thy neighbor," are the "two breasts" on the chest of the believing Soul. "A garden enclosed is my *Sister*, my *Spouse*; a spring shut up, a fountain sealed" (Song 4:12–15). The Soul should become a Sister and a Spouse turned in love to God. "Spouse" refers to the Soul as being different in nature from the Bridegroom yet subject to conjugal deification, while the word "Sister" shows Her human affinity with him. Kindled by Sophia and Agape, faith gives wine and milk to the human soul, the "prince's daughter" raised by the Law and the Prophets. But Israel, although "the heir, as long as he is a child, differeth nothing from a servant" (Gal 4:1), and the Spouse, peering into the cloudy heights of Love, calls to the Bridegroom to deepen and strengthen her emotionally unstable love: "Make haste, my Beloved, and be thou like to a roe or to a young hart upon the mountains of spices" (Song 8:14). In breathless expectation, Israel waits for the first coming of the Messiah; the same extreme tension, according to the Book of Revelation, will occur before the Second Coming: "And the Spirit and the Bride say, Come. And let him that heareth say, Come" (Rev 22:17), "Even so, come, Lord Jesus" (Rev 22:20), as the Messiah of the universal Resurrection. In *The Apocalypse of John*, Archpriest Sergei Bulgakov comments on this verse as follows:

> If it is the Church, the Spirit and the Bride, who says this, it does so in the Holy Spirit on behalf of all its living members. Each one of them, doing so in the name and on behalf of the Church, becomes a bride in relation to the Heavenly Bridegroom, the God-Man in His

God-manhood. However, if this conclusion is applicable to every member of the Church, this is predominantly and supremely applicable to the Ever-Virgin Mary as the personal head of the Church which is always inseparable from Her.

"The Song of Songs is a certain spiritual pleasure of holy minds, in the marriage of that King and Queen,"[57] because chosen are Jehovah the Bridegroom and Israel the Bride, and the people is chosen and invited to inherit God's Chamber. He says, "My bride, come from Lebanon: thou shalt come and pass from the top of Faith" (Song 4:8, Slavonic version), having rejected the other "suitors" leading to idolatry, to Me in My City. In this interpretation, presumably, there is the "beginning" of existence in God's City, which in the New Testament will be called "new Jerusalem, coming down from God out of heaven, prepared as a bride adorned for her husband" (Rev 21:2). Looking into these conceptual depths, we can see where and how true faith originates not only in the minds of the ancient Jews, but also in contemporary individuals who still pass through different stages of development of love from the Old Testament "infancy" to seeing the New Testament sacrifice. This is the usual way of formation of Eros, Philia, and Agape on the paths of ascension of faith, where the soul becomes now closer to God, now farther away from Him, now arduously searching for God, now unexpectedly meeting Him. Historical and mystical interpretations lead us to a deeper understanding of the people's metahistory in its relation to the Heavenly Bridegroom who, before the wedding ceremony, offers the soul special dogmatic terms: purification, formation, and catching fire. These are necessary steps for preparing and beautifying the Bride, and then the Bridegroom visits her and exclaims: "Behold, thou art fair, My love; behold, thou art fair" (Song 4:1).

3. The *messianic and ecclesiological* interpretation — the iconological mystery of the *image* of the re-unifying Love of the founder and head of the Church, Christ the Logos, and the *united* Church of believers. The analogy with the Temple: *the Court of the Priests.*

---

57 St. Augustine, *The City of God.*

Logos—Miraculous Angel in the Manifestation of Energies

The God-Man Bridegroom exists in two natures, while His Bride—the Church, as the Soul, exists as His *Sister* by human nature and His *Bride* by Divine nature. At present, among many called souls there are chosen souls—those who devote their souls' inclinations only to God. The Church Soul royally enters the court designed for sacrificing "lambs" and "calves," repudiating (just like the repudiation of Satan during baptism) the "erotic" movements of this animal nature and washing oneself with water from "the molten sea" (1 Kgs 7:23–26; 2 Chr 4:2–5). This is the *beginning* of the Christian understanding of love in its dogmatic aspect. The Bride *betroths herself* to Christ by the dignity of the Queen of the cosmos, while the Bridegroom, as "the King of kings and Lord of lords," calls upon her to mount the throne.

Theodoret, interpreting the Song of Songs in terms of relations between Christ and the Church, said,

> So, as soon as the Bride began to know her Bridegroom's beauty, power, wealth, reign over all, and His eternal, indestructible, and endless might; she immediately desired to see (know) Him, plunge into His arms, and give Him spiritual kisses: "Let Him kiss me with the kisses of His mouth: for Thy love is better than wine" (Song 1:1).

St. Jerome explains the same words said by the Bride as follows: "Not through the patriarchs, Moses and the prophets, but let Him accept my body and live in my flesh. Let the Logos be in the flesh, and so let him kiss me, dwelling in me as Emmanuel." In this early yet very deep interpretation, Christ is already understood as both the Bridegroom of the whole Church and a personal Bridegroom-Logos who dwells in the human soul under the enigmatic biblical name "Emmanuel." Here, we can find two discrepancies, and the second one relates to the next, fourth, stage of realization of God's Love. The Bride calls for the fulfillment of the prophecies, because she can already see: "Behold, he stood upon a wall of adamant, and in his hand was an adamant" (Amos 7:7). An adamant is a diamond, which is the hardest gemstone and the symbol of strong faith, virginal purity, and transparency of the soul.

THE ANGEL OF THE COUNTENANCE OF GOD

In different names (little breast, bosom, and breasts) denoting the same thing, Origen sees three levels of ascending to or approaching Christ:

> When a sacrifice is offered in the Law, the Divine Word says: "The *little breast* that is set apart." But when someone reclines with Jesus and enjoys full fellowship of thought with Him, then the expression is, not "little breast," but "bosom." And again, when the Bride speaks to the Bridegroom, the word used is not "little breast," as in the sacrifice, not "bosom," as in the case of the disciple John, but "breasts": "Thy breasts are better than wine."[58]

According to G. Fast's explanation of these words, there are three degrees of Bridal initiation: sacrifice (little breast), disciplemaking (bosom), spiritual marriage and becoming the Bride (breasts).

4. The *spiritual and psychological* interpretation shows intimate (prayerful) relations between Christ the Logos and the Soul (Greek: Ψυχή). These relations are hidden from the outside world in the temple of the human heart. This is the beginning of iconological Love forming Man "in the image of God," and Its actions are effected in a spiral motion and directed to the soul. The analogy with the Temple: *the Sanctuary*. In the sanctuary, i.e., in the inner world of the believer, incense is always burned on the golden altar, the light of the seven-branched candlestick shines, and the bloodless showbread, instead of the sacrificed animals of the "Court of the Priests," is on the communion table. Standing in the Church, the soul personally calls for its Bridegroom, asking Him to be touched. How to see the Lord "face to Face" is the *God-seeing revelation* of the Sophia of Christ. In addition, we should understand that "kisses of the mouth to the Mouth of the Lord" is the *God-knowing revelation* of the Agape of the Holy Spirit. During the Holy Communion, the believer kisses, as it were, the body of Christ and then kisses the Chalice, while the priest at this time says, "Lo, this hath touched my lips and mine iniquity is taken away and my sins are purged." Therefore, whenever God's grace touches the soul, it is equal to

---

58   Origen, *Homily* I *on the Song of Songs*.

His *kiss*. A kiss is a symbol of the Logos mysteriously touching the mouth of the Soul. According to St. Gregory of Nyssa,[59] "a kiss is given through the sense of touch, because kissing mouths touch one another. But there is a certain soul touch, for feeling the Word through spiritual rather than physical contact." Through this mystical connection of energies of created and uncreated "mouths," the soul is elevated to the *ekstasis* of the Kingdom of God. With God's Agape in mind, St. Gregory of Nyssa further explains:

> Why does the Bride say "Thy breasts are better than wine," by "breasts" meaning "heart" in terms of its location? It surely would not be erroneous to use the word "heart" to denote the innermost and ineffable Divine power; it would be equally correct to say "breasts" to imply the divine Power's beneficial actions (energies) used by God to sustain everyone's life.

Life is sustained by love in its *Eros*, *Philia*, and *Agape* forms, whose nutrient juices provide the human body, soul, and mind with growth and measure in the Knowledge of God. But it must be remembered that Agape should first and foremost serve as the inspiration for Eros in the body. It should be an active energy in the human Eros, not vice versa. The knowledge of God is gained through the intelligent heart rather than the intellect, and the polysemantic term "to know" in all its meanings — from the words "And Adam *knew* Eve his wife" to the theology of the *knowledge* of God — truly reveals the vital force of Agape at all levels of the intellect and heart *ekstasis*.

In prayers, God is known through Man's spiritual heart. So, St. Jerome, somewhat breaking the architecture of speech, interprets "Thy breasts are better..." as describing the Bridegroom, interpreting the "two breasts" as the two Testaments available to the Bride Church "to deliver the milk of the word," because "Thy name is as ointment poured forth" (Song 1:2). As we remember, the term "outpouring" refers to the divine Energy *pouring out* of the essence of God. For the Soul, this outpouring brings aroma and fragrance perceived as "the sweetest name of Jesus" in the prayer of the heart. At this stage,

---

59 *An Exact Exposition of the Song of Songs.*

it is necessary to know the name of the Bridegroom, and then a prayer *pours out* of the heart of the believer just like a loving breath of the Bride. Gregory of Nyssa compares an aroma emanating from a substance with the energies of Theophanies. The inconceivability of God's essence is revealed in the spiritual gifts of energy poured out of His essence, and these aromas conceal all the names of the Bridegroom with which, as with savor, He provides the Soul that has become His Bride, "for there is none other name under heaven given among men, whereby we must be saved" (Acts 4:12). According to Theodoret, *"ointment poured forth"* refers to Chrismation and the revelation of the Lord's Name in it. Let us recall the "sixth gift" from the Revelation of St. John the Divine: "Him that overcometh will I make a pillar in the temple of My God . . . and I will write upon him the name of My God, and the name of the city of My God . . . and *My new name*" (Rev 3:12).

5. The *ascetical and anagogical* interpretation concerns the relations between the Logos and the Soul which has chosen a direct path of ascension to the Mount of the Lord as the path to the wedding in the Wedding Chamber of the Bridegroom. This is the beginning of contemplative theological Love experienced in the course of circular centripetal movements of the Soul. This movement can be compared with recurrent Resurrection of the Soul enclosed in the *ekstasis* of the circular cycle of the Holy Pascha.

The analogy with the Temple: the Holy of Holies. Once a year, the High Priest passed through the sanctuary veil and entered the Holy of Holies; but, according to St. Silouan the Athonite, "God Himself looks for a person before a person finds Him." Similarly, the Soul enters the secret royal Chambers only when the Logos Himself calls for it: "The king hath brought me into his chambers" (Song 1:4). "It is not written that He brought many into *His* chamber. Many remain outside, and only the Bride enters the chamber to see hidden and secret treasures and announce to the virgins: 'The king hath brought me into his chambers'" (Origen, Jerome). He brought His Bride, chosen from many, to make her a "special virgin," the ark of the Logos, and give her an image of distinctive beauty; but before that can be, the Soul has to accomplish a feat of purification and make a long search for the Bridegroom. "In the future, not all those who believe will be in the same degree of glory."[60] "By the term *virgins*, the Scripture (Song 1:2) means virtues, owing to their conjunction with the soul, resulting in their being contemplated as one spirit and body."[61] On this ascetical and anagogical path, the Soul pines away, its love growing very faint, but it is still identified with mental and corporeal emotions, finding it hard to reunify, and be kindled in the fire of Agape. At this point Sophia helps the Soul, and then *"Uprightness hath loved thee."* Uprightness, according to some church fathers' interpretations, is also a name of the Bridegroom: "God is called Love, and also Uprightness."[62] In addition, "uprightness" is one of the energemas of the Sophia of Christ, who said, "I am the [*right*] Way, the [*straight*] Truth, and the [*pure*] Life." The Right Way is the one illuminated with Light; straightness of the Truth belongs to those who speak with the mouth of Wisdom; and the pure Life is the Tree of Love, which is evergreen in bloom and bearing fruit in sweetness. And none of these images should be omitted in the search for the Bridegroom, or changed by the Soul named by the Logos as His Bride.

Exhausted in its search, the Soul cries out to the Logos: "Tell me, O Thou whom my soul loveth, where Thou pastureth Thy flock, where Thou makest Thy flock to rest at noon?" (Song 1:7) This is a prayer. Not every soul can cry out in this way with prayerful boldness, but only a soul moved by Agape in its heart can do so. Hermits felt such a deep sorrow when they lost sight of the Bridegroom. Origen, who experienced this, exclaims: "and sometimes He comes again; but when He appears to be embraced by me He disappears again, and I search for Him again after he disappears." According to St. John Climacus, "Love is an infinitude of radiance; Love a source of fire in the heart, and the more is poured out, the more inflamed a thirsty person becomes." On the path to spiritual marriage, however, the Bride often needs help from her sister, Sophia, which, like the midday Sun, illuminates all the

---

60 Theodoret.
61 St. Gregory of Sinai.
62 St. John Climacus.

soul's movements, making them clear, true, and right. For the Soul can easily go astray if she is not enlightened by God's Wisdom and does not know where her Bridegroom feeds and makes His flock to rest at noon: this is how the Bride's exclamation is interpreted by St. Gregory of Nyssa and Origen. St. Athanasius of Alexandria says that "Having hearkened to her prayer, the Logos teaches her as follows: no one can know God without knowing oneself first." "To know oneself," according to the Orthodox Christian interpretation, means to belittle one's physicality and see in oneself, as in a mirror, the inner beauty of God's Image with Christ's Sophia and Agape acting in it. That is why *"My Kinsman is to me a bundle of myrrh; he shall lie between my breasts"* (Song 1:13). A bunch of myrrh was worn by women between the breasts for fragrance. The Bride, while still in the "image of a sister," compares her Beloved, calling Him *"my Kinsman,"* with a bundle of the purest fragrant myrrh. According to St. Gregory of Nyssa,

> the Lord Himself reclines as *stakte* [myrrh] in the bundle of my conscience, having settled in my very heart; because the local position of the (*prayerful*) heart, according to observers of such things, is between the breasts. And owing to the appearance of Your divinity in the flesh, You are perfectly well named *Kinsman* by Your loving Soul.[63]

The Bride's trial on her way to the Wedding Chamber of the Logos, as well as her passage along a narrow path over an abyss, is challenging. This requires harmonizing the three natural powers of the mind, body, and soul. If they "are enraptured by celestial spiritual mysteries and captivated by the diversity of God's beauty, seeking in a great thirst for the best and greatest things,"[64] the Soul is helped during this ascent by the diamond-like shining Sophia and the fiery-eyed Agape. According to the Church Fathers, both iconological energies are at work in Theophanies. Elias Ekdikos writes: "And the contemplative mind (Greek: Νους), when descending from the sky, being drawn by natural needs, can proclaim the same words as the one who has said,

---

63 St. Gregory of Nyssa.
64 St. Macarius the Great.

'Is there anything more marvelous than the divine Beauty?'" And St. Basil the Great says that "the inscrutable and ineffable kindness of the Word is the Beauty of Wisdom and God's glance in the image of His Love."[65] God's Wisdom and Love embrace the Soul like the Bridegroom's two mystical hands: "His left hand is under my head, and His right hand doth embrace me" (Song 2:6).

Being kindled, the Bride implored: *"Set Love (Agape) before me.* Strengthen me with perfumes, stay me with apples: for I am wounded with love" (Song 1:4). According to the Church Fathers, the primary meaning of the words *"set Love before me"* lies in the Christian doctrine emphasizing the necessity for sophianic orderliness and intelligence in the sense of love. Love is not anarchy of emotions or a tree-felling hurricane. Wisdom inclines the uncontrollable passion of human love towards divine Providence, urging that it set its feelings on the spiritual path. Similarly, St. Gregory of Nyssa says, "It is important to realize the order of love for which the Law is a guide: how one should love God, neighbor, wife, and enemy, lest the practice of love be disordered and perverted."

The spiritual asceticism of the one who enters the Holy of Holies once a year is an act of pure transfigured love on all its levels — Eros, Philia, and Agape — in the Name of the Lord. They prepare Man to be the Ark of the Covenant; in them, the grace of incarnation in the body, transformation in the soul, and resurrection in the spirit is fully fulfilled; this is the deiparous state of faith, but it is ideally required by the Church for all Christians. This is also the anagogy (path) of the Soul ascending into the Wedding Chamber. From infancy, the Soul should reach the "perfect age" and become a spiritualized image of the Bride, which is adequate to the Logos — "unto the measure of the stature of the fullness of Christ" (Eph 4:13). The age of Christ is not measured by years, but by the depth of the Bride's mystical perceptiveness of, and willingness for, a spiritual Marriage in Heaven. This Path is called the "Pascha" or "Ladder" (such as the one described by St. John Climacus), giving thirty steps of virtuous ascent to the age of Christ. In the same context, Origen says: "Have you awakened

---

65   *Commentary on Psalm* 45.

and restored your existing love?" Seeing the Bride's willingness, the Bridegroom calls: "*Rise up, come, My companion, My fair one, My dove*" (Song 2:10–14). In this enumeration, St. Gregory of Nyssa sees a certain spiritual sequence of steps of the heavenly Ladder, and this is the Logos calling for the Bride Soul who, while strenuously searching for virtues and collecting them in her heart, is capable of becoming a Mother—an animate Ark. If a Virgin Soul does not conceive from the Holy Spirit, she still stands outside the Chamber at His gate as an "image of a woman" facing the outside world.

6. The *mariological and matrimonial* interpretation: a "marriage" between the Logos and the Soul—a cyclic circular (i.e., constant) movement of the loving Soul "around" the Logos. The analogy with the Temple: the "*Ark of the Covenant.*" Chosen from among brides and virgins, the Immaculate Virgin Mary, the Unwedded Bride, became a living Ark into which the Logos placed himself instead of the stone tables of the Old Testament. The image of the Virgin is reunited with the image of the Mother nursing the Infant God. From then on, the iconological image of the Holy Virgin Mother has reminded believers of the conception and birth in their hearts of Logos Emmanuel sown by the Holy Spirit rather than the flesh. Since then, "My kinsman is to me a [*fragrant*] bundle of myrrh; he shall lie between my breasts [*in the heart*]" (Song 1:13). We justify our lives only by conceiving from the seed of God and living in harmony with the meaning of the creation of the world and Man. While Adam and Eve lost this chance of "spiritual conception," in history it happened that the Son of God was born from the Virgin Mary. From then on, she really became the Virgin Theotokos, the Virgin Mother of Christ, rather than a product of myth-making. We do not know the exact words of God's Word written by God Himself for Moses on the stone tablets, because they were destroyed. However, we know that the incarnate Living Word was placed into the Living Ark of His Bride Mary, who was then called the "Mother of the Light." The other believers in Christ from then on have been given the spermatic Logos of the Light; and those who have discovered, accepted, and cultivated their inner *seed* in themselves are called "children of the Light" and "brides of the Logos" in the Scripture.

Logos—Miraculous Angel in the Manifestation of Energies

The marriage of the Lamb and the Bride is crowned with the *ekstasis* of communion of the Bride. "Bring me into the *house of wine*; set love before me" (Song 2:4). The annunciation to the Soul engulfed in the flames of Love transforms itself into the act of knowledge of God and of conception from the Holy Spirit. However, not only does the Soul come to know the mystery of God's Love, but also God to the same degree deeply immerses Himself into the Soul and comes to know the mystery of the human heart. According to Gregory of Nyssa, this verse is about the wisdom-loving Virgin, the Soul, who is filled with such a strong Love that she is not satisfied with the cup prepared by Wisdom and, to quench her thirst of love, asks to be *brought into the house of wine* to set her mouth to the very winepress pouring out the spiritual drink of Agape. This daring rise to the heights of Love can be compared with the state of the Virgin Mary at the Annunciation. Only she who passed through this fire of immeasurable Love of seedless conception could boldly ask her Son to turn water into wine at the marriage(!) feast in Cana. The divine Logos Himself was present at the wedding, but was not recognized by the earthly bride and bridegroom. Therefore, He said to His Mother Bride: "Woman, what have I to do with thee?" However, He worked the miracle for the sake of the all-encompassing Love between the Bridegroom and the Bride as symbolized in its earthly aspect. Here, we see the convergence of conceptual aspects of "wine" at the earthly wedding (Eros) and then at the wedding of heavenly Communion (Agape).

The state of sober Love is always under the care of the heart: the Bride says, "I sleep, but my heart waketh" (Song 5:2). As compared with the eternal action of the Logos of God within us, which is always turned to the heart of His beloved Bride Soul, all our "spiritual" mental activity resembles a state of drowsiness. If the heart suddenly feels the Presence of God, the Soul immediately glorifies the Lord and is ready to wake up from "sleep" having suddenly realized itself to be a Bride who is willing to accept the Bridegroom. "Therefore, once imprinted as a seal in the domineering power of the soul, the thought of God can be called a praise to God, which is always present in the soul."[66] Thereby every believing soul comes to resemble the

---

66 St. Basil the Great, *Commentary on Psalm* 34:1.

Virgin Mary who said to the Angel in front of the simultaneously opened gates of the Annunciation and the Incarnation, "Behold the handmaid of the Lord," and was immediately named the Theotokos and the Mother of the Unapproachable Light. This is the mariological "mouth-to-mouth" "marriage" consummated by the beauty and power of Agape between the Logos and the Soul during the mystical Sacrament of Marriage.

In the Song of Songs, the Bridegroom praises the beauty of His Bride (4:1–5), and the Bride praises the beauty of His Image (5:10–16).

> With the Bride, *seven* parts of her body were named and praised, which meant the fullness of grace of the Church, because the Church is the Body of Christ, while the number *seven*, according to the Fathers, is the church number of this century. With Christ the Bridegroom, *nine* parts of His body were praised and *three* characteristic features were described, making a total of *twelve* (9+3=12) comparisons. With the Bride, the number *seven* refers to the fullness of grace of the visible and earthly Church. With Christ the Bridegroom, the number *twelve*, consisting of nine and three, refers to the *nine* angelic orders (of the *Heavenly Church*) and the Divinity of the Holy Trinity glorified by the visible and invisible Church: *Holy, Holy, Holy, the Lord of Sabaoth; heaven and earth are filled with Your Glory.*[67]

7. The *Christological and soteriological* interpretation, the unraveled mystery of the *Seventh Day*. The analogy with the Temple: "the Tables of the Covenant." Once written by God on the stone tablets of law and placed by Moses in the Ark of the Covenant, the Word was inscribed and depicted in matter again. This time, however, this was done through the "conception" in an acheiropoetos and living ark—the Virgin Mary, and the Word was made Man. Christ's human nature, reunited *inseparably and discretely* in the Prosopon of humankind with the Hypostasis of His Divinity, is interpreted as the "ark" of the New Testament. Similarly, the human "flesh" into

---

67   Fast, *Commentary on the Song of Songs*.

which He immersed Himself is named the "Bride" of God the Son and Christ by some Church fathers. St. Athanasius writes: "The Song is interpreted as a Song, because it sings a wedding song for the marriage between the Logos and the Flesh." Christ's body is not some abstract created nature, but a human essence with all its feelings and its mind, with all its will and the soul with its natural impulses, being reunited (Greek: enhypostatized) with His Divinity, possesses the fullness, and hence immortality, of Life — "For in him dwelleth all the fullness of the Godhead bodily" (Col 2:9). Having a perfect human bodily organization, Jesus grew in Wisdom and Love through a gradual and humble perception of His divine energies rather than through external "schooling." "Gradually" means in accordance with His age and with the Providence of the Grand Council of the Trinity, not to break the law of Creation. "However, by reason of the identity of person and the inseparable union, the Lord's soul enjoyed the knowledge of future events as well as the other signs of divinity."[68] In addition, we can recall His human nature from His Agony in the Garden: "nevertheless not My will, but Thine, be done" (Lk 22:42).

So, the theological, seventh, and final interpretation of the Song of Songs, yet mystically preceding all other interpretations, is the marital union between the Son of God and *His* own human *Soul*, the Bride of ineffable beauty and wisdom. Uncreated energies of the Shekinah, Sophia, and Agape acted freely in the fullness of the Incarnation in His Soul and became creative *beginnings* of the dispensation of the Church in His Body. Similarly, in the eucharistic communion with the Body and Blood of Christ, in accordance with the Church dogma of "the essence and energy," we continue to take communion with the uncreated Light of Sophia and Agape given by the God-Man Christ to those who acknowledge the incarnate Hypostatic Son. In the Divine Liturgy, the revelation of the Eucharist explains the full depth of God's Love for the created world in particular, because the whole world is given the opportunity to enter into this Love; however, Agape operates only in the holy marriage between Christ and the Church of all who believe in Him.

---

68   St. John of Damascus, *Exposition of the Orthodox Faith*.

THE ANGEL OF THE COUNTENANCE OF GOD

Having entered into His own Garden of Creation, the Son Logos was incarnate from the Holy Spirit and the Virgin and became Man. The flesh of the divine Bridegroom is His beautiful Bride. "My beloved, the eternal Logos, began to say to me, His Flesh: My beloved Flesh, My fair one, for there is no spot or vice in You, You have not inherited Adam's sin, you are deified having united with Me."[69] And His Bride agrees: "My Beloved, the Son of God, is Mine and I am His: He feedeth My virtues among the lilies, among the six senses of my heart." The best of what happened in the relations between God and Man earlier—the marriage of two natures—then mysteriously and perfectly happened in the God-Man. In accordance with the image of this union between the "Spirit" and the "Flesh," the Church of believers was born and grew. The Bride who entered into the Holy of Holies of the internal states of the Logos united with the Flesh, became His Sister too. After all, all souls are united in accordance with this, the Lord's word: "He that eateth my flesh, and drinketh my blood, dwelleth in me, and I in him" (Jn 6:56). The Logos was made flesh. In other words, He entered into the cosmic Garden of His Flesh, having restored and renovated the example of His habitation—Paradise. Receiving communion, a Christian accepts and is blessed by all the fullness of the Godhead; being driven and deflected by his/her (gnomic) will, however, he/she should repeat this Sacrament again and again, gradually growing "from a particle" "unto the measure of the stature of the fullness of the Bridegroom," and being transformed into the Sister according to the flesh and into the Bride according to the Soul.

This interpretation also points to the number seven, corresponding to the seven churches which are different in the nature of their actions and united into the "one Holy and Apostolic Church" of Christ. Their seven "color domes" illuminated by the seven uncreated stars, the Angels—the seven Spirits of God, make up the Rainbow of the last Covenant of God (cf. Revelation) and the sevenfold fullness of the Church. The seventh interpretation of the Song of Songs discusses the Bride Soul. In this case, the "Soul" should be understood in the sense of fullness of a churched person, where the

---

69   Fast, *Commentary on the Song of Songs*.

Church, the *Soul*, and the *Logos* are not only inseparable in terms of space, but also as indistinguishable as the *body*, *soul*, and *spirit*. Every Soul in the Church has all those things that the whole Church has. While the Church is a gathering of souls who "unanimously acknowledge" Christ, every individual soul partakes of the transfiguring wine of Agape in the same way as all the others, because the Bridegroom is one and the communion is one. But whether every Soul who has partaken of God's Love heads for the Chamber or "meditatively and dreamily" looks at the world after Communion, is another matter. Distinguished as the personal Logos of His chosen Soul, He never moves away from the Soul in action, time, or space, remaining in Man's tropos (method) of practicing a perfect faith. He becomes incarnated and humanized in every person, while every soul retains the intimate mystery of sacrificial Love after the image of reunification of the two heterogeneous (created and uncreated) natures of the God-Man. "The mystery of the Incarnation of the Word (Logos) contains in itself the whole meaning (τὴν δύναμιν) of the riddles and symbols of Scripture, the whole significance of visible and invisible creatures."[70] The two *natures* are antinomic by their distinction, but they reunite and fuse in the fire of Agape to create the conditions to *meet* God. In this distinction, the Song of Songs compares the two natures with the aromas of *myrrh* and *frankincense*: myrrh is burned at burials, while frankincense is blessed in honor of God and burned as a sign of serving Him.[71] Theodoret interprets this in the same way: "The best of all incenses are *myrrh* and *frankincense*, that is, the knowledge of the Bridegroom's Divine and Human Natures."

Therefore, every believing Soul called upon and chosen by God in a noble harmony of its body, soul, and mind is a Virgin Sister, according to human nature, and a Virgin Bride, according to the Divine Nature. As a Sister, the Soul should necessarily create *virtuous* conditions for the Logos to be "made flesh" in it. According to St. Ambrose of Milan: "She is a virgin, who is the bride of God, a harlot, who makes

---

70 St. Maximus the Confessor.
71 St. Gregory of Nyssa.

gods for herself."[72] Considering the Bridegroom's words urging us to be simultaneously in the world and "not of this world," we can also understand virginity as sobering asceticism. "And so he is truly dispassionate, and is recognized as dispassionate, who has made his flesh incorruptible, who has raised his mind above creatures and has subdued all his senses to it, and who keeps his soul in the presence of the Lord, ever reaching out to Him even beyond his strength."[73]

The Divinity of the Trinity is reunited with the churched Humanity through the sacrifice of Christ the Lamb, because Christ enhypostatized the *"first fruits"* of our created nature, brought them closer to Himself, and deified them. Similarly, the Church of all the souls, as the Bride, is enhypostatized and deified in Christ. The words said during the Sacrament of Marriage "and they shall be one flesh" indicate that Christ (the head) is the *Hypostasis*, while the Church (the body) is His *Prosopon*, and no one can sever this relationship, because God's "love is strong as death" (Song 8:6). In the Ladder of St. John Climacus, the twenty-ninth step of dispassion is followed by the final thirtieth step of God's Agape. Using the analogy of these steps, we can say that the Sister should be dispassionate, i.e., sober, but the Bride is always on fire with Love while waiting, because "Behold, the Bridegroom comes at midnight, and blessed is the servant [*in terms of the body*] whom He shall find [*in terms of the soul*] watching."[74]

The image of the immaculate Bride — Christ's body and soul — is described by the Bridegroom in the Song of Songs (4:1–5; 6:5–7; 7:2–10). These features are iconologically depictable and could be personified in icons of the Angel of the Countenance of God, characterizing Light, Wisdom, and Love. If the Bridegroom is the *Logos*, it is natural that His Bride is an *Image* woven from His *own actions*, the light energies of Sophia and Agape. This iconographic form can be used to describe the forms of the Bride's virginal *body*. In other words, according to the seventh (*spiritual*) interpretation, through the symbolism of Christian icon realism, the Image of Christ can be interpreted as the virginal, maidenly, and Sophianic-Agapian Image

---

72 St. Ambrose of Milan, *On Virginity*, Book 1, Chapter 9.
73 St. John Climacus, *The Ladder of Divine Ascent*, Step 29, 3.
74 From the Midnight Office prayers.

of His human nature: His mystical Bride. In the Song of Songs, the Bridegroom himself so colorfully describes the Bride in the virginal body of His true Incarnation.

> And we should not be confused that the body or flesh of Christ, "a man approved of God" (Acts 2:22), is described using a *feminine* (or rather, *virginal*) image of the Bride. In this case, the image of the Bride is a common (in biblical language) anthropomorphism used to describe God and the mysteries of His Kingdom. In addition, God's entire creation is in some sense God's Bride (regardless of gender). Similarly, the human flesh received by the divine Logos became His Bride.[75]

How much more appropriate it is to recognize the divine energies of God's unapproachable Light around Christ the Lord which operate iconographically as the personification of His virginity and divinity, especially in such dramatic cases as Theophanies of Sophia-Wisdom, or Agape-Love. In mystical distinctions between the Virgins Sophia and Agape, when God's Kingdom and Power and Glory are meant, their actions are iconographically depictable and recognizable as the Archetype in the Icon of the Revelation.

Such sublime poetic descriptions as "Behold, Thou art fair, My love; behold, Thou art fair. Thy lips are like a thread of scarlet, and Thy speech is comely. The roof of Thy mouth is like the best wine. Thy stature is like to a palm tree, and Thy breasts to clusters of grapes. The smell of Thy nose is like apples. Thy navel is like a round goblet, which wanteth not liquor. Thou art all fair, My love; there is no spot in Thee" are the images of the New Testament doctrine of the churched Bride-Soul who abides in the Love of the Logos, mystically embodied in it. Bearing in mind that the Son of God was incarnated not without His uncreated *Image* of essential Energy, the earthly Bride (the Soul in terms of the flesh) in Christ united with the heavenly Archetype is truly capable of recognizing and accepting the Bridegroom. Consequently, "God's Image" is iconographically depictable in terms of not only the human appearance of Jesus, but

---

[75] Fast, *Commentary on the Song of Songs*.

also His creative Energy personified in the iconography of the regal Virgin Sophia and the fiery Virgin Agape who represent the executive divine virginity of the Hypostatic Christ.

So, the seventh (*Christological and dispensational*) interpretation of the Song of Songs combines different interpretations: *Christ and the Church*—uncreated and divine, heavenly and earthly; *Christ and the Soul*—the Bride of Christ's flesh having all the abilities and capabilities of the material world; *Christ and the soul* of every individual as a "small" (personal) church.

8. The spiritual and *literal* interpretation, the "Omega" of the future state of faith after the general Resurrection. It has *no* analogies with the Temple, because in the future there will be no Temple or symbolic worship of God; instead, there will be married Life with God, and then "the Spirit will breathe Its multivarious power where It wishes and in whom It wishes." Not the Temple, but the City of the Kingdom, having "straight" (human) and "reverse" (heavenly) perspectives, will be built and become a place of human habitation; in the City, there will be a fragrant Garden in whose center the Tree of Seeing God in Sophia and the Tree of Knowledge of God in Agape will bear fruit.

And the Soul illuminated in the Kingdom of Theophanies exclaims: "My Beloved is gone down into His Garden, to the beds of spices, to feed in the gardens, and to gather lilies" (Song 6:2–3). Not the Tablets of the Covenant, but the Logos within the heart, awakened in Baptism and grown in the Communion gifts, now elevates Man directly, without any symbols or veils, to the Eighth Sacrament: Deification in front of the Heavenly Father. The eighth interpretation reveals the image of action of the future Eighth Day—the eschatological and paschal Sabbath of the Lord, and the Spirit of God, the Bride Church exclaims: "Even so, come, Lord."

ICONOLOGY AND ICONOGRAPHY OF THE SONG OF SOLOMON

> When you happen to hear about the communication between the bridegroom and the bride, about countenances, feasts, do not imagine anything material or earthly, because these things are discussed only by way of example.

Logos—Miraculous Angel in the Manifestation of Energies

> Inasmuch as all these things are ineffably spiritual and untouchable to carnal eyes, yet understandable to a faithful and holy soul (the communication of the Holy Spirit, the heavenly treasures, and the countenances and feasts of holy Angels are visible only to those who have experienced these things, while being unimaginable to uninitiated ones), listen to these things reverently until you gain this knowledge through faith; and then through actual experience your mental eyes will see what other good things can Christian souls commune with here.[76]

The images of the Bridegroom and the Bride in the Song of Songs, as we see, are primarily the symbols of Christ and the Church. They symbolize the matrimonial Love between Christ and the churched Soul, and in a more specific sense between Christ and the Virgin Mary. In addition, the theological image of the Bridegroom Logos and His Body, in which He became an angel and a man and which is understood as His Bride, is paramount for understanding the Christological ways of Theophany and, therefore, has an important iconographic significance. The divine Logos and His created Image, assumed by Him from the Mother's pure blood without a father's seed, is the most mysterious kind of spiritual "intercourse" representing the initial stage of ontological formation of the Church. Human bodies are male and female, but any Soul in relation to the Bridegroom Logos is an image of the Virgin, His Bride. Every matrimonial relation concerning Christ in all these symbolizations can only be *distinctions*, not differentiations determined by different "characters" of Brides. The Church is the Virgin created by Christ after the image of the eternal Church, the heavenly Tabernacle (Shekinah) of the presence, incarnation, and habitation of the Trihypostatic God. In this sense, the Church is the Image of God, or, iconologically, the Icon in which all of God's Revelations are iconographically depicted and fulfilled in the Liturgy of the Holy Communion.

The St. Ferapont Monastery is home to a fresco by the icon painter Dionisy depicting the Wedding Chamber with Emmanuel the

---

76 St. Macarius the Great, *Homily 6, On Love.*

THE ANGEL OF THE COUNTENANCE OF GOD

Bridegroom sitting on an elevated throne, and blessing the five wise virgins (who personify the five senses of the soul). The five maidens are not five "brides." They symbolize the Soul with its five senses entering into the abode of Love. Facing the Logos on both sides, there are two Angels (His uncreated images): the Virgin Sophia and the Virgin Agape. An early depiction of the young Logos featured in the parable about the ten maidens can be found in a fresco in the third-century Catacombs of St. Agnes (whose name means "pure," "chaste"). In the service dedicated to St. Agnes, she calls herself Christ's Bride: "He clothed me in a robe woven with gold. Already, His Body has been united with my body, and His Blood has adorned my cheeks."

An illustration of this parable can be seen in the fourth-century Catacomb of Ciriaca (St. Lorenzo). The theme from the Song of Songs is depicted in the mosaics of the Basilica of St. Mary the Greater, "Santa Maria Maggiore" (AD 432) and the Basilica of St. Mary in Trastevere (AD 1135) in Rome. Many paintings relating to the theme of "love marriage" (for example, the Marriage at Cana) can be found in paintings housed in Greek and Russian churches. Especially the theme of *heavenly love* began to develop in the seventeenth to the nineteenth centuries in frescoes created by Yaroslavl and Kostroma painters. These examples are indicative of the interest, shown by the ancient and modern churches, in the theme of King Solomon who glorifies the young Christ (in the image of the mystic Bridegroom) and the Soul (being deified in the Feast Chamber in the image of the Bride). The hymn to the Love between Solomon ("peaceful") and the Shulamite ("peaceful") is part of the Church's liturgical theology, waiting for its full symbolic revelation in iconography as a spiritual iconology of faith.

The Miraculous Angel of the Prosopon, who appeared to the biblical patriarchs and prophets, is now recognized as the Bridegroom, the Logos, who had matured by the time of the New Testament and who is willing to enter into a mystical marriage with the Church and with every Soul willing to be a Christian Bride. Depicted in hundreds of icons, Sophia is already a revelation of the New Testament Bride of the incarnate Logos. Christ's Wisdom is iconographically depicted as an enthroned regal Virgin symbolizing the virginal image of Christ's

Logos—Miraculous Angel in the Manifestation of Energies

Body and Blood. The body in which salvation was brought to human souls, and an example of bodily union with God, was given as the "firstfruits" of the Sacrament of Deification. Indeed, receiving communion, a person unites with God not in terms of essence or Hypostasis, but with His likeness—the Logos Lamb giving communion with sophianic and agapean energies:

> Participation in supranatural Divine goods consists in the participant becoming like (ὁμοίωσις) that in which he participates (Christ). Such likeness involves, so far as this is possible, an identity with respect to energy (κατ'ἐνεργείαν) between the participant and that in which he participates by virtue of the likeness.[77]

Developed into a certain symbolic appearance, energies become icons, visually bringing us back to the primary divine Idea of both "incarnation" for the sake of salvation and salvational "deification." Indeed, if it is possible to see the Church and Christ in the images of the Bride Shulamite and Solomon, why is it not possible to depict Sophia and Agape, the Bridegroom's everlasting and virginal Bride and Sister, in the sacramental art of icons? In fact, even at church weddings the choir sings verses from the Song of Songs: "*Come with me from Lebanon, My spouse...,*" and when the Bride enters into the church, they sing: "*Rise up, My love, My fair one, and come away... for sweet is thy voice* and THY COUNTENANCE is comely."

The Song of Songs is a piece of iconological poetry written in the mystical language of previously experienced Love of God. Between all of its lines invisibly and mysteriously hovers the Angel of Agape, the most enigmatic and hidden of all the Divine wonders bestowed out of superabundance to the world. "From the beginning (*alpha*) to the end (*omega*), the Song of Songs is written mysteriously with an enigmatic allegory of the dogmatic sense concealed under the literal sense. However, we will find it if we look for it."[78] What kind of art can express the height of the divine Power and God's Beauty?

---

77 St. Maximus the Confessor.
78 St. Athanasius, *A Brief Overview of the Holy Scriptures of the Old and New Testaments.*

THE ANGEL OF THE COUNTENANCE OF GOD

"No man hath seen God at any time,"[79] but iconography, just like mystical poetry, is an adequately figurative symbolic material made to show the beauty of the Bride and the Power of the Logos. To do so, however, it is necessary to step beyond the Old Testament laws that "prohibit images," beyond discursive opinions, and beyond that dogmatic theological thought which often does not even touch mystical theology nor bears the fruit of mystical theological *images*. Only mystical theology can solve issues relating to contemplation in the iconographic Revelations of God. In the case of modern iconography, we can talk not so much about "impossibilities" of depiction as about *some* "iconographic prohibitions." God is the Miracle of Freedom, and any laws and prohibitions are given by Him to people temporarily on account of their weakness, so that they would not hurt themselves, being unable to discern things accurately due to the simplicity of their hearts. But things may change when a certain level of consciousness of faith is reached and when believers fully understand the words: "Let us make man in Our Image, after Our Likeness." The pagan world fully "mastered" the depiction of "gods," so to speak. In the Old Testament there appeared a faith-related law and a prohibition demanding that the One God be acknowledged. But the Old Testament prophets said nothing about God in the Hypostatic Trinity. So, whom do we acknowledge in the New Testament? We acknowledge the One God, but in cataphatic theology we depict the Trinity of Hypostases, because in Christ there were revealed the depths of mystical contemplation of the Trinity as the *mode of existence* of God, while Contemplation of God became the criterion and symbol of faith and the art of symbolic icon-realism.

With the internal understanding (revealed in iconological mysticism) of God's uncreated Image, what appeared to be apophatically unattainable became possible in the Icon's cataphatic principles: God is present *in everything, everywhere, and always*. *Iconologically*, the Judaic idea of "indepictability" falls away on all planes of the Christian religious consciousness. The Orthodox icon does not depict God in terms of nature, or essence, or even hypostasis, not being naturalistically *co-natural* with Him yet being *after His image*; and besides, to

---

[79] John 1:18.

put it dogmatically correctly, here we mean God's Divinity rather than God. With faith and its tenets expressed iconologically, this type of icon strengthens rather than falls away from faith, illustrating not only hagiography, but also the edifying Revelation of His actions, which means that it reveals the deeds of the Divine Economy more clearly and distinctly. The icon — being attuned to *the image of* God's ability to step out of His inaccessibility and be visible, and to *the image of* Man's ability to use the method of symbolic realism — becomes not only a religious revelation of God's mysteries, but also, inversely, a key to the vision of God. From the beginning, Man was created after the image of the Divinity, which means that the Divinity must be visible in Man and, through Man, in the man-made icon for clarity. "After the image" means "in accordance with His Image." That is why Man is called the "mirror of God's Revelations." But then, any "*image*" in its etymological sense is a depiction. Is Christ in the likeness of the young Logos Emmanuel only a historical fact in which we remember the days of His youth or is He simultaneously also an image of the mystical and timeless state of the Soul? The method of symbolic realism claims to be able to depict not only "portraits," but also *divine ideas*. Has anyone ever seen the young Emmanuel having wings? However, there are such images. Liturgically revealed iconology should be understood in the spirit of the Divine Economy, whose images, ideas, and eide are useful for the deepening and strengthening of faith.

The acting energies by which the image of Jesus Christ is read are *enhypostatized* by Him. Just as the wife is an "active" *image* of the "contemplative" husband, so these actions represent the Image of God Who contemplates us. Through them and in them we can see with His "eye" of contemplative faith, and in the icon we depict exactly these actions rather than God, whose Name is hidden in the depths of His own angelic Image. God is unknowable, but the light-images of His actions are knowable and iconographically depictable, which means that all theological postulates are depictable, because they are "God's sayings" which are depicted from the "actions" of the uncreated Divinity and, therefore, are of educational importance. In accordance with the perception of their symbolism and meaning, believers reveal the movements of these divine energies in themselves. Is the image of the Angel of the Countenance of God less significant than the iconography of the Holy Spirit "in the form of a dove"? But surely, every word, phenomenon, and action should have its appropriate iconographic "appearance." So, everything that is described with words in the Bible and in the service books of the Church is depictable as well. By arguing the opposite point of view, we would break the mystical connection between the "word" and the "image" and, in the internal system of faith, the connection between the Logos and the Bride who live in our body, because "the Spirit and the Bride say, Come" (Rev 22:17). In icons, "depictability" is understood mystically rather than literally. Therefore, with respect to certain "prohibitions" in iconography, it would be appropriate to ask how much longer we shall stay "in the Court of the Gentiles and Jews" and interpret the contents of the Icon directly. Is not this the time to find a way and a method whose correctness would express the Presence of God not only in the "theological mind," but also in the "iconological heart"?

In the One God, icon painters should necessarily differentiate between His inaccessible and indepictable *Essence* and His *Energy of Revelations*, which is an important comprehensible icon-painting factor for faith; and that is why Christians know that the Energy with which they commune, lives and is depicted in them. For a more detailed consideration of this issue, it is desirable to further expound the term "enhypostatic" (Greek: Ἐνυπόστατον, ἐνυποστατικόν) which we have already used. Philosophers hold that it is necessary to see the *whole* before starting to distinguish particulars.

"In Trinitarian theology, we think that 'the whole' and 'distinguishable things' represent one nature and one essence, one Image and one Divinity, one grace and one equality, one glory, one concordance, and one power."[80] "I know one beginning of one Divinity, one kingdom, one authority, power, and action, one counsel, one will, one dominion and one supremacy of one essence and nature in three Persons and Hypostases."[81] We should clarify one more aspect of special interest: What is "the only *Image* of the Trinity"? One

---

80 Michael Psellos, *Dogmatic Theology.*
81 St. Niketas Stethatos, *Confession of Faith.*

means essential: God is one and His essential Image is one, but in that case He is unknowable and surely undepictable. On the other hand, when we talk about His Image in *actions*, about God's *oeconomy* Whose actions are directed toward our world, this issue passes over to another category: Theophanies, where the iconographically depictable energies of the Divinity, by the will of God, "come out" to the created world in general and to our three-dimensional world in particular, which is called "Revelation." It may be logically deduced that God Himself is indepictable, but God's Divinity understood as God's Prosopon "contemplated around His essence (περιτην ουσιαν) in many images, i.e., *goodness, wisdom, power*, divinity, that is, majesty" is depictable.[82] This is depictable not in a vague or abstract manner, but in a certain picture of Light acting with *meaning* and *beauty*, because the Divinity contains all the specific "models" of creation and mysteriously conceals the hypostatic Creator Himself. Therefore, the term "person" (Greek: *prosopon*), which is quite frequently used in the Scripture to denote the Hypostasis, means the Divinity—the *Image* and *Likeness*—of God acting in energies.

The term "enhypostatic" means that the energies of God's single Image are inseparably reunited with God's Hypostases—they are *enhypostatized*. John of Damascus says that every bodily or bodiless *enhypostatic* being exists in accordance with, and owing to, that in which it is inherent to have existence. According to this concept, we can specify, by way of example, that a person is a *hypostasis*, but his outwardly expressed character traits, inherent individual life orientation, and perception of the world exemplify his enhypostatized personality whose properties do not have their own separate existence, but depend on the immutable inner "self," which the given person's Logos Emmanuel actually has. On the other hand, the never-changing essence really is the "hypostasis" with the "personality" enhypostatized in it and with energies enhypostatized in the personality, which is usually called a person's "character." There is no existence of one without the other, but at the same time, especially in terms of religion, this is not a mixture, and it is necessary to distinguish between them, because Man will meet with God "face-to-face" as a *hypostasis*, while

---

82 St. Gregory Palamas, *Concerning Divine Union and Separation*.

the rest is the *image of his actions* as a kind of "decoration," a professional imprint of his personality, or, in other words, his *individuality*.

In Christ, according to the dogma of the Holy Church, one hypostasis exists in two natures: "Christ's human flesh, being subject to suffering, exists (ἐνυποστάναι) in the dispassionate Word," or, in other words, "the Word enhypostatized (ἐνυπέστησεν) the human nature into Its own Hypostasis."[83] So, "combined with the soul and mind, the body itself assumed by the Lord is not called a 'hypostasis,' but it is called '*enhypostatic*' as being one with the Hypostasis rather than existing as a separate hypostasis."[84] In another passage, Michael Psellos says that "the notion *enhypostatized* is a unifying basis — in case of differences — in relation to essence for the composition of one person (prosopon) and for the existence of one hypostasis." The church dictionary defines the term "enhypostatic" as "personalized," "having assumed a hypostatic appearance," and "contemplated in a hypostasis rather than in and of itself or in essence."[85] "Enhypostatic" is an epithet given by Gregory Palamas to "the divine uncreated Light which is named 'divinity,' 'thearchy,' and is generally called by all the names given by saints to the worshipful gift of the Spirit."[86] These words are directly suitable for the determination of the Theophanic images under consideration, especially the image of the Angel of the Countenance of God which is the *enhypostatic image of the Logos*, or, according to the Bible, "the Image bearing God's Name." The image is combined with the Hypostasis to such an extent that they become one "person": "hypostasis + prosopon" = Theophany. Meaning a complete unity of *prosopon* and *hypostasis* by the term "enhypostaticity," we can say that all kinds of Theophanies are depictable, because God's Presence is in every iconographically manifested energy of God. In fact, this *Presence* is surely depictable in a symbolic form. In this case, the purpose of iconography as a devotional art is to find corresponding symbolic images — Eide — *personifying* the Christological and Trinitarian Ideas of divine Revelation, to make God's "invisibility"

---

83 Leontius of Jerusalem, *Against the Nestorians*.
84 Psellos, *Dogmatic Theology*.
85 St. Gregory Palamas, *The Triads in Defense of the Holy Hesychasts*.
86 Ibid.

visible and (more or less) understandable. In icons, *actions* are not depicted in chronological sequence; they are depicted as if frozen for a moment, remaining in a certain *"image of narration"* in accordance with specific *ideas* of dispensation of enhypostatic energies, because it is important for iconography to convey in them the meaning of Revelation rather than movement. This can be compared with scrutinizing an individual motion-picture image depicting a certain event of a whole movie. On the other hand, variations of God's energies revealed in icons in the form of "a dove," "fire," "a cloud," "dew," etc., are not symbols proper. They are signs and energemata of God's anthropomorphic Symbol. The Church dogmas equally operate according to the "words" and "images" of confession, "because the Divine Voice shows visible deeds, and the words of promise are fulfilled, as the prophet says: *As we have heard, so have we seen* (Ps 48:8)."[87] The soul, plunged into a state of mystical ecstasy by Agape acting in it, can both hear and see simultaneously: "The *voice* of my beloved! *Behold, he cometh leaping upon the mountains*" (Song 2:8). The direct and living Symbols of the Divine "volitions" and "sayings" will be Logos Emmanuel, Agape, and Sophia—the true "mirrors of God's actions" manifested in the human and angelic form.

Sophia and Agape are the two movements of the essential *"Unsleeping Eye"* of the Logos through which He fulfills His Providence in Man. One of them sees to it that the Soul's adamantine facets retain their true power and undistorted *form* and clarity in the *refraction of Light*: this is the way of God-Seeing; the other one watches over the purity of the color of feelings depicted in the beauty of *radiance of Light*, and this is the way of knowledge of God. Christian philosopher Michael Psellos says that "Man's whole life depends on God's Providence and decision, and there is nothing unreasonable [*non-sophian*] or imageless [*non-agapean*]. And the Unsleeping Eye of the essential Logos Emmanuel watches over everything." In an entire person there shines this Lamp of the Seventh Day, and in iconography: Emmanuel, the Unsleeping Eye (Greek: Αναπεσών). He sends His Light into the prism of the human Soul and then, as it happened to the Virgin Mary, it happens to the

---

87 St. Gregory of Nyssa, *An Exact Explanation of the Song of Solomon.*

Soul: "the Babe leaped in her womb." The divine and spiritual "eye" of the intracardial Logos is mentioned in the Gospel: "The light of the body is the *eye*" (Mt 6:22). St. Symeon the New Theologian exclaims: "What else does He mean by 'the eye' than simply the mind (νους) which will never become simple unless it contemplates the simple (uncreated) Light? The simple Light is Christ. He who has His [*sophian-agapean*] Light shining in his mind (νους) is said to have the Mind of Christ."[88] In addition, the Holy Fathers also referred to the mind as God's Divinity. Therefore, he who has this Light acting inside him lives with Wisdom and Love and is called the Bride espoused to Christ, the Logos of the Church.

St. Gregory of Nyssa bases his interpretation of the Song of Songs on the words of Paul the Apostle: he refers to the transition from the bodily [*eros*] to the mental [*philia*] as "turning to the Lord and *taking away the veil* [*agape*]," not to stop at the letter, but to move on to the immaterial and noetic view, "for the letter killeth, but the spirit giveth life" (2 Cor 3:6). Christ teaches his disciples "the subtleties of understanding, using secret words in parables, likenesses, dark sayings, and stories offered in a mysterious manner, yet interpreting things in private and explaining obscure locutions to them, and sometimes blaming them for their slowness and inability to understand."[89] All these are iconological definitions of verbal expressions that can be used in icon painting as a method for translating literary words into pictorial language. In the past, there was a law "having a *shadow of good things to come*" without indicating "*the very IMAGE of the things*" (Heb 10:1). At present, the ideas and eide of Christ's incarnation are enhypostatized and become "trinitarily" visible in the Icon. Where there is no place for "idols," there is no limit to the veneration of icons; and where there is an adequate veneration of icons, art transforms the ideas of dogmas into pictorial forms of cataphatic theology.

For example, how mysterious and yet absolutely iconological the icon of the regal Virgin Sophia is! She is not an "idol"; being a depiction of an anthropomorphic symbol of oeconomic actions, She is Christ's image acting instructionally for Man in the physical

---

88 *Discourse* 59.
89 St. Gregory of Nyssa, *The Commentary on the Song of Songs.*

dimension. Another example is the Infant held in the immaculate arms of the Theotokos; He represents Jesus historically and Emmanuel symbolically. Solemnly sitting on the *bed* in the Wedding Chamber, however, He represents the young Bridegroom from the Song of Songs for every Soul. All these are the iconographic images of events taking place in Man's religious life, while their actors are God's Light, Wisdom, and Love. Those who rule out the possibility of depicting them in icons should also reject their action in themselves, because the icon tells only the truth about the possibility of perfect faith. The main thing that is peculiar to the icon is not the illustration of physical actions or the depiction of historical events, but the clear demonstration of Divine Revelation's mystical energies enhypostatized in the iconographic symbolism of the icon, because from this perspective alone is it possible to talk about "holy icons."

Described in the biblical parables as the Bride of Christ, Sophia instructs the human *heart* to ardently love the Logos (Prov 4:6). Agape, Her Sister, kindles the mind and directs it to a love for the wisdom of understanding the Logos. St. Gregory of Nyssa expresses the main feature of icon painting as follows:

> So, inasmuch as we desire and it is in our power to *conform* to what we desire, the Logos says to the one who became beautiful: you [*the Soul*] approached Me and, having approached the unapproachable Beauty, became beautiful yourself, *reflecting My features in yourself* like some *mirror*.[90]

Metaphorically, the icon can be called the *couch* on which the Bridegroom rests, and in the marital union between the human nature (the Virgin-Color) and the Deity (the Bridegroom-Light) there arises the *conformity* in which "they two shall be one flesh" (Eph 5:32). Such is also the Mystery of Marriage in the likeness of the relations between Christ and the Church: "Because of this mystery, the Virgin Soul names the union with God a *'bed'* [*i.e., the icon*]."[91] While the prophetic river is filled with *water* and the evangelical rivers are filled

---

90 Ibid.
91 Ibid.

with *spices*, as the visionaries say, the iconological river is filled with *images* of the proportions and perspectives of Sophia the icon-painter, and with the beauty and harmony of Agape the comforter. It is with them that "the Lord is clothed" and "hath girded Himself" (Ps 93:1) while creating the Church.

"The human soul has two natures: the incorporeal, intellectual, and pure on the one hand; the bodily, material, and irrational on the other. Wisdom limits our comprehension of God and is the sole divine *operation* which descends to our mortal existence for the purpose of giving us life."[92] To experience God's actions inside and outside the soul means to direct attention to the *conformity* of the three kinds of heteronatural existence: material, noetic, and divine. Meanwhile, in the iconography of God's personifications, the *conformity of actions* is revealed as a liturgical meaning of icon painting. And if someone turns oneself into a living Icon of the Lord, the symbolic veils will be taken away by the power of the Holy Spirit, because "the veil shall be taken away. Now the Lord is that Spirit" (2 Cor 3:16–17). Then, as a pure color of radiant energy rather than through colors or the symbolism of ideas, the Soul hastens directly to meet the Bridegroom.

In the iconological poetry of icons or books, the Bridegroom's Voice is figuratively conveyed and revealed to the Soul which really is multiform in terms of feelings yet uniform in terms of oneness of faith. "In absolute accordance with diverse volitions [*images of action*], God accepts everyone in his own rank, doing to each according to his deserts."[93] We *know* the Lord through iconology in which the action of Light, Wisdom, and Love mystically unfolds, and "there is nothing more valuable than the *knowledge of God*, for knowledge is the Light of the rational soul."[94] "Knowledge" becomes synonymous with "icon painting," because it is done as a visible action of the known, embodying that which has earlier been contemplated in ideas.

"How many times the Bridegroom repeats '*rise up*' and '*come*,' and how many times He gives strength to the Soul Bride to ascend to a greater perfection in Love, for the end of what was earlier achieved

---

92 Ibid.
93 Ibid.
94 St. John of Damascus, *Dialectic.*

becomes the beginning of guidance to the highest."⁹⁵ So, in *conformity* with the Deity, the Soul ascends to the knowledge of His names until It hears and sees the only Name, having touched the Logos in the Wedding Chamber of deification. The Soul enters

> into the divine sanctuary by means of the Song of Songs. What is described there is a marriage; but what is understood is the union of the human Soul with God. Because of this, the son in Proverbs (*of Solomon*) is named a bride (*in the Song of Songs*), and Wisdom is changed into the role of a Bridegroom so that a person might be espoused to God by becoming a pure Virgin instead of a bridegroom.⁹⁶

---

95 St. Gregory of Nyssa, *Commentary on the Song of Songs.*
96 Ibid.

CONTINUATION OF THE SONG OF SOLOMON
THEOPHANIES OF AGAPE IN THE NEW TESTAMENT

8
Continuation of the Song of Solomon:
THEOPHANIES OF AGAPE IN THE NEW TESTAMENT

Who shall separate us from the love of Christ? Shall tribulation, or distress, or persecution, or famine, or nakedness, or peril, or sword? As it is written, for thy sake we are killed all the day long; we are accounted as sheep for the slaughter.
Romans 8:35–36

THE NEW TESTAMENT APPEARANCES OF God's miraculous Angel in the images of action of the divine Love, Agape, are the Theophanies of the Holy Spirit who descended in tongues of fire first upon the Apostles, and then descends upon all the baptized in the Chrismation of a "personal" Pentecost. Since then, "sacrificial Love" has been a reality of the beauty of Agape depicted in Man, rather than a philosophical idea. From the Alpha of the Annunciation to the Omega of the Pentecost, iconographic divine actions are directed towards the creation of the Church and the salvation of humankind in it—by the Son through Sophia and by the Holy Spirit through Agape.

Baptism in the fiery element of Love concludes the Trinity cycle of New Testament salvation. God the Father revealed his *Will* having chosen Israel and through the Angel of His Divinity brought the people out of the midst of the pagan world. God the Son came into the world, was truly incarnated in the holy land of promise, and through the Angel of Sophia gave the people the Beatitudes and the rule of spiritual anagogy. God the Holy Spirit descended, and the people prepared by Christ were pierced and kindled with the divine fire of Love; from then on, the baptized in the name of the Trinity have been "sealed unto the day of redemption" (Eph 4:30) by the Holy Spirit. The Holy Spirit kindled in believers' hearts the firstfruits of deification, elevating Man from the *image* of general righteousness by law to the blessed *likeness* to the Divine Logos. From then on, the spermatic Logos became an active and guiding principle in human lives, and God's Name began to speak in Man through Baptism and Chrismation. The day of the descent of the Holy Spirit became the Eighth Day in the spiritual calendar of monotheistic faith and the First day of the living Kingdom anticipated in the Coming of Christ — the King, Prophet, and Priest.

The history of Theophanies of the Trinity shows not three ways, but one way of Man's deification in the Light of the Father, the Wisdom of the Son, and the Love of the Holy Spirit. Even though Christ outlines many life-affirming lines for Man through the Beatitudes, "there really is only one Way which is divided in accordance with every person's strength and volition," as St. Symeon the New Theologian said. To love *God* and the *neighbor* as *oneself* is the necessary requirement to be met for the Soul to attain the living levels of conscious faith: *agape, philia,* and *eros*. On these commandments "hang all the law and the prophets," because "Now there are diversities of gifts, but the same Spirit" (1 Cor 12:4) of Love. The Agapean gift is a sacrificial and selfless love in a state of total devotion. Etymologically, the Greek word Αγάπη is related to the Hebrew word חסד (Chesed) and means a "love" for those who "do not deserve love," which acts despite disappointments and rejection. In the full sense of the word, this is God's Love for every person; in fact, this is what Man's love for God should be. Despite woes, sufferings, and hatred among people, it should be remembered that all people are created after the Image of God and always live in the sphere of God's unconditional Love. All the negative things happening in the world should not be correlated with Agape, thereby terminating its access to the human heart. Paul the Apostle says, "God is not mocked" and "Quench not the Spirit." Through our neighbors, whatever they may be, and most of all through our "enemies," we perceive in ourselves the harmony of essential "all-encompassing unity," mysteriously finding ourselves

Continuation of the Song of Solomon

in Christ who took upon Himself the sins of not only the "chosen" people, but the whole world. The world can be made right only by God's Love-Agape, from which all energies that are not consistent with it run away. This means that Man's personality itself can be changed in this way.

The Agapean path of Love predestined as early as the Old Testament indicates *betrothal*: "And I will betroth thee unto Me for ever; yea, I will betroth thee unto Me in righteousness, and in judgment, and in loving kindness, and in mercies. I will even betroth thee unto Me in faithfulness: and thou shalt *know* the Lord" (Hos 2:19–20). This implies that "betrothal" is a "rite of the Church," while "knowledge" is a "sacrament of Life." Some go to the betrothal with the Lord by doing His *will*, while others go by *wisdom*, but the fastest and most direct way on the Christian path is an unselfish and sacrificial *love*. No wonder that Paul the Apostle dedicated his great hymn to Love portrayed as if It were some creature living in Man, while St. Symeon the New Theologian wrote:

> All faith comes from it [*Love*] and is built on its foundation; on it, hope is based. Without love no thing has ever taken shape, nor ever will. Its names and actions are numerous. Even more so are its distinctive features; its properties are divine and innumerable. Yet it is one in nature, wholly beyond the ken of angels or men or any other creatures, even those which are unknown to us. Reason cannot tell of it; its glory is inaccessible; its counsels unsearchable. It is eternal and beyond time, and beyond sight, though it may be perceived [*it is iconographically depictable but essentially inconceivable*].[1]

Mental visualizations are those hymnographic properties of ideas and eide on whose basis the *images* of action of God's Agape are composed into a certain order and iconographic form.

Love is Light, and he who is born into the world and lives in the love of God is called the "son of Light." The New Testament offers Love in the grace of Christ's *gifts* and the Holy Spirit's *fruits* rather than by

---

[1] *Homily* 53.

the law and by the merit of gained life experience. Christians must not only know the three commandments of love, but also invoke God's Love, so that Its transforming actions can help them become again and entirely not only born children of Light by grace, but also the *image of action* of His *Beauty*. "Beloved, let us love one another: for Love is of God; and every one that loveth is *born* of God, and *knoweth* God" (1 Jn 4:7). "He that feareth is not made perfect in love," and "There is no fear in love" (1 Jn 4:18). A sincere aspiration to God reveals to the soul necessary conditions for a perfect faith: a) to *be born* and to *grow* in the Spirit of Love time and time again, b) to constantly *contemplate* and *comprehend experience* in the Spirit of Wisdom.

In this present eon, first the Sophia of Christ acts and then the Agape of the Holy Spirit revives our faith. In the future to come, however, the action will take place in reverse order: first Agape will kindle the creative flame in Man for the Knowledge of God and then Sophia will lead Man to new comprehensions of multifaceted complexity and to the depth of God-Seeing. In this co-creation, the prospect of the future Life takes shape. Sophia and Agape are the two angels leading a new humanity out onto diverse paths of the iconological way. Portrayed in the iconography of the Ascension in white robes of the Shekinah, they point at the Source of Life—Christ risen to the Heavenly Kingdom. The Logos of the Church is risen to the Father, while His Sophia and Agape, as the Angels of dispensation of the Church, act in grace to restore the fallen nature and to straighten the ways of deification. "The Love of God is shed abroad in our hearts by the Holy Ghost which is given unto us. For when we were yet without strength, . . . Christ died for the ungodly" and "God commendeth his Love toward us, in that, while we were yet sinners, Christ died for us" (Rom 5:5–8), and everyone born in God's Agape conquers the world with Sophia. "For there are three that bear record in heaven, the Father, the Word, and the Holy Ghost: and these three are one" (1 Jn 5:7). Death still reigns over the bodies of all people, even righteous ones, governing the worldly life until the Second Coming, but it departs from the Virgin Soul clothed with the Wisdom of the Son and with the Love of the Holy Spirit, "For if we have been planted together [*by the*

Continuation of the Song of Solomon

Logos] in the likeness of His death, we shall be [*through Agape*] also in the likeness [*Sophia*] of his Resurrection" (Rom 6:5).

The presence of the Trinity's energy is evidenced by the dispensation by God's Son of the *gifts* of grace, through which Man's actions are brought into *conformity* with the Trihypostatic God, which is followed by *their* turning into the *fruit of the Holy Spirit* during the eternal and heavenly life.

Gifts of St. Sophia are revived time and again in the Chalice of Communion with the Body and Blood of Christ:

1) the fear of the Lord, 2) piety, 3) knowledge, 4) strength, 5) counsel, 6) understanding, 7) God's Wisdom, Sophia.

Wisdom says about Itself: "Counsel is mine, and sound wisdom: I am understanding; I have strength" (Prov 8:14).

Fruits of St. Agape are the sacred and divine sacraments of the Trinity:

1) Faith, 2) mercy, 3) gentleness, 4) longsuffering, 5) peace — hesychia, 6) joy, 7) God's Love, Agape.

According to Paul the Apostle, "the fruit of the Spirit is love, joy, peace, longsuffering, gentleness, goodness, faith, meekness, temperance: against such there is no law" (Gal 5:22–23). In addition, the intracardial Logos revives the Soul with gifts and fruit

> to be strengthened with might by his Spirit in the *inner* man; that Christ may dwell in your hearts by faith; that ye, being rooted and grounded in Love, may be able to comprehend with all saints what is the breadth, and length, and depth, and height [*of faith*]; and to know the Love [*Agape*] of Christ, which passeth knowledge, that ye might be filled with all the fullness of God. (Eph 3:16–19)

Ancient Theophanies, which were in symbolic images, terminated in the reality of the Lord Jesus Christ who was *crucified, resurrected* in power, and *rose* in beauty in the flesh. God's gifts and fruit created conditions for every soul to gain the prayerful experience of knowing and seeing God. Experiencing this *ekstasis*, the rejuvenated Soul can be the Bride of the Logos. The Light of the Revelation is focused in the soul by Agape's actions until a flame flares up to temper faith which is prepared for asceticism in the struggle "against the wiles of the devil. For we wrestle not against flesh and blood, but against principalities, against powers, against the rulers of the darkness of this world, against spiritual wickedness in high places" (Eph 6:12). Otherwise, the soul cannot pass through the "spirit" of this world to raise the banner of faith over its own world. "And the Lord direct your hearts into the Love of God, and into the patient waiting for Christ" (2 Thess 3:5). And if we rise with Christ in Wisdom, we kindle our life in the Holy Spirit, "and above all these things *put on* Charity, which is the bond of perfectness," and this means that we "seek those things which are above, where Christ sitteth on the right hand of God" (Col 3:1).

Sung by all the peoples under different guises and glorified by many poets, Agape is God's life-giving flame, the non-burning Fire, and it is necessary to expose oneself to its action like a "dry billet," because, as Paul the Apostle said, "Though I speak with the tongues of men and of angels, and have not Charity, I am become as sounding brass, or a tinkling cymbal" (1 Cor 13:1). Paul the Apostle's Love theme, in the criteria of perfect faith, resounds as an anthem of the New Testament and a continuation of the biblical Song of Songs:

> And though I have the gift of prophecy [*or all gifts*], and understand all mysteries, and all knowledge; and though I have all faith, so that I could remove mountains, and have not charity, I am nothing. And though I bestow all my goods to feed the poor, and though I give my body to be burned, and have not charity, it profiteth me nothing. Charity suffereth long, and is kind; charity envieth not; charity vaunteth not itself, is not puffed up, doth not behave itself unseemly, seeketh not her own, is not easily provoked, thinketh no evil; rejoiceth not in iniquity, but rejoiceth in the truth; beareth all things, believeth all things, hopeth all things, endureth all things. Charity never faileth: but whether there be prophecies, they shall fail; whether there be tongues, they shall cease; whether there be knowledge, it shall vanish away. For now we see [*and love*] through a

Continuation of the Song of Solomon

glass, darkly; but then face to face: now I know in part; but then shall I know even as also I am known [*by God*]. And now abideth faith, hope, charity, these three; but the greatest of these is Charity. (1 Cor 13:2–13)

Three divine and life-giving elements — Light, Wisdom, and Love — create conditions for Christian asceticism, by God's will reuniting the Soul with its inner Logos. Through an iconological revelation of one's own life, through purification, enlightenment, and deification, Man opens access to his intracardial Icon, because God's Name mysteriously dwells in It. In fact, the seven Sacraments of the Church are the seven gates to the revelation of this mysterious Icon, while various Sacramental Actions (energies) of the Church give believers the power to open these gates.

The Song of Songs continues to echo in the exploits of the New Testament saints who are focused on the uncreated bedewing Fire of Love. In the New Testament, the Soul re-embarks upon the path of returning to Paradise, finding the full breath of God just like in the first days of Creation when "Adam became a living soul." In the experience of transformation "of the soul before the resurrection of the body," devotees used the word "mysticism," which basically is not a doctrine, or even a faith, but a reality of inner emotion, an experience of *ecstasy* (ἐκστασις), and a "conversion" from created energies to the Divine Love and Wisdom. The return to Paradise *is a turning to God* (Greek: μετάνοια — literally, "a turn of the mind" at 90 degrees, and the repentance called for by John the Forerunner). This is the idea put by God into the essence of the created world, and Man should be the first one to return-turn to the Creator, fearlessly stepping into the stream of God's sacrificial Agape.

During the betrothal and wedding to the Logos, the Bride Soul, according to the teachings of the Church Fathers, must pass through three mystical actions:

1. *Purification* (κάθαρσις) from a deep emotional state of material "color" to the state of being white and transparent;

2. *Contemplation* (θεωρία), which is carried out through: a) a denial of external thoughts, b) a weakening of active relations between

the rational soul and the bodily eros, c) a weakening of relations among the mind and the five senses of the heart, d) the hesychia of heart-and-noetic reunification of the mind-nous, e) a liberation of consciousness from everything that is not God;

3. *Standing outside one's senses and mind*, the *ekstasis* (ἔκστασις) and *hesychia* of a dynamically tense pose of prayerful intercession before the gates of the Marital Chamber while "hearing" and "seeing" the Word. The Bridegroom's voice, like the sound of bells calling to worship, will proclaim, "The doors, the doors," which will swing open to the Soul. This is followed by the mystical Liturgy of marriage between the heavenly Bridegroom and the earthly Bride. Long is the way to God by doing the Father's will, shorter is the way by following the Son's Wisdom, but God shows "the most perfect and blessed way of salvation, the way, I say, of Love" of the Holy Spirit.[2] The Mystic Marriage between the created Soul and the uncreated Spirit gives rise to a miracle of iconographically depicted Life—the *theology* of the Spirit and the *iconology* of the Soul unite in one sacred Icon of Existence. According to St. Macarius the Great, the whole individual in all his triad—the body (through resurrection), the soul (through transfiguration), and the mind (after ascension to heaven)—will receive a new Life in deification.

The mystical experience of "most pure betrothal and marriage" indicates the fullness of faith, because "for the fathers of the Church, deification is first and foremost the fact of their inner life, rather than an idea, a theory, or a dogma."[3] On the way to the reunification of the heart and the Logos, prayerful experience takes us into the realm of fiery and flaming religious feelings. The melody of the wedding Song begins to sound in the individual Sacrament of mystical experience of every person. "The kingdom of God is within" (Lk 17:21) us, and the Bridegroom, the Kingdom, is within our heart temple. St. Gregory of Nyssa says, "Love ardently, because in the bodiless this passion is unreproachful and passionless." And then, illumined with divine Agape, the eros of our usual psycho-corporeal state becomes an ardent desire of the soul for eternal, good, and beautiful things,

---

2 St. Gregory of Nyssa, *Commentary on the Song of Songs* 1:1–3.
3 Pyotr Minin, *Mysticism and Its Nature*.

Continuation of the Song of Solomon

which is characterized by unusually intense feelings. It is possible that this wonderful union of physiological Eros and passionless Agape gives rise to an extreme antinomy of sublime states of love, which is inherent only in Man. Probably this is how Fyodor Dostoyevsky felt this: the extreme, sometimes bordering on madness, flaring up of erotic passions in his works; then suddenly transforming them into extremely elevated feelings leading to a religious awakening. With the elevating Eros tuned to the divine spirit, the soul connected with the body undergoes a life-giving and worshipful transformation, turning into "the first resurrection" of eternal Life.

Origen was the first to interpret the poetics of the Song of Songs in the Christian sense of relations between the Bride Soul and the Heavenly Bridegroom Christ. Then, this theme and image was scrutinized and developed by many Holy Fathers, especially by Methodius of Patara in his *Symposium*, a mystical treatise on the virginity of the Soul aspiring to unite with Christ in a constant desire to contemplate the regal and divine beauty of the Bridegroom; later, by Athanasius of Alexandria in his *Commentary on the Song of Songs*, Gregory of Nyssa, and other Holy Fathers. The idea that the Soul is a Virgin and the Bride of Christ became a solid foundation of the mystical experience of subsequent devout fathers, and found particularly vivid expression in the mysticism of *love* of the fourth-century Egyptian hermit Macarius the Great. Later, the doctrine of the spermatic Logos sown in the human soul was developed by Maximus the Confessor in the eighth century, and in practice it was further developed in the mystical theological works of St. Symeon the New Theologian in the eleventh century. The doctrine of the life-giving Logos of sophian and agapean Light hidden in the sacramental depths of the human heart paved the way for the mysticism of late Hesychasm (fourteenth century), which was iconologically developed by St. Gregory Palamas in the orthodox doctrine of uncreated energies and God's Divinity.

* * *

St. Macarius distinguishes between Man's *Heavenly Image* and *natural image*-form (μόρφη) in his doctrine of "embodying" of the Logos, or of His descent into the depths of the soul in the likeness of the

THE ANGEL OF THE COUNTENANCE OF GOD

Divine Light. The "Heavenly Image" is "the dwelling of the Logos in the human soul," so the Christian life is based on one principle — the impact of the personal Logos on the human soul; and if the soul responds to the call of this Annunciation, it is ready to become His Bride.

> How much more cannot He, who is as He wills and what He wills, through His unspeakable kindness and inconceivable goodness change and diminish and assimilate Himself, *embodying* Himself according to their capacity in holy and worthy faithful souls, ... and that they might ... enjoy in real experience the goodness of the Light of that ineffable [agapean] enjoyment?[4]

Like the Old Testament Angel of the Countenance of God, the agapean Light of Christ is the mediating force that acts between the Soul and the spermatic Logos. The Miraculous Angel who appeared to three youths in the fiery furnace is referred to by St. Macarius as the appearance of God's uncreated Fire:

> But the Three Children, because of their righteousness, while they were in the visible fire, had in their hearts the divine and heavenly Fire ministering within their thoughts and exerting its energy in them. That very *Fire showed itself outside them. It (the Angel) stood between them and the visible fire*, and restrained it, that it should not burn the righteous.... As, then, the Three Children, having thoughts of righteousness, received in themselves the Fire of God, and worshipped the Lord in truth, so now faithful souls receive that divine and heavenly Fire, in this world, in secret; and that Fire forms a heavenly image upon their humanity.[5]

The actions of Christ and the Spirit equally have the energy of Light, Wisdom, and Love, which *give birth to and enlighten* the soul. Logos Emmanuel teaches, instructs (let us recall the iconography of

---

4 St. Macarius the Great, *Fifty Spiritual Homilies*, Homily 4, 11.
5 Macarius, *Homily* 11, 2.

Continuation of the Song of Solomon

"Mid-Pentecost"), and caresses the soul, as if she were a child, until she comes of age, to be a Bride. Then, "by His own power God receives her to Himself, gradually accommodating Himself to her changes, until He has increased her with His own increase. For He stretches her out and lengthens her to an endless and immeasurable increase, until she becomes a Bride without blemish and worthy of Him."[6] In the active practice of pious ascetics, luminous *Will* reveals itself as a method of *increasing* the soul, while *Wisdom* and *Love* are part of the *contemplative* and *deifying* practice of seeing and knowing God. The Light of Wisdom and the Fire of God's Love form "the vessel of the human soul" and "the Lord, who copies the intentions of faithful and good souls, and forms an Image even now in the soul according to their desire, and at the Resurrection it appears external to them, and glorifies their bodies within and without."[7]

* * *

Active and contemplative practices were beneficially reunited in the experience of St. Isaac the Syrian who became a singer of pure contemplative silent prayers offered in the heart. The teachings of St. Isaac feature practical parallels of *knowledge* and *speculation*: the practice (πράξις) of active faith purifies the passionate part of the soul, while contemplation (θεωρία) illuminates its intelligent side. Kindled by faith, the soul ascends to the Kingdom from material life to divine Life through three degrees of paired "elements" of the mind and the heart: "Gnosis — Eros," "Episteme — Philia," and "Sophia — Agape."

Entering through the first gate of knowledge ("gnosis"), the soul reveals the sensitivity ("eros") of its own heart; reaching the gates of heavenly intuition ("episteme"), it can be enveloped in a universal sense of delight and a feeling of unity of the private (personal) world and the general (universal) world. This is the state Philia; becoming silent at the gates of the divine Chamber, the soul, enlightened by Sophia and kindled by Agape, contemplates her Bridegroom as if from afar. But He calls her by the name corresponding to her beauty and she approaches. The Bride Soul receives a spiritual unalterable Name

---

6 Macarius, *Homily* 47, 17.
7 Macarius, *Homily* 11, 3.

of *re-unification* with, and conformity to, the Bridegroom Logos. Transformed in the early stages, Gnosis-Eros and Philia-Episteme escort the Soul only to the "holy of holies" of the Chamber. Further, behind its gates, however, there operate the Sophia and Agape of the Bridegroom's "embraces and kisses."

* * *

The mystical experience of St. Maximus the Confessor combined both trends in the teaching of the universal Logos. Professor S. Averintsev describes the significance of this great saint as follows:

> Against the background of these bewildering times, there towers the lonely figure of Maximus the Confessor, the original philosopher and theologian who for the last time embodied something of the intellectual audacity of Origen, the subtlety of Gregory of Nyssa, and the system-forming breadth of Dionysius the Areopagite.[8]

St. Maximus placed special emphasis on the personal spermatic Logos sown into the human heart, increasing in faith and confidence in accordance with the disposition of the heart and mind.

Despite the "intricacies" of pagan mythology, the entire pre-Christian history is a monotheistic descent of the Logos to the creation. Direct Theophanies pass through both Testaments, from Abraham's meeting with three Angels, to Jesus Christ who "was incarnate and became man." Having repeatedly appeared under different forms and names in the Old Testament, He actually showed in the Transfiguration, just like the Angel of the Countenance of God, the angelic, luminous, and essential nature of His Divinity. Theophanies continue to change the world and, from the Resurrection of Christ and the Descent of the Holy Spirit, have formed an inverse perspective of the Way of the Divine Economy not only to arouse people's religious memory and kindle the fire of faith, but also to clear the way for returning to the "Garden and City" of the Heavenly Kingdom.

The Holy Spirit's actions kindle the fiery intracardial seed of Christ, and the soul receives again a Light *Image*, in accordance with the

---

8 *Byzantine Culture.*

providence and iconography of the uncreated Icon. According to the saints, Logos Emmanuel henceforth shines brightly and can be visible (as the Icon) even in the physical heart of the believer.

> In our hearts, He is formed incorporeally, but as it befits God. However, just as a woman having a child in her womb clearly knows that because the child moves in her womb, so the one who has Christ formed in oneself knows His movements and leaps, that is, His radiance and brightness, and sees Christ formed in oneself. Just as a lamp's light can be seen in a mirror, so in a person Christ can be seen like the Light that is essential, invisibly visible, inconceivably conceivable, in an imageless *image* and in a formless *form*.[9]

Every person baptized in the Name of the Trinity is a participant in the sacrament of Annunciation, because at that time a person becomes fertilized by the Spirit of God. It should be noted that every baptized person is washed and reborn in the sacrament of Baptism. However, we should also admit that not every person then creates conditions for growing the Child Emmanuel in the mystical heart; with the result that the union between the Soul and the Logos is delayed for many years and sometimes never results in a mystical Marriage, while faith — in which the soul becomes deified and the Logos becomes finally humanized — remains fruitless.

According to St. Maximus the Confessor, the knowledge of God is gained through the following stages:

1. the knowledge of logoi (λόγοι) of the visible nature;

2. the study of the Holy Scriptures, with the obligatory participation of the heavenly Mind (Nous);

3. the direct intuitive contemplation of the Light of one's own intracardial Logos Emmanuel;

4. the return of the Soul together with Logos Emmanuel to Hypostatic Christ, the Logos to the Church (because Christ, as the "Father of the Christian race," is the Father of the intracardial seed of every Soul);

---

9 St. Symeon the New Theologian, *Homily* 57.

5. the mystical reunion, first between the human "image" and Christ by His human nature and then, having gained the heavenly "likeness," the reunion with Christ by His Divine Nature. In this reunion, a person will receive the gift of contemplation of the Trinity in *God*'s Kingdom.

Entering into the Life of the transfiguring Light, a believer combines all existing things and is mysteriously elevated together with the Logos to the Divinity of the Holy Trinity. Maximus the Confessor writes that a Christian, while ascending, reunites five spheres of existence:

1. *Created* and *uncreated* natures, becoming conformable to the energies of God's Divinity;

2. in created nature—*intelligible* (noetic) and sensual *material* natures;

3. in sensual space—the *heaven* (metaphysical) and the *earth* (physical);

4. on earth—*paradise* and *Man*;

5. in Man—the *male* and *female principles*.

This reunion presents to us, at least partly, the idea of realization by Man of agapean and sophian completeness for those who prepare themselves to live in the Eighth Day of Creation.

* * *

A special place among the later representatives of mystical theology is held by St. Symeon the New Theologian (eleventh century). His hymns and homilies variously continue the theme of the Old Testament's Song of Songs in the personal experience of Love reuniting Man with God. In this case, however, we can see Love from a strongly pronounced perspective of the New Testament. It is enhypostatized and reunited with Christ, having become His creative Image, in the enhypostatic unity between the Soul and the Logos that is inherent in Christian theology and iconology. St. Symeon called upon believers to experience the action of the Holy Spirit and the mystically increasing Child Emmanuel in their real lives. "A Christian is a person who has experienced the grace of the Deity and who has felt, through the Soul's *intelligent sense*, the action of

Continuation of the Song of Solomon

God within oneself." The recognizable sign of this grace is illumination of the soul with uncreated Light, sometimes formless, like an intelligent cloud, and sometimes in an angelic personification of the Virgin — Love or Wisdom. In this light-bearing illumination, the Logos is reborn in the soul, and

> we accept Him, and He is in us *as a seed*. This is how we conceive Him, not physically, as the Virgin Mary conceived once, but spiritually, yet essentially. This spiritual birth administers a sacrament of renovation (*deification*) within us, *uniting and joining* us with the incarnate (*in the soul as well*) Son of God by the grace of the Holy Spirit.

St. Symeon places particular emphasis on the fact that deification is an internal action giving rise to a new "heavenly Image," rather than something external and communicated to Man, as in the Old Testament. The Soul and the Logos spermatikos, in the fullness of their union, mysteriously increase in the heart ("embodying," according to St. Macarius), and "then Christ Himself comes down from heaven, comes into us as into a coffin, uniting with the soul and resurrecting it."[10] In the experience of the Church Fathers, this event is called "the first resurrection" or "the Transfiguration of the soul before the general Resurrection in the body."

In St. Symeon's writings, the meeting between the Soul and the Logos is filled with a feeling of irrepressible and personal attraction to Love itself, whose description is similar to that of the ancient Angel of the Countenance of God. It reveals, or conceals, in itself the hypostatic God, the Lord and the Bridegroom. Agape, the marital energy of Christ, is enhypostatized in Him so specifically that the bodily Soul, being lovelorn, turns to His personified Love as if to a person and asks: "Where do you hide Christ?" Similarly, in the Song of Solomon, the Shulamite asked the virgins: "Where is my Bridegroom hiding himself?" The poetic styles of the biblical book and the New Testament singer of Light are very similar in the height of feelings: "When I recalled the *beauty* of undefiled love, its Light suddenly appeared in my heart. I was ravished with its sweetness

---

10   St. Symeon the New Theologian, *Homilies*.

and lost my senses."[11] This song is not a poetic metaphor, because it pours out from the ascetic heart of a devout person who is serious in his perfect faith, because his heart is filled with real experience of mystical kindlings. St. Symeon fully relies on the iconology of symbolic realism when he refers to Love as some Virgin Bride hiding "behind the veils" of her Bridegroom. In this speculation, however, it is important to understand that it is not *hypostatic* or abstract; as a revelation of the Prosopon, Agape is a depictable Image, a virginally energetic and iconographically real Image of Christ's Divinity. Let us recall the words of the prophet Isaiah: God forms the light, and creates darkness. The Logos always dwells in the Light and is absent in the darkness. But then the uncreated Light is intelligent and "formed" into Theophany through revelation. In the religious sense, to form means to depict, personalize, and give a recognizable appearance, to Him Who is invisible by nature. Divine Agape and Sophia *form* the mystical appearance of the Son of God, so in contemplations He is recognized not only by human traits, as the Jews once saw, and did not believe that He was the Messiah, but as the "Image of the invisible God." In mystical theology, it is natural to assume that Christ should be recognized not only by His human appearance, but He is recognized by the Soul by His Divinity and directly iconographed in His royal energies of Virgin Sophia and Virgin Agape. This iconography is understandable, because the marital union between the Soul and Christ is formed not by human or divine nature, but by the *Prosopon* of the thrice-radiant Light whose iconographic personifications are notable in the images of "the bride and the sister"—Sophia and Agape.

St. Symeon could not keep Christ's enhypostatized Agape with him: "I do not know how it departed from me again and left me to mourn my infirmity all alone," because it is so written: "The wind bloweth where it listeth, and thou hearest the sound thereof, but canst not tell whence it cometh, and whither it goeth" (Jn 3:8). It is appropriate to mention a distinction between two concepts: a) "energy of Love" and b) "energy-Love." St. Symeon never lost the *energy* of Love in his spiritual life, constantly living in grace and holiness, but he

---

[11] St. Symeon the New Theologian, *Homily* 53.

speaks about the very personification of Love, rather than its energies as properties, or more precisely, he speaks not about energemata (rays), but about their iconographic Source, about the most iconographically enhypostatized Agape. As the image of the *appearance* of Christ, It is self-willed and free to approach or retreat, to hide or reveal the Lord. "A garden enclosed is My Sister, My Spouse" exclaims the Bridegroom in the Song of Songs, describing His image of attraction to the Bride. These actions — or, as the saints say, appearances —

> are the *Energy* that is essential and life-giving, making us wise and creative, and maintaining created beings in existence. So, divine appearances and energemata of fulfillment and vivification are God's uncreated *providences* (*pronoiai*) and *goodnesses*. And they are God Himself, although not by essence.[12]

The Angel of the Countenance of Christ is the Light of oeconomy of God's sophian and agapean actions: "God is Light, and those who are worthy to set eyes on Him see Him as Light; and those who have received Him receive Him as Light." However, "although Christ is called the Light and the Sun, He is above them as their Creator and Lord."[13] Agape is a *Prosopon* (*Image*), while Christ is a *Hypostasis*, and there is no confusion in this distinction, because the former expresses itself in the iconology of Prosopon, whilst the latter is expressed in the theology of the Hypostasis.

Personified energies of the divine *providence* express the hypostatic idea of God's "omnipresence," which includes material life, despite the heteronaturality of existence. "Providence is nothing other than God's turning (Speech) to inferior beings and His good will." "For this reason, the one *Providence* through which God takes care of His inferior (human) beings is not just *ONE*, but is called by theologians *MANY* providences and goodnesses, because energy is a *movement* of essence rather than essence (let alone hypostasis) itself."[14] The New Testament hymn to Love, to which St. Symeon appeals in search of

---

12 St. Gregory Palamas, *Treatises*.
13 St. Symeon the New Theologian, *Homily 79*.
14 St. Gregory Palamas, *The Triads in Defense of the Holy Hesychasts*.

THE ANGEL OF THE COUNTENANCE OF GOD

the Lord who has hidden from view, is very similar in meaning to St. Dionysius the Areopagite's description of God's appearances in His holy names. Speaking very highly of Dionysius, Gregory Palamas says that "the entire *Divine Names* is a *hymn* glorifying these appearances and God's energies."[15]

Glorifying God's figurative *appearances*, Dionysius ascribes glory to Christ in his hymns. Referring to the "seven spirits" of the prophet Isaiah as the "seven energies" of the Holy Spirit, John the Apostle ascribes their actions to the Father and the Son too, while clearly distinguishing them from the Holy Spirit itself when he says: "Grace be unto you, and peace, from *him which is, and which was, and which is to come*; and from *the seven Spirits*...; and from *Jesus Christ*" (Rev 1:4–5, 5:6). Gregory Palamas clarifies: "but in the spirit he also sees Christ as a *Lamb* having *seven horns and seven eyes*." So, "the Sacred Science (*theology*) sometimes employs a method of *Undifference* and sometimes one of *Differentiation*; and that we must neither separate those things which are Undifferentiated nor confuse those which are Differentiated."[16] In icons, it is permissible to depict *hypostatic* things as an "image and likeness" *united* in one Person (for example, Christ Pantocrator), while *prosoponic* things are permissible to be depicted *separately* (for example, the Angel Sophia is Christ's "Image," energy, but Christ blessing Sophia's actions should be depicted at the top to avoid referring to the angel as a "person"). Not distinguishing between the inseparable combinations of a *prosopon* and a *hypostasis*, where God is both knowable and unknowable, we annihilate one thing with the help of the other thing. Gregory Palamas writes that

> *those who have not the knowledge of God* do not even understand that negative statements in relation to God do not contradict positive ones, because He is both the Existing and the Non-Existent, both the Many-Named [*cataphatic theology*] and the Unnameable [*apophatic theology*]. Thus, the Divinity is one and is not one, so both

---

15   Ibid.
16   Dionysius the Areopagite, *On the Divine Names*.

statements are godly, and each of them *has many and different meanings*. So, the One God inseparably worshiped in Three Hypostasis and in one Essence is also inseparably separated into different energies, because, according to the divine Maximus (Scholia on *The Divine Names*): "God, from a desire to bring every existent being to deification, multiplies and manifoldly increases through providential emanations."[17]

This "providential emanation" can be found in the Miraculous Angel of the Lord of Sabaoth, be it the image of Logos Emmanuel, Sophia, or Agape.

So, the Church Fathers said enough to understand that wonderful *appearances*, or Theophanies, are related to the iconological and iconographical rather than theological side of faith and belong to dispensational argumentation. The image of the Angel Agape, whose presence kindles believers with the life of faith, indicates not only the presence of God, but also the state of spiritual health of believers themselves. This icon instructs the one who contemplates it, and from the depths of the heart the Soul cries out and asks: "Where is my beloved Bridegroom, O Love hiding Him from me?" Let us have a look at the whole text of St. Symeon's hymn. This is a New Testament hymn to the Virgin Agape personified in ascetic iconography. In this hymn, now Christ becomes Love, now Love becomes Christ, and this perichoresis has no space, or separation, or fusion. It describes the *appearances* of prosoponic Love instructing the Soul with its energies in the *beatitude* of the future betrothal. This can be heard in the love dialogue between the Bride and the Bridegroom in the Song of Songs, in Sophia's evidence in the Proverbs of Solomon, in the words of Agape — the gracious Image of Christ's kenosis — in the evangelical Beatitudes, and in the hymns of the Holy Fathers. This hymn has a timeless and spaceless combination of symbolic forms of poetry, iconology of symbolic realism, and mystical theology. The song of the New Testament hymn ineffably contains the interwoven meanings and the spirit of Holy Scripture and Tradition. In this hymn,

---

17 St. Gregory Palamas, *Treatises*.

God's essential and unapproachable image manifestly and animatedly appears in the form of the Angel of enhypostatic incarnate Love that can appear before the believer as an uncreated Icon of God's ways, like the ancient shining Angel of Jehovah or the New Testament Sophia.

This is the mystical Way, the path formed as the angelic Ladder of "Man's ascent and God's descent," which was described by St. Isaac the Syrian, and St. John Climacus in "The Ladder of Divine Ascent." This ascent is promoted by the assistants and guides who descended from Christ in the hypostatic Holy Spirit for the dispensation of the Church and Man — Sophia and Agape, the *enhypostatic* and *figurative* energies of the Divinity. "What God forms in us [*as the Logos*] essentially concerns the fact that He recreates, renews, and transforms us after the *Image* of His Divinity."[18]

THE HYMN TO LOVE BY SYMEON THE NEW THEOLOGIAN. HOMILY 53

When I recalled the beauty of undefiled love, its light suddenly appeared in my heart. I was ravished with its sweetness and lost my senses; I lost all perception of this life and forgot all the things of this world.

Love desired, how fortunate are those who have *embraced you*, for they will no longer have a yearning to embrace any human beauty.

How fortunate are they who are moved by divine love to cling to *you*.

How fortunate are those who caress *your* beauty and delight in it with great desire, for their souls will be sanctified by the undefiled blood and water which issue from *you*.

How fortunate are those who passionately embrace *you*, for they will be altered for the better in spirit and will exult in their souls, because *you* are inexpressible Joy.

How fortunate are they who gain possession of *you*, for they will count the treasures of the world as nothing, for *you* are indeed wealth "beyond the dreams of avarice."

How blessed and thrice-blessed are they whom *you* accept, for though they be apparently without any glory, they will be more glorious than those who are glorious, more honored than those who are honored.

---

18 St. Symeon the New Theologian, *Homily* 80.

Continuation of the Song of Solomon

How worthy of praise are those who pursue *you*; even more so those who have found *you*. Most blessed are those who are loved by *you*, received by *you*, taught by *you*, those who have dwelt in *you* and been fed by *you* with immortal food, that is the Lord, Jesus Christ.

Love divine, where are *you* holding Christ? Where are *you* concealing Him? Why have *you* taken the Redeemer of the world and departed from us? Open a wicket gate for us, so that we also may see Christ Who suffered for us, and so hope in His mercy that we will die no more when we once have seen Him. Open up to us, *you* who became the door allowing Him to be made manifest in the flesh. Love, *you* who have forced the unforced and abundant compassion of our Master to bear the sins and infirmities of all people, do not reject us by saying, "I do not know you."

Be with us, so that *you* may come to know us, for we are not known to *you*. Dwell in us, so that, for *your* sake, the Master may visit even us, who are lowly; go before us to meet Him, since we are wholly unworthy. So that He will pause on His way, to converse with *you* and will permit even us sinners to fall at His unblemished feet. *You* will intercede on our behalf and plead with Him to forgive the debt of our sins, so that through *you* we may again be found worthy to serve Him, our Master, and be sustained and nourished by Him.

Holy Love, may we then be pardoned through *you* and may we enter into the enjoyment of the good things of our Master, since no one will taste their sweetness except through *you*. Those who do not love *you* as they ought and are not, as they should be, the object of *your* love, may well run, but have not yet reached the goal. It is far from certain that somebody who is running will actually complete the race. But for those who have laid hold on *you*, or on whom *you* have laid hold, victory is certain, since *you* are the end of the Law. It is *you* who surround me and inflame me, *you* who, by the pangs of my heart, kindle me with boundless desire for God and for others.

You are the teacher of the prophets, the co-traveler with the apostles, the power of the martyrs, the inspiration of the Church fathers and teachers, the perfection of all the saints, and the commission for my own present task of obedience.

When I recalled *Love* [*Agape*], my heart rejoiced and I hastened to sing the praise of *its* marvels.

Because any zeal and any ascetic effort is in vain and with no useful outcome, unless they end in *Love*, with a contrite spirit.

"By this shall all men know that ye are my disciples, if ye have *Love* one to another" (Jn 13:35).

* * *

Sung by Symeon the New Theologian in the poetic style of the New Testament, the hymn of "beatitudes" dedicated to Agape, God's Love, is part of Christian theology, when read and understood from the iconological, i.e., liturgical, perspective. Love is seen as divine Energy of paramount importance, as God's Image appealed to in prayers, as a dynamic Image of the Logos that can revive the human soul and bring it to the object of love—Christ, the Son of God. Agape is a type of extremely mystical image of the Guardian Angel who guards the human Orthodox Spirit, rather than the soul and the body as a created Angel does. In this hymn, it is interesting to consider the believer's attitude to God's Love-Agape in terms of its iconological depictability as a "person." It is clear from the context of this song that Agape, being God's Prosopon and Life, is different from the Hypostasis of Christ, and this distinction makes it possible for the saint to appeal personally to Agape without any fear of confusion, which is consistent with the Church Fathers' teaching on the distinction among essence, hypostasis, and prosopon (face).

We have italicized the pronoun "you" to emphasize the appeal to Agape and its personal ability to enter into prayerful communion with the soul, helping it gain a creative ability to always see the Bridegroom. If we understand the conceptual difference between the terms "image-prosopon" and "logos-hypostasis," we should not worry about the personification of Love in St. Symeon's hymn. After all, we pray to the Holy Cross and appeal to it as to a living being, "O life-giving Cross of the Lord! *Help* us together with the Holy Lady Theotokos..."[19] In this prayer, the Image of the Cross is equated with the personality of the Virgin Mary. In "Adam's

---

19 *A Canon of the Cross.*

Lament," Paradise is appealed to as a person, "O Paradise, my Paradise, help me..." This is not "idolatry," but the personification of the Presence of the living God in religious symbols, in images of God's actions. The prayerful invocation is addressed not to the "wood" of the Cross or to "the place" of Paradise, but to the Shekinah, the energy of the Cross and Paradise. The Mother of God is also a symbol of the presence of God, and She is a living Symbol. We honor and worship not the "Virgin," but the *actions* of the Holy Spirit in Her. Both Sophia and Agape are enhypostatized images, uncreated "mirrors" in which God contemplates Himself and wants to contemplate "reflections" of the world and Man in them. St. Symeon exclaims to Agape as to a living being: "Be with us, so that you may *come to know* us, so that He will converse *with you* and permit *even us* to contemplate Him through *you*. Dwell in us, so that, *for your sake*, the Master may visit *even us*, those who are received by *you*." In this hymn, Agape is personified, because by nature It can be described as follows: "Reason cannot tell of It; Its glory is inaccessible; Its counsels unsearchable." It is attained by us in the search for the Trihypostatic God, but it is Agape that, like a miraculous Guardian Angel, brings the Soul, previously formed and faceted by Sophia, into the Marital Chamber of Christ, for It is "the door allowing Him to be made manifest in the flesh." Only by abiding in Agape's energies does the believer come to know the Truth, calling Him the Lord, and this is what is said: "No man can say that Jesus is the Lord, but by the Holy Ghost."

Love prepares us

> by the grace of the All-Holy Spirit, clothes us in Christ, kindles a lamp and makes us children of the Light. Only then the soul leaves this (corruptible) world, resembling some kind of dark womb, and enters into the mental and heavenly Light, somehow penetrating further into this divine Light and getting filled with unspeakable joy.[20]

In search of God's Love, through the cloudy mist of ignorance, the Soul cries out,

---

20 St. Symeon the New Theologian, *Homily* 54.

> O desired divine Love! How fortunate are those who have embraced *you*, how fortunate are they who gain possession of *you*. Where are *you* holding Christ? Be with us, so that *you* may come to know us. Dwell in us. For *you* are the end of the Law. It is *you* who surround me and inflame me, *you* who, by the pangs of my heart, kindle me with boundless desire for God and for others.

So, before we love the Lord, asceticism requires that we love His Wisdom and His Love, for only they can maintain the *perspective* of pure faith, and the *proportion* of the reunification of created and uncreated things into an integral whole of the *Image of Life*, which then reveals the *harmony* of a non-false state of the Knowledge of God. The Soul, following these three principles, is kindled with the fire of Agape, and becomes Light.

> When a man has within him the light of the all-holy Spirit (*Logos*), he cannot bear the sight and so he falls prostrate on the ground. He cries out and shouts, driven out of his senses by immense fear. He is like someone who sees or feels something beyond nature, reason, and understanding. It is as if his entrails were touched by fire and scorched with flames. He cannot bear this burning and becomes like someone outside himself, and because he does not have the strength [to endure], he pours out an endless flood of tears which refreshes him and rouses up the flame of his desire. His tears become more abundant and, when he is purified in their flood, he shines with greater brilliance. Then, entirely on fire, he becomes like light and fulfills the saying (*of the Theologian*): "God is made one with the gods and becomes known," maybe so much as he has connected with those united with Him and as he has known Him.[21]

In this illumination by the Holy Spirit, they achieve a harmony of a living Icon painted with "light" and "color," which is followed by its sanctification by the Spirit of the Lord. "Illumination by the Spirit is

---

21 St. Symeon the New Theologian, *The Practical and Theological Chapters*.

the endless end of every virtue and whoever attains this illumination by the Spirit has finished with everything sensory and has begun to live with his consciousness in spiritual things alone."²²

John the Apostle's words "that which is born of the Spirit is spirit" (Jn 3:6) should be understood as a mystery of *agapean conception* and then sophianically "Christ is formed [*i.e., mystically born*] in our hearts" (Gal 4:19).

> Incorporeally in the soul, but as it befits God. However, just as a woman having a child in her womb clearly knows that because the child moves in her womb, so the one who has Christ formed in oneself knows His *movements* and leaps, that is, His radiance and brightness, and sees Christ *formed* in oneself. Just as a lamp's light can be seen in a mirror, so in a person Christ can be seen like the Light that is essential, invisibly visible, inconceivably conceivable, in an imageless Image and in a formless Form (Eidos).²³

What is meant by this iconographic and "essential and invisibly visible" appearance of Christ is His *image* not only by human nature; emphasis is placed exactly on His mystical image that can be revealed (or concealed) by the actions of Sophia and Agape. This relation between *prosopon* and *hypostasis* shows us the possibility of the existence of the icon of Jehovah's Angel, be it the New Testament depiction of Emmanuel, the personification of Light, or many-eyed Sophia, or many-flamed Agape. At present, Theophanies, which started as early as the Old Testament in the likeness of Jehovah's Angel, are imprinted in the heart of the Christian faith, through the embodiment of the Logos, directly in every soul turned to its Bridegroom. In the ancient Song of Songs, the Bride exclaims, "How long will my Bridegroom send me kisses through Moses and the prophets?" At present, through the grace of Christ-revealing Agape, the Bride says, "Thy Name is as ointment poured forth. Let Him kiss me with the kisses of His mouth. He hath brought me into the Chambers of His Love."²⁴

---

22 St. Symeon the New Theologian, *Homily* 56.
23 St. Symeon the New Theologian, *Homily* 57.
24 Priest Gennady Fast, *A Supplicatory Canon of the Song of Songs.*

THE ANGEL OF THE COUNTENANCE OF GOD

Icons and frescoes depicting Logos Emmanuel seated on a throne in the Chamber are the evidence of the Bridegroom waiting for His Bride until the Kingdom's gates close after the "Last Judgment." Emmanuel's variously shining Light guiding the Soul to the glory of transfiguration may have a direct and personal meaning in the Christian interpretation: "God is with *me*."

> This is how, brethren, incomprehensible things are comprehended in our faith! This is how the Father, and the Son, and the Holy Spirit are *seen and certainly mentally conceived* by those Christians to whom the Father, and the Son, and the Holy Spirit *come* and make Their abode in them, being knowable in one indivisible Light [of Wisdom and Love]. Therefore, those who have not become worthy of achieving this, let them blame themselves instead of saying that it is impossible or that it is beyond our consciousness; that is, we do not know about that. May they find proof in the Divine Scriptures and may they know that this thing is possible and true and happens knowingly to us in such a way that we cannot but know about that.[25]

In the context of New Testament, we can now see and re-evaluate the meaning and truth of the Old Testament Theophanies, for example, the meal of the three angels at the home of righteous Abraham, and, following the tradition of the Church, we undoubtedly recognize in those appearances the Trihypostatic God, yet not by essence, but by the *eidos* of God's three Energies forming the Revelation. In the experience of hospitality, Abraham received an extra letter in his name (A-*alpha-image*) and future promises, while we, inheriting the faith of the patriarchs, acquired in our hearts a special gift of the *seed* (O-*omega-likeness*) of God incarnate. If the seed grows in our intelligent heart to reach Christ's age and dwells in our whole being, the youth Emmanuel will become a Bridegroom grown from the seed in every Soul, transforming it into a heavenly beauty and taking it "by the hand" as a Bride to bring it to the hypostatic Jesus Christ, the Bridegroom of the whole Church, for a blessing. He is

---

25 St. Symeon the New Theologian, *Homily* 57.

our Prototype, "the brightness of His glory, and the express Image of His Person" (Heb 1:3). The ability to contemplate and understand this statement depends on the full development of the talent to see first symbolically, and then directly, the uncreated Icon of God, while understanding that all types of the Icon contain the meaning given by the Church fathers: "it is possible to see God as He is." And we should learn this iconology even now. To approach God and to strengthen our faith, there is a Church canon acting as a kind of liturgical path of iconology and iconography.

> For your own spirit, or your whole soul, is in your whole mind, and your whole mind [*reason*] is in your whole word; and your whole word [*nous*] is in your whole [*intellect and heart*] Spirit, inseparable and ununited. This is God's image [*Icon*], and we are enriched with it from above to be *in the likeness* of God and *in the Image* of Him Who Created us. Therefore, when we bow to a person, we present our regards to the person as having the mind, the soul, and the logos (in terms of the Icon), without separating them or preferring one to another.[26]

We come to know God's commandments through three types of Love: in the body—through Eros, in the rational soul—through Philia, and in the intelligent spirit—through Agape. "He that hath My commandments, and keepeth them, he it is that loveth Me: and he that loveth Me shall be loved of My Father, and I will love him, and *will manifest Myself to him*" (Jn 14:21). For Christ so loved Man, that He, having become incarnate and Man, "in accordance with the promise, manifests Himself to those who love Him and gives them the Spirit of God along with His manifestation, so the Father and the Son are with us through the Spirit."[27] In this sense, Love acts as a renewing, life-giving, and life-asserting Energy (Prosopon) of the hypostatic Holy Spirit. Filling the believer's heart, Agape is felt in it as a transfigured Eros; then It forms an intellect-and-heart sphere of Philia and, permeating all the microcosms in Man, dwells inside as a

---

26 St. Symeon the New Theologian, *Homily* 61.
27 St. Symeon the New Theologian, *Homily* 63.

mystic power and a sacrament of faith. Prepared by it for Deification, the believer attains

> the *fruit of faith*, which is the holy unfading Light [*Logos*]; the Light, on its part, applies and multiplies faith. The brighter the Light shines, the more faith grows and the higher it ascends. And again, the more faith grows, the more the fruit [*in Agape*] of the Spirit multiplies. And what God forms in us is essentially about the fact that He recreates, renews, and transforms us *after the Image of His Divinity*.[28]

Developing the theme of "the Image of God's Divinity" and its substantial significance in the development of anthropology in the context of iconology, we should note that it is spreading wider and deeper, intensively manifesting itself and growing from the root of the ancient culture of the orthodox art of the Icon. No matter whether modern iconoclasts "of all hues" want it or not, existing canonical icons reveal and show the natural connection between every soul and the Prototype in accordance with which every person is given the opportunity to become a *child of Light*, for "God is Light, and in Him is no darkness at all." Iconologically, it becomes clear that "mysticism and asceticism, rather than theology and dogmatics, reveal a special and integral view of Man and his destination. On the way to this destination, there opens up a truly integral experience-based anthropology, an established doctrine of Man in his everlasting being," because anthropology, designated after the image of God, "reveals in the entire Man a living Icon of his state of faith."[29]

To better understand such a complicated point concerning the relationship between the incomprehensibility of God and the depictability of His Divinity, we should remember that, while supporting both statements, the Orthodox Tradition, in a single movement of thought directed toward Him, distinguishes among several transitional stages in the goals, practice, and theory of comprehension of Divine Providence. Contemplating the *integral whole*, we should see

---

28 St. Symeon the New Theologian, *Homily* 80.
29 Sergey Horuzhy, *The Diptych of Silence*.

that "the former" belongs to theology, while "the latter" belongs to iconology. In this pair of concepts, the former is *intellectually conceivable* in accordance with the *likeness* of the Logos, while the latter is *iconographically depictable* in accordance with the *image* of the Logos. For example, while theology discusses a subject of apophatic content and avoids all kinds of names and definitions of God, iconology can in the same subject find and realize, "on the other end of the scale," images in accordance and *conformity* with a cataphatic content, whose understanding is symbolically expressed in our ordinary life inscribed in the iconography of a particular icon. Understanding theology and iconology only as two perspectives and two states of unidirectional faith—"upward and downward" (toward "deification" and "incarnation"), we need to train our minds and hearts in the piety of religious *discernment*. In addition, it is necessary to choose an "instrument" of discernment, knowing that the earthly "mind" is an instrument of philosophy, while Man's "heavenly mind" (νους) is an instrument of theology; Man's heart "eros" is an instrument of painting, while heavenly "Agape" is an instrument of icon painting. By making proper emphases, we will not sin against the truth in any consideration of both theological and anthropological "details." When contemplating, diverse categories of thought will become more understandable as essential differences, for example:

1. between everyday reasoning (business, politics, sports, etc.) and philosophy;

2. between philosophy and theology;

3. between the two ways of knowing God (apophatic and cataphatic)—in theology;

4. between dogmatic theology and mystical theology;

5. between the theology of knowing God and the iconology of seeing God; besides, both philosophy and mythology as methods of reflection on God's Divinity equally participate in iconology, making their respective contributions of associative, sound logic into the icon.

It seems that in modern times there is a slow return to some ancient "primordial" conditions of faith cultivated from philosophical reflections on the Universe, because, as Archimandrite Cyprian (Kern) says, "with extraordinary audacity not typical of the present state of church theologizing, ancient Church fathers and teachers adopted the teachings of Hellenic and other philosophers and were not afraid of extracting grains of truth from their works."[30] Concerning the theme of Theophanies, an essential point is the practice of distinguishing between things related to Divine incomprehensibility, and those possibilities of knowing God that are constantly expanded by human boldness. The key received nowadays to unlock these antinomian problems is in the "hands" of *iconology*, and this key has already helped to reveal something in the iconography of icons. St. Symeon focuses on the iconological aspect of the soul-forming faith in the asceticism of seeing the uncreated Image of God's action. This bold viewpoint becomes possible when a distinction is made between God's "hypostasis" and His "prosopon," for the human spirit is *conformable* (rather than *connatural*) to the Spirit of God, and can recognize and distinguish between the "images of action" of visible Theophanies and the "modes of Existence" of God. In St. Symeon's Song of divine Agape, the visible distinction between God's "hypostasis" and His "prosopon" sometimes nearly disappears, but they are never confused: "If you allow hatred and enmity against someone to enter you, the *One Who Is named* and is self-existent and hypostatic Love [*Agape*], immediately runs away."[31] These are the iconological subtleties of distinction when it is said: "God is Love" and "God is known in Love."

A rational principle — the uncreated spermatic *Logos* — is placed (or, better to say, *sown*) into Man's spiritual heart. The seed that is preserved by God in Man and that grows in the pious soil of a "cultivated garden" is not an allegory or metaphor of lofty ideas, but an absolutely icon-like *law, canon and freedom* of God's Presence in a body whose nature is different from His nature. The spermatic Logos is sometimes called a divine "spark," which, according to the Gospel, is the sole and precious "pearl of the heart" — "the Logos was with God, and the Logos was God," and, according to Gregory of Nazianzus, He is what should be "made *God* and the *spirit* in the *soul*." This is the idea of a holy person strengthened with a complete faith — he is "a god," "a spirit," "a soul," and "a body." In this state,

---

30 *Anthropology of Palamas.*
31 *Homily* 82.

the body is so permeated with the soul that it stops being subject to the law of "consolidation." This is the idea of a deified person — he is in a body that is not of "bodily" origin, because he is already born of the Spirit, the Logos of God. According to Theodoret, God's image is in Man's free and rational spirit; but the human *spirit* was referred to by the Church Fathers as the "angelic" mind (νους), which is surely united and permeated with the *uncreated Light*. In the treatise titled *On the Incarnation of the Lord*, Theodoret writes that the two natures of Christ "are united in one Person, in the unity of life, ἐν πρόσωπον; it is noteworthy that Theodoret expressly distinguishes between the term 'person' and the term 'hypostasis,' and considers ὑπόστασις to be synonymous to φύσις."[32] The statement to the effect that there is one Person in the God-Man was generally characteristic of the theology of the Antiochian school. "Distinguishing between these terms, however, he decidedly insisted on their unity in Christ, considering 'prosopon' to be a necessary and self-understandable term to be used in Christological discussions."[33] Eventually, the Council of Chalcedon recognized the rightness of both the Alexandrian school, which insisted on a greater fullness of the union of natures in the hypostasis of the Son, and the Antiochian school, and proclaimed in its Oros 4: "at no point was the difference between the natures taken away through the union, but rather the property of both natures is preserved and comes together into a single Person (*Prosopon*) and a single Subsistent Being (*Hypostasis*)."

Christ is God and the God-Man, and in Him we should distinguish not only between His two natures, but also between His two energies that express them: a directly visible energy as a created image (Person) of human nature, and an energy that is visible through the mystical *eye* as a divine Face woven from uncreated Light. Uniting un-unitedly and differing inseparably, both energies, connecting without confusion and differences indivisible, provide an integral Icon of "Theandric Action" (a term devised by St. Dionysius the Areopagite). According to the interpretation of St. Maximus the Confessor, this Theandric action

---

32 Georges Florovsky, *The Byzantine Fathers of the Sixth to Eighth Century*.
33 Nikolai Glubokovsky, *Theodoret, the Bishop of Cyrrhus*.

means not a single action, but a new and ineffable *form of manifestation of* Christ's *natural actions* in accordance with the ineffable form of interpenetration of Christ's natures, and His human living—which is marvelous, extraordinary, and unknown to the nature of things—, and a form of interchange in an ineffable union.[34]

"Union," as defined in the Chalcedonian Council Oros, is a single Prosopon of Christ.

"Speculation in colors" is essential and extremely important for icon painters who have placed themselves next to the "vertical" of the Spirit in the art of iconological service for the Logos of God. According to St. Anastasius of Sinai, "Christ's presence in the human soul is an outwardly invisible and mysterious fact of mystical life," while St. Gregory Palamas says that "the Angel of Great Counsel (*the Logos-Son*) created Man not only after His Image, but also after His Likeness."[35]

Iconologically and theologically, it appears that Man gains *two kinds of* the one Deification: a) "according to the image"—the human nature gains *deification* for its body and rational soul through Christ's Transfiguration mystically continuing in eternity; b) "according to the likeness"—the intelligent (noetic) human nature, growing in the Spirit, gains *deification* through the mystical continuing Resurrection of Christ by partaking in His Divinity.

Aimed at the dispensation of salvation, Divine Love creates conditions for the possibility of iconographic images. If saints prayerfully appealed to Love personally, as to a Person, and if the prayerful experience "gained and lived in the freedom of Wisdom and Love leads to deification" (according to St. Maximus), the necessity of iconographic depiction of Sophia and Agape does not have to be proved—"the icon shows what is said in words."[36] This is the symbolic realism of the Church, and in this symbolism (referred to by St. Gregory Palamas as "the processions of God") they solve the issue of seeing and, therefore, depicting God's "appearances," His "processions," for which Dionysius the Areopagite uses the term πρόοδοι.

---

34 *Disputation with Pyrrhus.*
35 *Homily* 4.
36 St. John of Damascus.

Continuation of the Song of Solomon

St. Maximus came to the conclusion that there were two ways of deification: sacramental and ecstatic, which refers to the experience gained while *understanding* Wisdom and *feeling* Love. Deification was made possible only after the Incarnation of the Logos, and "deification itself should be accepted and experienced in *freedom* [*Sophia of Christ*], in *love* [*Agape of the Holy Spirit*]."[37] "Mystically representing" as is sung in the Cherubic Hymn, the actions of Christ's Wisdom are preparations for the perception of the Logos-Lamb, while Love's actions are the "seraphic" *kindling* of the Spirit of Life experienced in Communion.

Describing their "divine inspirations," the Church fathers usually use expressions showing both an un-united union between God in His Hypostasis and His Prosopon (for example, "God is Light," or "God is Love") and a mystical state in which God's Image is personified. For example, Solomon describes the words of personified Wisdom Itself; Paul the Apostle writes about a direct appeal to the Wisdom of Christ; prayer canons feature appeals to the Cross as a living being; and St. Symeon appeals to Light and Love. This "life-giving" symbolization arises from *prosopon*'s inseparable penetrations into *hypostasis* and from a mystical "betrothal" of the Image and Likeness in the names of the essential Logos (for example, the Angel who spoke with Moses from the burning bush, or the Miraculous Angel who wrestled with Jacob). These inseparable combinations of "prosopon" and "hypostasis" are clearly manifested in the person of the God-Man Jesus Christ. In addition, they are often featured in composite icons, where the concepts "image and likeness" are dogmatically united into a single idea of Divine Economy. Even the names of divine energies often "change places" and are exchanged in the image of God's actions. For example, Sophia, being Christ's direct energy, also acts as Agape in the dispensation of the Church. On the other hand, Agape, being the life-giving energy of the Holy Spirit, is also mentioned as an image of Christ's self-sacrifice, so Christ is inseparably both the Wisdom and Love of God. If the words about the "fear of God" are understood as God's Light and Will, Light becomes the beginning of Wisdom, while Wisdom becomes the beginning of Love; on the other hand,

---

37   St. Maximus the Confessor, *Mystagogy*.

THE ANGEL OF THE COUNTENANCE OF GOD

Love, being the fullness of all things, returns to God's essential Light together with the holy bearer of this Love in accordance with his power of confession. And there is neither beginning nor end in this circle of God's mercy; all energies interpenetrate each other, revealing a uniform *Image* of actions of God who *forms* in this circle a habitat for a perfected human being. God's thrice-radiant uncreated Image is the image of Agape acting incorporeally and being open to Man in a mystical understanding of "fear," and "he who is imbued with the fear of God is not afraid of being among malevolent people."[38]

Man's heavenly mind is retained within the body by the power of love, and "he who strives to confine his incorporeal being within his bodily house is a hesychast" who enters into the essential Logos.[39] According to St. Gregory Palamas, a hesychast is he who comes to unite with the Logos and to see God by clearing his active will with "*deeds*," his cognitive wisdom with "*knowledge*," and his contemplative love with "*prayers*." He who keeps his mind in heaven, for he is of angelic nature, and his heart on earth, for he is of sensual nature, is a hesychast, silent in himself yet great in theology.

According to the Holy Fathers, the human *mind* (νους) is a reflection of the Eternal and the First Mind (Deity) of God, in whose likeness it is organized.

> Those who have accepted [*intelligent*] Christ as their internal treasure invisibly contemplate His ineffable Beauty [*Energy*], without holding, hold Him, inconceivably conceive His [*Idea and*] invisible Image [*Divinity*], His formless form [*Eidos*], and His indepictable Face [*the essential Logos*] which while being unembellished, is embellished with invisible vision and unartificial Beauty. So what do they perceive and contemplate? It is the simple Light of His Divinity [*Prosopon*]. This is what they richly contemplate with their intelligent eyes.[40]

In this quotation, we italicized the iconological terms that correspond

---

38 St. Symeon the New Theologian.
39 St. John Climacus.
40 St. Symeon the New Theologian, *Homily* 84.

Continuation of the Song of Solomon

to St. Symeon's words, because they are given here in full compliance with the content of icon-painting practice.

While creating an icon, painters pass through external (on a wooden panel) and internal (within themselves) stages of real icon-painting. They understand icon-painting as a path from a "sign" to a "symbol" and from a symbol, through the method of symbolic realism, to a real contemplation of God's Image reflected in themselves. This understanding depends on manual, mental, and heart practice, which should proceed through:

- the clearing and relaxation of the discursive mind (intellect and reason) from worldly concerns;
- the purification of the heart with its five senses and with the sixth sense of holistic cosmic consciousness;
- the bringing of the mind-νους to the temple of the heart and their union;
- a continual self-moving prayer—the source of creativity;
- the experience of attention, sobriety, and silence in the heart while contemplating the images and eide of Life;
- the invocation of God's Name and the feeling of Its mystical power through which the Word of the Divine Logos can be heard;
- the distinction between a) iconological manifestations and actions of God in the images of Light, Wisdom, and Love of God and b) theological manifestations of the Trihypostatic God in the likeness of the Logos. These distinctions reveal the hypostatic meaning of any "images of action";
- the discovery and contemplation of the spheres of seeing and knowing God.

The main instrument in the knowledge of God is the heart capable of letting in the energies of the noetic mind. Actually, the human heart is the center of Man's mystical life; the heart is home to a Cross where the horizontal physical nature and the vertical noetic nature intersect, and there, at the point of intersection, God's Presence is depicted. According to Russian philosopher Boris Vysheslavtsev, "The heart signifies some hidden center, hidden depth (*emptiness*), which is beyond the reach of an ordinary glance; it is like a light center from which infinitely diverse (*color*) rays can emanate."⁴¹ Distinguishing between the concepts "soul-horizontal" and "spirit-vertical" in the "intelligent heart," which unite in the symbolism of the geometry of the Cross, saints see condensed light, the logos Seed, which is traditionally called Emmanuel. So, the image of the Cross inscribed in the heart is the main organ of religious experience and mystical *ekstasis* of the human spirit. St. Macarius the Great says, "the heart governs and reigns over the whole bodily organism; and when grace possesses the ranges of the heart, it reigns over all the members and the thoughts." "The heart is the shrine of the intelligence and the chief intellectual organ of the body."⁴² The heart, if it becomes a "shrine," becomes a place of reunion of the noetic (angelic) mind and the energy of the six senses of the physical mind. In addition, the intelligent heart is the main body and the center of human love; through the heart, as through a point of contact between the two worlds, there "trickle" the divine energemata of God's Agape itself with its life-giving action coming from the Holy Spirit, which is the "Spirit of Life and knowledge, the revealer of divine mysteries, the betrothal of the Kingdom of Heaven."⁴³ The correct and pure proportion among the cardiac mind, the noetic mind, and the divine Mind result in seeing incredible depths and diverse dimensions of the heart, and in its mystical space reveals the logos Light of God's infinite Hesychia. In Orthodox asceticism, the term "heart" denotes the "center" of all things which is capable of aggregating all things in itself. On the other hand, the mind (νους) is a pure non-material energy, the conductor of divine Revelations which sends God's Light into the innermost recesses of the physical heart of the six senses. The sign showing the presence of the divine Light in ourselves is described by St. Symeon as follows: "When your 'eye,' that is your mind (νους), is simple and bright, your bodiless body, your soul, will be bright too," because your Logos will shine for you.⁴⁴

---

41 *The Heart in Christian and Indian Mysticism.*
42 St. Gregory Palamas, *The Triads.*
43 St. Symeon the New Theologian, *Homily* 62.
44 St. Symeon the New Theologian, *Homily* 59.

Continuation of the Song of Solomon

The New Testament saints see the reality of religion not in the fulfillment of God's "commands" and "orders," forming their lives under the control of the *law* of faith, but rather in the visitation and habitation of the life-giving and gracious Light within the soul, so that their own *Image*, truly transfigured by the visitations of grace, could shine like a mirror of God's Ways in the *Likeness* of the Logos. Many saints saw God's radiant Image and went into *ekstasis*, but many wanted to see more, God's "holy of holies," crying, "Holy Agape, may we then be pardoned through you and may we enter into the enjoyment of the good things of our Master, since no-one will taste their sweetness except through you." Appealing to Christ's Agape as to a being, *conformably* rather than hypostatically, St. Symeon establishes Their iconological unity: "Love desired, how fortunate are those who have *embraced you*!"

A prayerful appeal personally to Agape is not just a poetic metaphor — a saint prays to the really perceptible and iconographically recognizable Angel of Light, "Do not leave me deprived of Your divine grace. O Invisible One, may You desire to *form* [*in the form of Agape*] inside me, may I see Your beauty and Your incomparable kindness, may I bear *Your single Image*, Heavenly One."[45] This is truly a fact of mystical correspondence where "prosopon and hypostasis" are united in their actions, and this vision, like the vision of the Angel of Jehovah given to Moses, is Theophany. What is the discernment of the Lord's "beauty" in His incomparable Agape-Image? Beauty is the radiance of unconditional Love which *forms* the Lord, makes Him visible, and reveals the depth of relations between Him and the Bride-Soul. Christ is not only *formed* through His Agape; He also becomes visible in the human soul and is contemplated by the pure mind. Awakened by the movements of Sophia and Agape, the essential and unapproachable Light opens for Man a mystical *window* to the Kingdom of Heaven, because with their energies the Lord settles into Man and dwells in him.

> O excess of love! *He Who embraces* all things *makes His home* within a mortal corruptible man, He by Whose

---

45 Symeon the New Theologian, *Homily* 63.

> indwelling might all things are governed, and the man becomes as a woman heavy with child. O astonishing miracle and incomprehensible deeds and mysteries of the incomprehensible God! A man carries God consciously within himself as light, carries Him Who has brought all things into being and created them, including the one who carries Him now. He carries Him within as a treasure inexpressible, unspeakable, without quality, quantity, or form, immaterial, shapeless, yet with form in beauty inexplicable, altogether simple, like light, Him Who transcends all light.[46]

"God is Light, and those who are worthy to set eyes on Him see Him as Light; and those who have received Him receive Him as Light. The *Light of his glory streams from His Face (Prosopon), and therefore it is impossible to see Him otherwise than as Light.*"[47] In the mysticism of Theophanies, the Divine Light acts as a creator of iconographic action, iconographically describing the Lord. According to the Orthodox doctrine of God's all-pervading uncreated energy transforming the human spirit into a Temple for His dwelling, Logos Emmanuel, conceived in the mystical space of the heart, increases as a personal and uncreated Light, mysteriously embodying into the person himself, and mysteriously and inscrutably transforming the whole person into a *child of God*.

A WORD ON LOVE BY ST. MAXIMUS THE CONFESSOR

> The Purpose of divine Providence is to unify by an upright faith and spiritual love those who have been separated in diverse ways by vice. Indeed it was because of this that the Savior suffered, "to gather together in one the children of God who were scattered abroad" (Jn 11:52).[48]

"For nothing is more truly Godlike than Divine Love, nothing more mysterious, nothing more apt to raise up human beings to deification.

---

46 St. Symeon the New Theologian, *Homily* 82.
47 St. Symeon the New Theologian, *Homily* 79.
48 St. Maximus the Confessor, *Chapters on Love, Fourth Century*.

Continuation of the Song of Solomon

For it has gathered together in itself all good things that are recounted by the Logos of Truth in the form of virtue." Divine Love "makes gods out of human beings, and reduces the individual commandment to a *universal* meaning [*logos*]. Everything is circumscribed by Love according to God's good pleasure in a single form, and Love is dispensed in many forms in accordance with God's economy."[49] Agape is an action "raising up human beings to deification," and, according to St. Maximus, what Sophia "recounts," that is "distinguishes," in the form of virtue, is "gathered together" by Agape, with the result that things go into the *ekstasis* of experiencing true Life. Love reunites all the diverse streams into a single "word," and this "word" is a sea of Love and the purest image of the Logos, because It is the only *Beginning of Life*.

> Does not Love grant enjoyment of those things believed in and hoped for, by itself making present the things to come? And what about humility... or meekness, through which we strike at censures and praises, and on a kind of diameter between evils, I mean glory and ignominy, drive away distress? And simply, Love is the goal of every good. Love gives faith the reality of what it believes, and hope the presence of what it hopes for, and the enjoyment of what is present. Love alone, properly speaking, proves that the human person is in the Image of the Creator, by making his self-determination submit to reason, not bending reason under it, and persuading the inclination [*gnome — conscious aspiration of free will*] to follow nature and not in any way to be at variance with the logos of nature. For out of ignorance concerning God there arises self-love. And out of this comes tyranny toward one's kin. For Love gathers together what has been separated, once again fashioning the human being in accordance with a single *meaning* (*logos*) and *mode*. It levels off and makes equal any inequality or difference in inclination in anything, by which each is so drawn to his neighbor in

---

49 St. Maximus the Confessor, *Letter 2, To John the Cubicularius, on Love.*

> preference to himself, and so honors him before himself, that he is eager to spurn any obstacle in his desire to excel. And in this God is understood: in him they are all beheld together and they are bound together and *raised* to him, as the source and maker. The (*spermatic*) Logos of being, of all beings, by nature preserves itself pure and inviolate for our attention, who, with conscious zeal through the virtues and the toils that accompany them, have been purified from the passions that rebel against it.[50]

In this passage, St. Maximus speaks about the "*spermatic* Logos" — the Logos of existence naturally contained in the human soul as the gift of the Spirit. Through it, Man is raised to God:

> So, each of the intelligent and verbal beings, i.e., angels and humans, by means of what he was created, the Logos, *existing in God* and *with God*, is and is called (in a person) a particle of the Divinity [*i.e., Prosopon*] owing to its Logos pre-existing in God. There is no doubt that, if he moves in accordance with it (i.e., the Logos), he will find himself in God, in Whom preexists the Logos of his existence as the beginning and the cause; and, if he does not desire something else other than his own beginning, he will not flow away (i.e., fall away) from God, but rather he will ascend to Him and become a god, and will be called a particle of God through what befittingly participates in God in accordance with our nature wisely and prudently.[51]

It is the Logos (Emmanuel) —

> peaceful and undisturbed, not at all primarily moved to any of those things that are after God — by which we have established that God is certainly manifest, and through which God is set forth as good, making the creatures His

---

50 Ibid.
51 St. Maximus the Confessor, *The Ambiguum to John, the Archbishop of Cyzicus*.

Continuation of the Song of Solomon

own, since creation cannot know God from Himself, as He is in Himself [*i.e., without the participation of the Logos*].[52]

It is necessary to properly embrace St. Maximus's idea, namely, his idea of the existence of the *spermatic Logos* in Man—Emmanuel directed "*toward God,*" to reunite with the *hypostatic Logos-Son* "pre-existing in God" or "*existing in God.*" Following the flow of this faith, Man, being of created nature that is different from that of the Logos, nevertheless unites with Him by Divinity rather than by nature, becoming a *deified child of Light* in the *Likeness of the Son and Christ, Jesus*. Actually, this is the constitutive essence of the saving dispensation of the Christian Church who in expectation of fulfillment exclaims "Even so, come, Lord Jesus!"

> Perhaps it was this that great Abraham achieved, restoring himself to nature's Logos of being, or reason [logos] to himself, and through this being given back to God, and receiving God [*the Trinity*]. As man he was made worthy to see God [*in an angelic Image*], and to receive him, since he lived naturally in accordance with the perfect *natural Logos* through love for humankind.[53]

Owing to his hospitable nature, Abraham unveiled the *inner Gift* actually possessed by every person who "contrives that the names and properties of those that have been united through love should be fitting to each other. So the human being is made god [*in accordance with the Logos*], and God is called and appears as human," and is recognized in the iconography of Theophanies. "For the 'hand' of each just man: that is, his ascetic struggle in accordance with virtue, in which and through which God *receives his likeness to human beings.*" Having sown the spermatic Logos in the womb of the Virgin Mary, the Son of God does not leave us without His Logos and through It invites us to Himself after His Ascension to Heaven.

According to St. Maximus, bodily love eventually weakens, moving away together with the space that separates people. "On the other

---

52 St. Maximus the Confessor, *Letter 2*.
53 Ibid.

hand, spiritual Love (*Agape*) in the (*cardiac*) mind always keeps together those who are united through it, having no limits in time or space."[54] This freedom of action regardless of time and space is characteristic of uncreated Agape, and divine Light's pictorial action in it is marked with holiness. For, according to St. Maximus, there are three things toward which Man moves, one way or another: God, nature (noetic theocosm), and the world (material cosmos); and each one of them diverts a person from the other two, because Man, in accordance with his choice, changes his action too and is named "carnal, psychical, or spiritual."[55]

Like Paul the Apostle and Symeon the New Theologian, St. Maximus enumerates the properties of God's deifying Agape:

- Love is the way of Truth.[56]
- Love is the door, through which the one who enters finds himself in the Holy of Holies, and is made worthy to behold the unapproachable beauty of the Holy and Royal Trinity.[57]
- Love is the true vine, in which he who is firmly rooted is made worthy of becoming a partaker of the divine quality.[58]
- Because of Love, the Creator of nature himself has clothed himself with our nature without change.[59]
- Love is the true and blameless divine wisdom of the faithful, the goal of which is the good and the truth. For it is good to *love humankind* and right to *love God* in accordance with faith. These are the marks of Love, which binds human beings to God and to one another, and therefore possesses an unfailing continuance of good things.[60]
- Spiritual Love (*Agape*) is characterized not only by doing good deeds to the needy when they are nearby, but also by consoling them in their absence, not letting souls and bodies part and preventing the power of the word, owing to which

---

54 St. Maximus the Confessor, *Letter* 8.
55 St. Maximus the Confessor, *Letter* 9.
56 St. Maximus the Confessor, *Letter* 2.
57 Ibid.
58 Ibid.
59 Ibid.
60 Ibid.

Continuation of the Song of Solomon

the soul bears the Image of the Creator, from being limited by space. For I know that direct communication with God and compassionate care for the weakest are not equally glorious deeds. However, this is not alien to God's determinations.[61]

- Love possesses God who is alone unfailing and unalterable. Love works in such a way in those who live in accordance with it, that it approves of you, saying through the prophet Jeremiah,

> She is the book of the commandments of God,
>   and the law that endureth for ever.
> All those who keep her will live,
> But those forsaking her will die....
> O Israel, we are blessed,
>   For the things that are pleasing to God
>   Are known to us. (Bar 4:1–4)
> Learn where is wisdom, where is strength, where is understanding,
>   That thou mayest know also where is length of days and life, where is the Light of the eyes and peace (Bar 3:14), and I have come to you in the way, and appeared to you from afar (Jer 31:3).
> 'Yea, I have loved thee with an everlasting Love [*Agape*],
>   Therefore I have continued my faithfulness to thee.
> Again I will build thee, and thou shalt be built,
> O virgin Israel!...
>   and shalt go forth in the dance of
>   the merrymakers (Jer 31:3, 4).[62]

- I believe that God is Love and that He is one and will never cease to be one. He also unites those who live in accordance with His Agape and gives them one heart and one soul so that they could know each other's hearts and not be bothered in uncertainty with being unaware of each other's state of mind.[63]

---

61 Ibid.
62 Ibid.
63 St. Maximus the Confessor, *Letter* 25.

THE ANGEL OF THE COUNTENANCE OF GOD

- Develop a living and active faith in Him that has the *power of the Cross* to abstain from sin, the *power of the death* to totally reject vice, the *power of the burial* to abandon psychical dreams of sensual things; the *power of the Resurrection* for the abundance of virtues and the true knowledge of God, mentally striving away from corruptible things toward heavenly things to become fellow heirs of the body and soul of the Lord Jesus Christ, and be like Him in everything other than natural identity with Him.[64]
- God became man, loving us as Himself, and more than Himself.[65]

LIFE AS LOVE. THE STORY OF PETER AND FEBRONIA

> The Spirit made them internally faultless and spotless. Therefore, it is impossible for them to produce outwardly the fruit of evil. At all times and in all circumstances the fruits of the Spirit shine forth in them.[66]

To consolidate the words said by the human heart about God's Love, I would like to tell a mystical story about Agape's extraordinary and wonderful actions in *The Story of Peter and Febronia*. Like the hagiography of St. George, the legend is filled with a sacred myth, where worldly events are intertwined with deep symbolism of spiritual significance. The life story of these saints, Prince Peter and divinely wise maiden Febronia, is so wonderful, coherent, and lofty that it clearly reveals the light-bearing action of *three* areas of the knowledge of God — Faith, Wisdom, and Love. Their story is a wonderful edifying example of symbolic coincidences of "theology and iconology" and "hypostasis and prosopon" against the background of physical life.

Seven centuries ago, the city of Murom was ruled by Prince Paul. He had a younger brother, Peter, and a wife, Princess Mary. The brothers got along very well. However, their favorite hunting trips to the forests of Murom often kept them away from home. So, a dragon,

---

64 Ibid.
65 St. Maximus the Confessor, *Letter* 44.
66 St. Macarius the Great, *Homily 6, On Love*.

taking advantage of their absence, fell into the habit of flying to their palace to visit Princess Mary, taking on the form of her husband Paul whenever he entered through a window. One day, the Prince noticed that the Princess had wasted away and lost some of her beauty. He asked her the reason for her change. So, Mary told him that in his absence a dragon in the form of Prince Paul had started visiting her and getting into her bed, exhausting her energy and beauty. The Prince was surprised, yet he believed her and ordered her to find out how to kill the dragon. When the dragon came to Mary again on the following day, she asked him whether he knew of some thing that could kill him. Despite his suspicions, the dragon trusted the woman and said, "I will die of Agrik's Sword held in Peter's hand." Prince Paul told his younger brother how his wife had been disgraced, and that the dragon could be slain with Agrik's Sword. Filled with courage, Peter immediately set out in search of the mysterious sword. Reaching the Church of the Exaltation of the Holy Cross, Peter went in and prayed. Suddenly, the Archangel Michael appeared to him and invited him to enter sanctuary of the altar, saying, "The miraculous sword is here, under the wall." The Archangel easily lifted up the wall, and beneath it Peter saw a long narrow sword gleaming with gold. When Peter returned home, he showed the sword to his brother and asked him to bless his battle with the dragon. As soon as evening came, Peter rushed into the Princess's chamber, his sword in hand, and suddenly saw his brother Paul sitting on her bed and embracing his wife, with a smile on his face. Surprised, Peter ran to his older brother's rooms. When he opened the door, he saw Paul kneeling and in front of his icon of the Theotokos and praying. Peter understood that he had been deceived by the dragon, because Paul had never left his room. So, Peter rushed back to Mary's chamber and without a moment of hesitation beheaded the dragon disguised as his brother with a mighty stroke of his wonderful sword. After that, a horrendous stench swept all over the city of Murom. When Peter took off his shirt stained with the dragon's blood, he saw that his whole body was covered with sores. The younger prince suffered from this disease for a long time, and no doctors could cleanse his body from the leprosy. One day, Prince Peter was lying in bed, exhausted by his disease, when a young monk entered his room, saying that he came at the request of the Father Superior of the Monastery of God. The monk read out the story of passion-bearer Job. Even though Peter's body was covered with sores, he was proud of having defeated the dragon to save his brother and, perhaps, the whole city of Murom from the beast. The monk made the sign of the cross over the Prince, gently giving a hint to Peter about his "pride," which was more dangerous than his bodily disease, and suddenly disappeared.

One day, Peter's servant, Anika, found out that in a remote village there lived a maiden named Febronia who was famed for being a fool for Christ's sake and a good doctor. Anika helped Peter to get into a carriage and drove to the village where Febronia lived. Before bringing the Prince to the maiden's log cabin, Anika decided to have a look at her first. When he entered her room, she was sitting at a weaver's loom and weaving a cloth, with a hare sitting in front of her on its hind legs. The maiden was the first to speak up: "It's absurd for a house to have no ears and for a room to have no eyes." Anika asked her, "Tell me, maiden, where your mother and father are?" She replied, "My father and mother went out to lend some weeping, and my brother is staring death straight in the eye between his legs." Seeing a puzzled look on Anika's face, she explained, "If we had a dog in our house, it would have barked at you. That is the ears of a house. And if we had a child, it would have seen you and warned me about your visit so that I wouldn't be caught all untidy like that. That is the eyes of the house. My mother and father went to a funeral to mourn for a deceased person. When they die, others will mourn for them. That's what I mean by lending some weeping. My brother is collecting some honey in the woods. When he climbs up a high tree, he looks at the ground between the legs so as not to fall down to his death. That is why I said that he was staring death straight in the eye between his legs."

Anika marveled at the wisdom of the simple maiden and told her what had happened to his master the prince, but Febronia already knew everything in advance, "Bring the Prince over here. If he is sincere and humble in his words, he will be healthy." The Prince promised to lavish gifts on her if she cured him. Febronia answered, "I don't need any gifts from you. However, I won't be able to cure you

Continuation of the Song of Solomon

if you don't marry me." Peter's first reaction was indignation, "How can I, a prince, marry a village maiden?" But finally he promised to marry her. Febronia took a ladle of kvass, blew on it, and said, "Heat up the bathhouse, take a steam bath, nice and hot, and rub this kvass over your body, yet leave one scab untouched."

Before going to the bathhouse, Prince Peter decided to test the maiden's skills. He gave his servant a bobbin of flax and ordered him to take it to Febronia and ask her to weave and sew a shirt, a pair of pants, and a handkerchief for him while he was taking a bath. In response, Febronia took a dry piece of wood lying near the stove and said to Anika, "While I'm combing this bobbin of flax, let your prince use this piece of wood to make a weaver's loom and all the other tools for me to weave the cloth for his clothes." Peter said that it was impossible, and Febronia just smiled for an answer. As instructed, the servant rubbed some kvass into Prince Peter's steaming body, leaving one scab untouched. As soon as the Prince's body dried out after the bath, all the scabs dried up too and fell off, except for one tiny scab on his shoulder. Delighted, Peter forgot all about his promise. He presented Febronia with some gold and silver and decided to return home, but Febronia returned the gifts to his servant, saying, "Give these gifts back to the Prince, for he abode not in the truth. Therefore, he will need these gifts for other doctors to treat him for the same disease." And she was right, for, as soon as Peter came back home, sores appeared on his body again, and they were even worse. He told his brother the story of maiden Febronia, and Paul ordered him to repent and ask forgiveness of her, "Mind you, Peter, God can show not only mercy, but also wrath. If you do not apologize to Febronia, God will not forgive you." But Peter was too proud to agree with his brother. So, Paul continued to instruct him, "Remember what John Chrysostom says, 'Pride is the most heinous sin. A proud person does not like to admit his sins, considering himself to be pure even though he is all soiled.'" Realizing that he was wrong, Peter repented of his sins in the church and went to Febronia. He apologized for his deception and vowed to marry her. Febronia again ordered Anika to give Peter a steam bath and spread the same kvass over his body. Completely healed by the morning, Prince Peter decided to get married immediately. Although it was summer, Febronia said that they would need a sledge rather than a carriage for their wedding. Peter laughed at her words for a long time. All the villagers laughed too, and felt sorry that the Prince was obliged to marry a holy fool.

On the morning of St. Peter's Day (June 29), however, it suddenly started to snow heavily, and soon everything was covered with snow and, indeed, they had to use a sledge to go to the church to get married. So, Peter stopped being ashamed of Febronia's simplicity and never laughed at her again. On the contrary, he became proud of her wisdom. In Murom, the newlyweds were met by Prince Paul holding the icon of the Theotokos. Yet, the quiet maiden Febronia was not to everyone's liking. It was her modest and simple style of dressing and the way she behaved in everyday life that was particularly resented by the rich boyars' wives. After a while, Prince Paul fell asleep in the Lord, and Murom came under the reign of Prince Peter. He ruled wisely, honestly, justly, and impartially, rewarding his subjects according to their merits and good deeds. The boyars did not like that, and, through their wives, started to blame Febronia for regarding them with disfavor and to malign her in front of Prince Peter. Once, during a meal, one of the boyars said that Febronia was in the habit of collecting bread crumbs in her hand and taking them away after meals as if she were always hungry. So, Peter unfolded her hand and saw some pieces of fragrant incense. From that moment, the Prince loved his wife even more, never tested her honesty, and did not trust his boyars any more. However, they did not stop there and finally demanded: "Peter, if you want to remain our prince, find yourself another princess, because we hate to be ruled by a peasant woman." The boyars came to Febronia and demanded that she leave Murom. For her part, she asked them for a favor in return, and they agreed. Then, Febronia said that she would leave the city together with her husband, Prince Peter. So, the wicked boyars banished Princess Febronia and Prince Peter from Murom. They boarded a ship and sailed on the Oka River away from Murom. When they disembarked, Peter started to harbor doubts and became pensive, "Did I do the right thing by abdicating as Prince of Murom?" Febronia hugged him and said, "Darling, can

Continuation of the Song of Solomon

you see those two small trees which were chopped up for firewood? I can tell you that tomorrow morning they will become big trees with branches and leaves, and that would be a sign from God that He has not abandoned us." Early in the morning, everybody was amazed at what they saw — the two trees miraculously grew new leaves and blossomed, filling the air with fragrance.

Meanwhile, Murom was in a state of commotion. Out of nowhere, there appeared a lot of handsome red-robed young men holding canes in their hands. They started beating the frightened boyars, saying: "What did you do to your Prince Peter and Princess Febronia? If you do nothing to allow them to come back to Murom, you'll all be flat broke and dead!" Scared out of their wits, the boyars boarded a ship and sailed to catch up with the Prince. When they came up to Peter, they fell down on their knees at his feet and begged him for forgiveness, imploring him to return to Murom together with the Princess and to rule over them. The Prince forgave them and said, "Ask the Princess, for it's up to her to decide." Febronia replied to Peter, "God gave us two equally precious abilities: to remember and to forget: when someone does good for us, Wisdom demands that we remember, and when they do evil things to us, Love impels us to forget that."

They began to rule in Murom, observing the Lord's commandments, loving their neighbors, governing the city in wisdom and meekness, and growing in the Spirit of God and in love for each other. Febronia, serving the Lord in fasts and prayers, continued to work miracles and take care of the poor. Prince Peter, seeing her meek light around him, gradually changed, showing mercy and doing good deeds. When they grew old, they prayed to God that they might die at the same time and never part with each other even after death. So, they willed that their bodies be buried in one coffin hewn out of a rock, with a thin partition in the middle. One day, the Prince came to the Princess's chamber, took her slender hand in his, and said, "Oh, my love, I want to retire from the world to a monastery. Will you follow suit?" Febronia bowed to her husband and said happily, "Oh, my beloved lord, I have been waiting for this moment for a long time, never daring to suggest that. Now I rejoice, and I want to be with you in God, inseparably." Peter took monastic vows and Febronia took the veil at the same time. Peter was given a new name, David, at the Savior Monastery, while Febronia was named Euphrosyne at the Assumption Convent. It is unknown what spiritual exploits they performed after that, but living in the world in Christ's Wisdom and Love they undoubtedly won the glory, and dignity, and peace of the Kingdom of Heaven.

One day, Euphrosyne was embroidering veils for the church, when a young monk knocked on the door of her cell and came in, saying, "Sister Euphrosyne, I'm here with a message from your brother in Christ, David—the time of his demise is near and he is waiting for you to go to the Lord together." "But I can't join him now," said Euphrosyne quietly. "Let him wait for me—I'll be with him as soon as I finish sewing these." When the Prince heard that, he said to the novice, "Go quickly to my beloved sister and tell her to hurry up, because I'm already at death's door." But again the Princess beseeched him to wait a little, so that she could finish embroidering just one more pattern. When the monk returned, he saw that the Prince was more dead than alive, whispering, "Run...tell her that...I can't wait for her any longer..." When Euphrosyne heard that her beloved husband had passed away, she raised her eyes to an icon of the Theotokos, crossed herself three times, stuck a needle into an unfinished cloth, sighed, and quietly departed to God. On June 25, 1228 (on St. Febronia's Day), after the funeral service, Murom residents thought that it was wrong to bury the monk and the nun in the same coffin. Therefore, they put their bodies in different places. They decided to bury Blessed Prince Peter near the Cathedral Church of the Most-Pure Theotokos in Murom, and Princess Febronia at the premises of a country convent. In the meantime, their bodies were left in different places until the morning, while their shared stone coffin remained empty in the Church of the Theotokos. In the morning, a lot of people, including bishops and priests, came to give the last honors to the saints. But when they opened their coffins for the last kiss, they saw that both coffins were empty. At that moment, a terrified sexton came running from the Church of the Theotokos and apologized for his negligence: it turned out that someone had secretly moved the bodies of Peter and Febronia to their shared coffin. They all rushed there and saw that the deceased married couple, covered with the veil embroidered by Febronia, were both in their coffin as they had willed. But the unreasonable Murom folk did not believe that they saw a miracle. So, they separated the bodies again, putting them in different coffins and in different churches. Moreover, they locked the churches until the morning to see whether the same thing would happen again. But in the morning, they discovered that the bodies of Peter and Febronia were together again in their stone coffin. Then everybody came to believe in their true love and buried them in one coffin, singing chants and praising God who gave them an example of holiness and inseparability in wedded love. For many a year, the bodies of Prince Peter and Princess Febronia cured worshippers.

"Rejoice, honest husband and wife, for Christ blessed you and your marriage with His grace, for even after death your bodies are inseparable in one tomb, while your inseparable souls are in Heaven in front of God! Amen."

Marriage is a symbol of the inseparable union between the "mind" and the "heart." While the practice of faith and trust can help achieve this union in Man, two persons separated by physical space become perfect in the love for God too. In love which has emerged between a man and a woman with so much trust that even after death their souls can meet, there operate the miraculous powers of divine Sophia and Agape; they transform the natural human gnosis and eros, showing the perfection of Faith even in this age, before the resurrection of the dead. Thus, Divine Revelations can be manifested not only visibly in *images*, *symbols*, and *signs*; they can be invisibly and mysteriously present in the lives of saints who inseparably unite their faith with God's Wisdom and Love. Such people are called "angels in the flesh," because they bear both an angelic image and a divine Image.

Reflections on the theme of "angelic image" should not be limited only to the "diversity" of nine created orders of angels, but should penetrate farther and deeper. Based on the biblical stories and Theophanies, it is advisable to see one's own tri-radiant "angelic" image of Light resembling the ancient appearance of the Angel of Jehovah. Because it remains an unchanging Christian tradition, the theme of Theophanies is still relevant. It was developed in some Church Fathers' teachings concerning the four *types* of Logos:

- the Son of God and Christ, the Logos by the hypostatic name;
- the essential unapproachable Logos of the Light of the whole Trinity;
- the spermatic Logos, the "spark" of the divine Light, the seed and the Lamb, sown into and growing in Man's spiritual heart;
- seminal logoi (λόγοι) of beings, light energemata dispersed throughout the created world.

Faith is the power of spiritual Life, and through its mystical effort Man lives in the Light of God's Wisdom and Love. Clothing themselves with the splendor of glory of the new Adam and preparing themselves spiritually, while their spermatic Logos is increasing, believers come nearer to the meeting with the hypostatic Logos, Christ. So, from ancient times the Old Testament Theophanies are gradually bringing us to the point that "someday" God will really dwell in Man, and the New Testament Logos will be fully developed in the hearts of Christians who have understood the meaning of the divine Word: "Emmanuel—God is with us." When Logos Emmanuel starts on its journey to the Father, Man will come to know God ever more closely, because "Emmanuel—God is with me and in me." Christ's Love on the Cross has become part of people's flesh and blood, and the soul, repeating a well-known Gospel saying, may sing in a new way the hymn: "In the Light of Your *Love and Wisdom*, O Lord, we will behold the Light of the *Will* of the Heavenly Father." Amen.

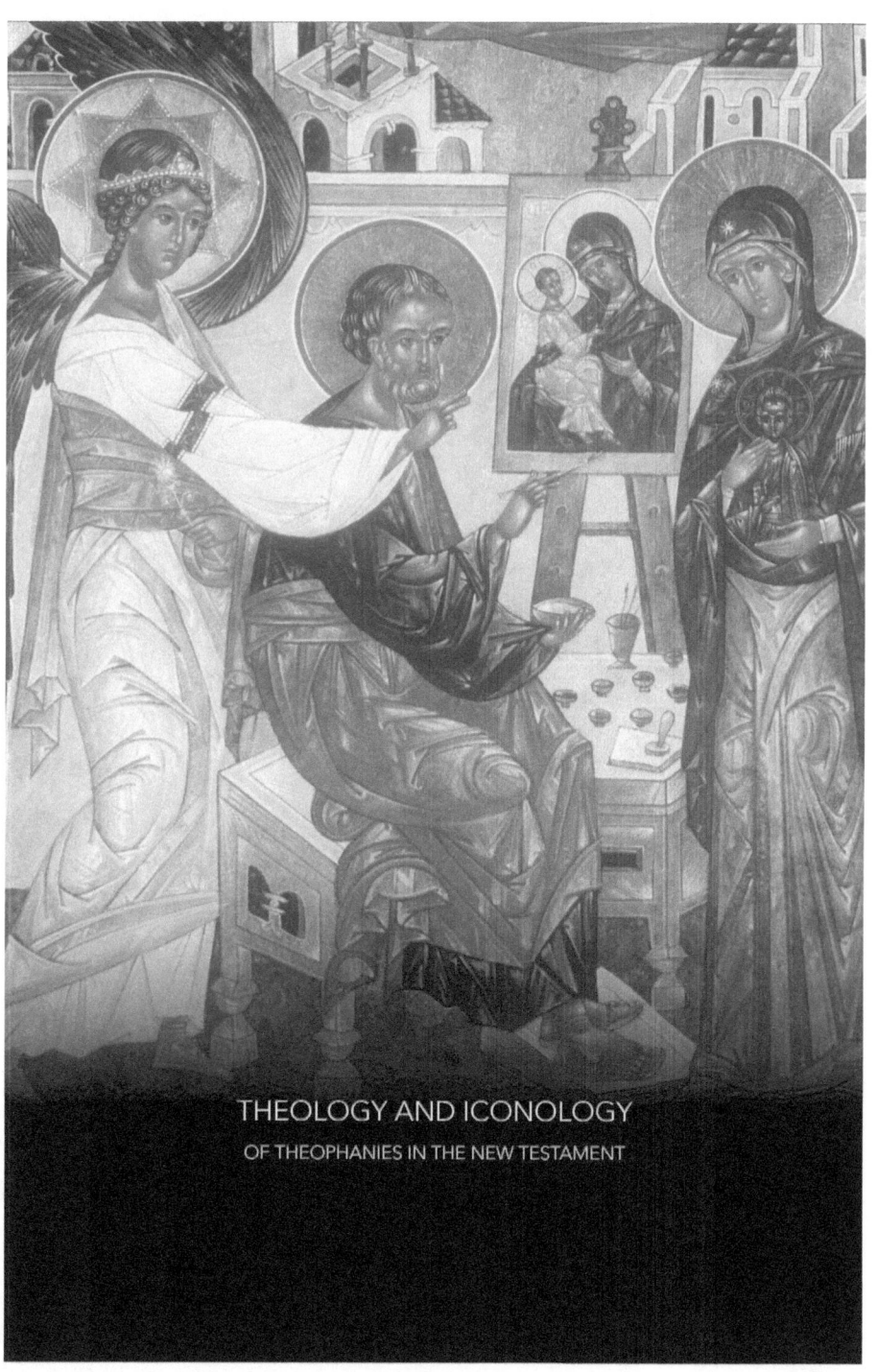

THEOLOGY AND ICONOLOGY
OF THEOPHANIES IN THE NEW TESTAMENT

9
Theology and Iconology of Theophanies in the New Testament

Behold My Servant, Whom I uphold;
Mine Elect, in Whom My soul delighteth;
I have put My Spirit upon Him:
He shall bring forth judgment to the Gentiles.
                              Isaiah 42:1

For there stood by me this night the Angel of God,
Whose I am, and Whom I serve.
                    Acts of the Apostles 27:23

THE TEACHINGS CONCERNING ANGELS, unlike the other dogmas of the Church, were not subject to much discussion, but the veneration and establishment of angels as hypostases rather than natural phenomena, and the determination of heavenly powers as spiritual incorporeal creatures rather than cosmic ones, was ultimately approved by the Seventh Ecumenical Council of Nicaea (AD 787). Before that, however, the Council of Constantinople (in AD 653) forbade the worship of angels and condemned the doctrine that they were all created equal in nature and power, which contradicted the Hierarchy of Minds.

> In the history of theological thought, there are different periods, or kinds of doctrinal cycles, in which some aspect of the Christian tradition gains exceptional importance as compared to other aspects, and in which all doctrinal themes are to some extent interpreted in correlation with some issue which becomes central for dogmatic consciousness.[1]

---

1 Vladimir Lossky, *The Vision of God*.

THE ANGEL OF THE COUNTENANCE OF GOD

At present, an issue of great importance is the possibility of iconography of images and types of Theophanies according to Old and New Testament interpretation. The verse from the Acts of the Apostles used by us as an epigraph speaks of a Theophany in the form of the Miraculous Angel of God. This is not an appearance of one of the created archangels, because Paul the Apostle's words, "Whose I am, and Whom I serve" refer to God.

Before passing on to the consideration of the iconology of Theophanies from the perspective of Christianity, we should understand these very important points serving as a clear basis for further definitions and distinctions:

> Israel in the Old Testament is a community, the chosen people, rather than the Church, and God directly appeared only to chosen patriarchs, prophets, and some individuals through whom He showed others the way to salvation;
>
> The New Testament opens with the idea of immediately embarking upon the path of salvation, where all believers who accept Christ become a new chosen "people" gathered into the Church of the incarnate God who said, "I will build My Church; and the gates of hell shall not prevail against it."

Grace bestowed upon all believers, irrespective of national identity as Jews through the Law of Moses, becomes the guiding principle for the religious life of believers gathered into the mystical Church of the Body of Christ. In the Church, all people are given equal grace, for now the *incarnate* Logos — the Word of God — is addressed directly to people. "Now are we the sons of God, and it doth not yet appear what we shall be: but we know that, when He shall appear, we shall be *like Him*; for *we shall see Him as He is*" (1 Jn 3:2). For the first time in the history of religions there appears an evangelical religious state of seeing God "face to Face," and there appears a new type and line of human "thought" — the *theology* of the Church rather than the philosophy of religion. It should be kept in mind that the evangelical *theology of Light* is just beginning, and this is clarified by Paul the Apostle as follows: "Now we see through a glass, darkly [*but we do see*]; but then [*during the Second Coming*] face to Face" (1 Cor 13:12). For then, the Apostle says, shall I know the Divinity even as also I am known and perceived now by the incarnate Christ. In this comparison, we are given a clear example of distinction:

> *God* gets to know Man, and Man perceives this in the Revelation of Enlightenment and, so to speak, enters into the *image of theology*;
>
> Man gets to know the *Divinity of God* and, trying to express his experience through some symbolism of events, enters into the *image of iconology*.

Until the Second Coming of Christ, our faith mainly operates and develops in accordance with the *canon of iconology*. It exists in the asceticism of actions aimed at "being" *in the Image* of Christ as the Son of Man. But in the future to come, faith will be thoroughly developing in the *freedom of the theology* of direct contemplation of the Trinity, because faith will be filled and strengthened by the experience of actions aimed at being *in the Likeness* of Christ as the Son of God. However, taking into consideration the diverse exploits of saints, it is impossible to dramatically distinguish between these two positions even in our times.

Theophanies primarily enable Man to see *something miraculous* "in the Light of God," to see and hear "talking icons" of Revelation. Theophanies can be expressed either in "signs" or "symbols," but a truly gracious vision experience is acquired only in the images of symbolic realism, which grows in the "iconographic" experience of the ratio (according to the Golden Section) of the "Man Icon": the "Divinity Icon." Principal comprehension of the Icon element reaches its maximal living glow of Glory in the practice of prayer, through the discipline of the mind, through the purification of the heart, and through the acquisition of the single "eye" (i.e., the intelligent heart). "To see the Light means to be in It and to be part of Its life-giving splendor. Therefore, those who see God in the Light are part of Life":[2] they are receivers and contemplators of the Icon of Divine Revelation. Therefore, Light should be expressed symbolically even

---

2   St. Irenaeus of Lyons, *Against Heresies*, 4.

in man-made icons so that a worshipper, seeing analogies, could look for the real Light of his Living Icon. For God is, in painted light, "somehow contemplated by energies," says St. Gregory Palamas. "By what energies? By desired, creative, substantive, and contemplative energies, by which He is called Theos. So, by them He is somehow comprehended and named [and, therefore, iconographed], while remaining nameless and ineffable in essence."[3]

In the history of the Holy Scriptures, there are three significant and pivotal Theophanies in which the Logos revealed the fullness of His Glory:

1. The "Divine vision" of the Angel of Jehovah on Mount Sinai, manifested to Moses in the Old Testament—"*stasis*" (Greek: "standing"), the *potency of promise*;
2. The "Divine vision" of the Logos Christ in His Glory on Mount Tabor, manifested to the Apostles in the New Testament—"*dynamis*," the *power of fulfillment*;
3. The "Divine vision" of the Lord Jesus Christ coming in Glory and Power, which will be manifested to all the nations in the Revelation of the Eighth Day—"*energy*," the *beauty of achieving perspective, proportion, and harmony* in the completion of the full salvation of Man.

In this example, we can see the three stages of God's Ways leading Man to full salvation and to Life in the goodness and truth of the Spirit. Like a hope born for salvation, the Angel of *Light* of the Burning Bush came out of "God's darkness [*gnophos*]" in the Old Testament events and flared up with a new irradiating Light of *Sophia* on Mount Tabor, establishing the iconological power of Theophanies; predicting the Second Coming of Christ, the two luminous Angels of the Resurrection, *Sophia* and *Agape*, pointing their fingers at the Ascension of Christ, established the promise and the beginning of the creation of the Church on earth. God's beauty and power came into the economy of the salvation of humankind as the Icon of Divine Providence, "and they shall see His Face [*Prosopon*]; and His Name [*Logos*] shall be in their foreheads" (Rev 22:4).

---

3   *Antirrhetici against Akindynos.*

Theology and Iconology of Theophanies in the New Testament

A new era began with the Theophany of the incarnate Logos and the Son of God who came in the image of Man, rather than in the Old Testament "image of an angel." The Angel of Great Counsel became the Son of Man. With His Incarnation, all the things that were earlier invisible—the cosmos and the angelic minds—became closer to earth. It became possible for the human race not only to communicate with some of the lower orders of Angels, but also to dwell in the Kingdom of the Heavenly Hierarchy. The Most Holy Virgin Theotokos, "more honorable than the Cherubim, and beyond compare more glorious than the Seraphim," was the first of the human race to establish this opportunity. The Church combines the uncreated, noetic, and material worlds, making it possible for every person who has reached the hypostatic faith to be a *god* by grace, an *angel* by his mind's conformity to the heavenly powers, and *Man* by the flesh of natural feelings correlated with the cosmos.

> For we have the mind by nature to search for God; and we are endowed with desire solely to desire Him; and we have the ability to be angry only to fight for Him. The end of this search is the true knowledge, the end of desire is constant passionate Love, and the end of the fight for God is Peace [*Prosopon*], which passeth all understanding (Phil 4:7).[4]

Continuing the theologian and philosopher's thought and clothing it in iconological "gilding," we can say that the icon-painting practice exists to determine, in the man-made icon, the sensual form of what rightly and truly belongs to the Icon of dispassionate Divinity. The man-made icon elevates the believer's mind to the symbolic heights of the knowledge of God, while the Theophanies themselves are revealed in the acheiropoetos Icon of the human spirit. *Iconographic* actions of creating icons, beyond the bounds of *icon-painting* symbolism itself, are transformed and enlightened by the pure *iconology* of Divinity, because it is "determined that the term 'divinity' denotes energy rather than nature."[5] If the Icon is understood as the principle of the true

---

4 St. Maximus the Confessor, *Letter* 31.
5 St. Gregory Palamas.

Life depicted in it, there visibly appear all the Old Testament prototypes of the dispensation and Incarnation of the Logos Christ who became a visible acheiropoetos Icon of the Christian race.

Every vision of God is threefold, because God is one and His essential Light is one, but He is named in the three energies of Revelation: Light : Logos, Light : Sophia, Light : Agape. This vision is iconological and should exist in canonical icon-painting. "Three Lights forming One Light is a united radiance," said St. Gregory the Theologian.[6] The contemplation of the Most Holy Trinity in the Image of dispensation, which replaces the vision of God's essence in the works of Gregory the Theologian, is the central theme in the exploit of seeing God. This is also the main theme for iconography, because we depict not God's essence, but Divinity in the icon-painted energies (life-giving actions) of the Father, and the Son, and the Holy Spirit. At present, the only reason why many people are confused by the issue of the depictability of the Father and the Holy Spirit is the lack of symbolic comprehension of the distinction between "essence" and "energy." According to Orthodoxy, God's energies (i.e., actions) are depictable. This means that the energy of the Father is one thing: the Light and Logos; the energy of the Son is another thing: Sophia; while the energy of the Holy Spirit is Agape. Being the "actions of the Trinity," all three are depictable in their own specific shades of content and beauty. All three uncreated energies are not an abstract notion, but they can be depicted in the enhypostatized reality of personification of the three luminous Angels of God. Images do not have an independent existence of their own, and they are certainly not self-hypostatic; however, being the Prosopon of Theophanies of any given hypostasis of the Trinity, they can be personified in the icon. "Angelic personifications" are most appropriate for the iconological tradition, because created angels were created in accordance with the energies of the Divinity, i.e., they can be *personified*. "Angels take whatever form the Lord may command, and thus they appear to men and reveal the divine mysteries to them." If it is said that the created angels take the form corresponding to their appearance, changing in accordance with the

---

6   *Orat.* XXIII, *PG* 35.

Lord's will, what can be the transforming actions of God's uncreated Light in the diversity of His appearances? For example, would not the divine Light, manifested and depicted in the form of the Angel of Divine Providence erecting the building of the Church of Christ, be an attempt to create a new iconography?[7]

"In the third–fourth centuries AD (and even in the first half of the fifth century), the theological use of the term 'hypostasis' did not have a distinct or stable meaning, varying between the semantic fields of the concepts 'essence' and 'person' (prosopon)."[8] The hypostasis and the prosopon are always connected together (like the "particular" and the "special"), but God's real actions more often reveal the "special": the Prosopon, because it initially contains the "iconographic" beginning. In the New Testament, the Logos and the Son Himself incarnated and became Man, visible and describable. But the Incarnation changed the entire sphere of theological and iconological ideas concentrated on dogmatic concreteness. Christ Himself said, "I am the Light," but Christ's two creative energies, Sophia and Agape, continue to operate differently (like strength and beauty) in the Church as the Angels of Christ's Light.

With the union between the "hypostasis" and the "prosopon" in the God-Man, the human nature was enhypostatized, becoming a visible *image* in the divine Hypostasis of Christ and uniting with His unchangeable divine Image.

> The Orthodox Dyophysite confession of faith implies not a symmetrical addition of two natures, but their combination into a single Hypostasis which is pre-eternal and divine. The dualism of the two enhypostatic natures is never expressed in terms of *separation*; it is expressed only in terms of mental *distinction*, because the incarnate Logos is one being.[9]

As noted above, the Christological definition of the Fourth Ecumenical Council of Chalcedon uses two Greek terms — *hypostasis*

---

7   St. John of Damascus, *Orthodox Faith*.
8   A. Sidorov's note to John Meyendorff's works.
9   John Meyendorff, *Christ in Eastern Christian Thought*.

and *prosopon*: "Christ is in one prosopon (person) and one hypostasis," but the Church fathers also insist on the undeniable distinction between these terms. Modern theologian Pavel Evdokimov, in his book *Orthodoxy*, explains the difference as follows:

> Both of these terms denote a "person," but each one of them has different particularities. *Prosopon* is a psychological aspect of a being turned towards his own inner world, self-consciousness, and, as such, he follows his evolution, passing through the stages of his own knowledge and through the levels of his comprehension of the nature whose carrier he is. *Hypostasis* reflects the aspect of a being who is open and strives beyond his limits — towards God. It is the latter aspect that is crucial for understanding the theandric dimensions of a person. In addition, we should remember that Personality in the absolute sense exists only in God (with God and toward God) and that every human person is only His *image* (*prosopon*).[10]

A personality, in its turn, is not fully determined by the individual properties of the prosopon, but is its center, "*I*" in Man's entire material and noetic composition, which is closely related to, yet different from, the term "hypostasis." A person can be determined as "hypostatic" when his "*I*" is uttered from the depths of his heart, on behalf of the divine Word Emmanuel rather than on behalf of himself. In the case of "personality," "*I*" is uttered from an individual's areas closest to the hypostasis. "*I*" uttered by a "personality" consists of opinions of one's own created essence and can increase to correspond to the hypostasis, while always remaining limited and dependent on the environment. Only deification gives rise to an un-united reunion between the hypostasis and the personality, and such saints are called "venerable." In Man, only Logos Emmanuel can truthfully say "*I*" and he who has made this "*I*" part of his life becomes a hypostasis. In this case, he who has gained a perfect faith has the power to say, "You are the Lord, Thy will be done," because in this case this is said by the Spirit of the Logos.

---

10 *Orthodoxy*, Part 1, *Anthropology*.

"The hypostasis is going beyond oneself (*standing outside;* Greek: ἑκστασῃ), beyond all human things, and in this sense a personality is created by overcoming itself."[11] In this context of distinguishing between the "personality" and the "hypostasis," the Church Fathers understand the mystical meaning of "humility" and "obedience," which is necessary for a believer to grow spiritually and develop a sincere religious consciousness.

The distinction between these terms becomes very important from the perspective of anthropology, which means that it becomes absolutely necessary to unravel the general mystery of God's Image in Man through iconology. "In a natural state, the *prosopon* (person) is usually mixed with the *individual*, but it is just a possibility of a personality; if this possibility is actualized, the personality requires its own transition to the *hypostasis*."[12] In accordance with the understanding of the idea of the Logos, the hypostasis, being spiritual, is not a person's supreme part separated from his other parts (individual, prosopon, hypostasis), but it is contained in Man as his essence. The Spermatic Logos, like "The Unsleeping Eye," is in heart of the human Soul, which explains the Soul's ability to have and retain the gracious properties of God.

The *common and whole* is essence and nature, while the *particular and special* is hypostasis and prosopon.[13] *Essence* has the same relation to *hypostasis* as the *common* has to the *particular*. The difference between essence and hypostasis is the same as the difference between the *common* and the *individual*. "Every one of us both shares in existence by the common term of *essence*, and by his own properties (*of prosopon-image*) is such a one and such a one."[14]

This is the meaning of another patristic distinction: Eve, a woman (the *prosopon* of a man) is by nature an active *image*; Adam, a man (the *hypostasis* of a woman) is a contemplative *logos*, because the cause of the following *actions* is nature rather than hypostasis. "Nature has a 'female' predisposition to the incarnation of life, but for this purpose it

---

11   Pavel Evdokimov, *Orthodoxy*.
12   Ibid.
13   St. Maximus the Confessor, *Letter 14*.
14   St. Basil the Great, *Letter 214 to Count Terentius*.

needs a *seed* of the Logos."[15] Analogously, the enhypostatized human nature in Christ is His created prosopon having mystical properties, and His "Body" is mystically called the "Bride of Christ,"[16] while His hypostasis is of Divine nature. The Church of believers, by its "image of action," is also called the Bride of Christ; the Soul which in its faith has matured to a marriageable age is also a Bride; it is a created image, but inseparably enhypostatized in the Love of Christ. The Soul-Bride, knowing the hypostatic God through experience and becoming personified in Him, becomes inseparably, yet distinguishably, united; conformable (*in the image of the Logos*) to Christ, and *enhypostatized* with Him. According to St. Athanasius, "God is in everything with His love, and outside everything with His essence";[17] while St. John Climacus said, "Blessed is he who has obtained such love and yearning for God as an enraptured lover has for his beloved."[18]

"When I am talking about God, I light up with the one triune Light; three by particulars (*Will, Wisdom, and Love*) and one by the Logos of essence, or by the Logos of the Divinity."[19] Becoming enhypostatized in deification, Man becomes a *god* and a partaker in the Divinity of God rather than in God Himself.

> The Hypostasis is an entity having its special properties whose quantity distinguishes it from things of the same kind, while an enhypostatized thing is something that does not exist by itself, but can be seen in some other thing, or as added to some other thing of different nature so that a whole could emerge.[20]

This is what happens in iconographed Theophanies — we see something "enhypostatized," but we feel and hear God. Continuing the thought of Gregory Palamas, "it would be ridiculous for a person to admit the existence of the Sun, while denying the existence of

---

15 Christos Yannaras, *The Faith of the Church.*
16 *Commentaries on the Song of Songs.*
17 *De Decretis* 2.
18 *The Ladder of Divine Ascent,* Step 30, 11.
19 Gregory the Theologian as quoted by St. Maximus the Confessor in *Letter 15 to Cosmas.*
20 St. Maximus the Confessor, *Letter 15 to Cosmas.*

its light-giving rays," we would say that it would be ridiculous for a person to admit the existence of God by essence, while denying the existence of His life-giving rays and iconographed Theophanies, because "it is ridiculous to admit that God's essence exists, but God's grace and other (for example, figurative) energies do not exist." Personifying the divine Light (for example, in the form of an Angel), an icon painter depicts something by energy rather than by essence, "singing praises" like a psalmist to the Life-giving God. What "fear" can be seen here? Not that of God, to be sure, because saints say that "God is not mocked" (Gal 6:7) and that "God transcends *all* affirmation and *all* negation."[21] As a matter of fact, iconography helps restore human nature; moreover, according to Maximus the Confessor, "a deified person, who, by the gift of grace, has fully *clothed himself* with the entire God, will become everything that God is (in His Divinity), except for identity by essence,"[22] which means that iconography can to some extent express this "clothing" through images of symbolic realism.

The body of Jesus Christ, the Son of God, has not been identified with Him; His body

> is not the Hypostasis, but it has always been *enhypostatized*, because it began in Him and united with Him according to the Hypostasis by the *logos of particularity*, i.e., it *became* Christ's *own property* (*prosopon*). Indeed, the difference is the *logos* by which mutual otherness of signified things is intrinsically observed and which expresses the *mode of existence*, whereas the identity is a full coincidence (for example, of the Trinity in a single Logos), by which the logos of the signified thing has a perfect unity.[23]
>
> The Hypostasis is an entity having properties or containing each of all the properties contained in an individual oneness (*in the prosopon*), while the complex hypostasis is a complex entity having properties contained in a single

---

21 Dionysius the Areopagite, *On the Divine Names*.
22 *The Ambigua to John*.
23 St. Maximus the Confessor, *Letter* 15.

individual. Therefore, complexity primarily distinguishes the complex nature rather than the hypostasis.[24]

For the good, and truth, of iconological and spiritual speculation and the practice of prayer, it is necessary to distinguish between the meanings of the words *nature, essence, hypostasis, prosopon, logos,* and *energy,* without confusing or fusing them together, because, according to Maximus the Confessor, "if there be any difference in some terms, there is some difference in their meanings too." "For it is indispensable to have clear understanding of that, as he who fails to confess the community of the essence or substance falls into polytheism, so he who refuses to grant distinction of the hypostases is carried away into Judaism."[25]

> Therefore, since the difference in Christ is preserved as a mutual essential difference between the parts after their union [*just as in us the human triad united with the spermatic Logos after the Incarnation of Christ*], it is clear that by essence the number of united things has remained unimpaired after their union, preserving in the resulting *whole* both the definition and the *logos of the essence* of each part as distinguished from some other part, while the whole remains hypostatically identical to its own number too. Using the number only to explain the difference between things after their union, we do not separate the things designated by the number, but just *explain* them. For the essence is characterized by *action*, while incoming things or quality are characterized by being subject to action, because with every stated difference there necessarily emerges the quantity that expresses it.[26]

This point serves as a basis for the iconography of such "baffling" (at least as viewed by some "orthodox" critics) images as the Lord of Sabaoth, or Sophia/the uncreated Bride, or the enhypostatized

---

24 St. Maximus the Confessor, *Letter* 13.
25 *Letter* 210 by St. Basil the Great as quoted by St. Maximus the Confessor in *Letter* 15 *to Cosmas.*
26 St. Maximus the Confessor, *Letter* 15.

energy "body" of Christ. In these icons, iconographic depiction is not based on nature or essence, because they depict *actions*, "for (*let us reiterate*) with every (*verbally*) stated difference there necessarily emerges the thing that expresses it," i.e., iconography. We confess that Christ has two essentially different natures and that the *distinction* between them remains the same with absolutely no separation, because, according to Maximus the Confessor, "distinction and separation are not the same thing." When we depict the Sophia of Christ, do we separate them? No, we don't. According to Maximus the Confessor, we "explain" "the one thing" and "the other thing." Iconology raises the issue of depicting *in action* enhypostatized *things* standing "in front of" ("prosopon") of the hypostasis of various phenomena. In the Book of Isaiah, the *Angel of the Prosopon of God* can be determined as an enhypostatized and, therefore, *personified* Light of the Divinity, or, iconologically speaking, the *Angel bearing a visible iconography of the unapproachable essential Image of God*. The Icon expresses the light of intelligence of holy people, symbolically expressing what is occurring within them. As Basil the Great says in his Homily on Psalm 30:5, "visible only to those who have cleared their minds, true and desired kindness is what *surrounds* the divine and gracious nature, and those who strive for its radiance and beauty acquire something from it, as if it were some kind of paint shedding colorful reflections on their faces."

To see the "difference" is to know a method of spiritual reasoning in accordance with which things are differentiated from each other, showing the *image of action* differing from the *mode of existence*. For example, by the image of Christ's two (created and uncreated) natures we distinguish between our own *material* and *immaterial* (*noetic*) natures, as well as our "spark of God," the spermatic Logos, which guides us and unites us with the Divinity of God. And no sane person would think of separating this composition, otherwise the notion "Man" would be eliminated.

Just as in Christ "neither the Divinity becomes flesh (the body), nor is the flesh transformed into the nature of the Divinity," so the spermatic Logos, the *Gift* given to us, reclines in the pristine nature of our soul, not damaging the soul with the uncreated Fire or becoming

THE ANGEL OF THE COUNTENANCE OF GOD

created Itself. "The Fathers constantly teach that the logoi of the united natures remain unchanged: they themselves, as they are, have united together and both formed one prosopon of the Son and one Hypostasis."[27] Man, however, contains not the hypostasis of Jesus Christ, but the Logos Emmanuel, that is, His fertilizing seed, through whom the believer grows, becomes deified, and then meets the Hypostatic Christ, his Father.

> For it is obvious that the *logos* of the Divinity and that of humanity, as is the case with the body and the soul, is not the same. But the fact that the body and the soul are two things *according to the essential logos*, and different essences *according to the logos of existence*, does not deny the fact of what, from what, and in what, Man is.[28]

And the Son "came to us in His flesh [*and mystically dwells in our flesh with His seed*] according to the dispensation rather than the *logos* of our nature, having fully united with it [*our logos*] in the divine Hypostasis and renewed our nature."[29] Having incarnated, He revived again Man's spiritual breathing, once given to Adam, and "fanned" the "spark of Divinity" into hot flames of faith, turning humanity to the Source of Light. After all, Man breathes not only "air" (as is commonly believed scientifically), but also the divine emanation of Light. St. Cyril of Alexandria explains that

> the two essences do not "steal away" the *logos existence* from the parts composing a man who is *similar to us*—from the intelligent soul and body, or from the parts composing the mystery of Christ—the Divinity and humanity, even though the difference in nature of the things that are brought into unity is still present within the system of the composition.[30]

The anthropological conclusion to be drawn from the Fathers'

---

27 St. Maximus the Confessor, *Letter* 12.
28 Ibid.
29 Ibid.
30 As quoted by St. Maximus the Confessor in *Letter* 12.

Theology and Iconology of Theophanies in the New Testament

statements is that the Logos will accomplish the dispensation of the *mode* of Life of a deified person and, without impairing the created human nature, ascend together with the soul to the *likeness of the Hypostatic Logos*, Christ.

> So, not asserting that *essence and nature* are the same thing in the proper sense (just as *prosopon and hypostasis* are not the same thing), in Christ we see, in a godly manner, *identity and difference*: the former: by the *Logos* of a single Hypostasis, and the latter: by the *logos* of essential otherness [*in terms of conformity rather than connaturality: the uncreated Logos of the Divinity + the logos of Man*].[31]

Unlike Orthodoxy, heretics

> claim that nature and hypostasis are identical, turning *union* into *fusion* and turning *difference* into *separation*; thereby showing that the essential Logos of the whole Trinity is extended to four Persons, while the mystery of the Unity is dissected into two deities, sacrilegiously casting Christ out from all essential existence.[32]

Iconology, on its part, does not approve *separation* or *fusion* in the case where the Lord of Sabaoth is depicted in icons, provided that He is understood patristically: not as the Hypostasis of the Father, but as the "one Lord" of the essential and logos *Image* of the Power (δυνάμις), Glory, and Will acting in the Revelation of the hypostatic Trinity. The same can apply to the prosoponic images of Emmanuel and God's Sophia or Agape. Being an organic part of general theology, the doctrine of the icon of God shows iconographic differences in God without turning "metaphor" into "hypostasis," or *unions* of various concepts into *fusions*.

In accordance with the iconological theme related to Theophanies, these distinctions are important for both iconography and the experience of the strengthening of faith. Cyril of Alexandria says,

---

31 St. Maximus the Confessor, *Letter* 15.
32 Ibid.

THE ANGEL OF THE COUNTENANCE OF GOD

> In Christ's mystery revealed among us, unity is not alien to difference, yet separation rules it out; so, having received some part of flesh and blood, the Word-Logos is still considered to be the one and unchangeable Son of God and is named so. The Only Begotten Son according to the *logoi* of His own (divine and human) nature is again something else. But to know this does not mean to separate the natures after their union.[33]

Maximus the Confessor continues this thought: "Indeed, the fact that the *logos of existence* of the united natures is by no means impaired shows that they have not mixed in one Hypostasis, each remaining and retaining its essence."[34] It is important in this context to be able to translate theology, or rather Christology, into crucial concepts of icon-painting, wherein liturgical meanings arise and are imprinted in icons, alongside with hymn symbols, poetic allegories, and metaphors occurring throughout the Church services. The unity, preserved while translating some types of liturgical work into others, also helps us to understand the practice of uniting human and divine volitions in the prayer of the inner mind. After all, naming the Theotokos "the animate Ark" does not change the essence of things and does not impair the hypostasis, but creates additional associations in the mind in order to experience the idea of incarnation in greater depth. In icons, this idea can be expressed in some types of iconography: for example, in "The Annunciation of Ustyug," where the Divine Infant Jesus is depicted in line rather than in form, as if He were just conceived and still staying in the "womb-ark."

Perception of the inner life is realized in the fullness of action and clarity of icon images arising from experience, through a variety of spiritual associations and metaphors, and this method is liturgically valid, because some things are given "by creation," while others are given "by the gift of grace." The believer's life, where all things are distinguished according to number, but not separated or fused according to essence, becomes like a river — now rapid, now quiet, but always flowing to the sea.

---

33 *Acta Conciliorum Œcumenicorum*, Vol. 1 as quoted by St. Maximus the Confessor in *Letter* 12.
34 St. Maximus the Confessor, *Letter* 12.

Who, having some knowledge of the Fathers' Divine doctrine, does not know that any number, according to the God-bearing Gregory, explains countability of related things rather than their separateness? So, the explanation of some number does not create or introduce separation, but explains the acceptability of the number by introducing the *logos of the mode of existence*.[35]

Admitting that it is possible to depict Theophanies of personified Light, iconology, being "in obedience" to theology, does not accept any increase in the number of persons in the Trinity. Counting various "images," however, iconology distinguishes between the Prosopon of God and the Hypostasis of God. In fact, one thing is the "indepictability" of the Father, and another thing is the "depictability" of *His actions* which, being by nature the *logoi of existence* (according to St. Maximus the Confessor), become understandable *Icons* of Providence, and the revelation of His Will. The purpose of "symbols" is to unite the earthly, heavenly, and divine parts of our existence and make them visible, that is, figurative and understandable. Furthermore, if a symbol also has a religious and mystical meaning, it will express Divine Revelation.

In regard to the *tropos of existence*, or the *mode of existence*, the number explains the difference in calculated things, rather than introducing their interrelation or interchangeability. In fact, if we do not utter a word explaining the difference, we reserve the possibility of fusing not only ideas, but also things. On the other hand, we should realize that if we do not use a statement denoting union we allow *separation*, because *difference and union* are not the same thing, even though they refer and are applied to the same subject.

In the context of the above, it would be appropriate to distinguish between the methods and the knowledge of God, of which *theology is the Mode* (tropos) of God's hypostatic *existence*, while iconology is the *Image* of God's prosoponic *action*, and "the *logoi* are different here" according to Maximus the Confessor. After all, the methods of the same action may be different too. For example, saying "Orthodoxy," the Church determines the *method* by which Christian

---

35 St. Maximus the Confessor, *Letter* 12, citing Gregory's *Homily* 31, *On Theology*.

faith is professed exactly. The traditional ancient-church method of icon-painting is *orthodox*, and every contemplator certainly recognizes ancient icons in it. However, it is obvious that icons painted using a different method will not look "orthos" (right), i.e., corresponding to the ancient canon of the Orthodox tradition developed by holy icon painters. Professor Ivan Ilyin explains according to the orthodox way the meaning and religious significance of the term "method":

> The word *method* is borrowed from the Greek language. Οδόσ is the Greek for *"way,"* or figuratively — *"mode, means"*; datively, ὁδῴ, this word is used to express a *right and proper way* ("going the right way"); in combination with the preposition μετά, which in this case indicates the objective and conformity, there arises the word μέθοδοσ — "a following after," acquiring in this case a religious connotation — *religiously following God.* [36]

In this sense, it is necessary to understand Revelations as a *method* for understanding the Will of God and as a method of *iconographic depiction* of the Logos of God's existence. In this interpretation, "method," "symbol," and "revelation" would be identical and Orthodox.

Iconology belongs to the order of God's dispensation (Greek: οἰκονομία) in the world and in Man. It transforms actions into "paintings," creating "visible" outlines of "invisible" things and filling the world with images of providential Theophanies. Theology, in a special sense, is a *contemplation* of the Revelations (ενέργεια) of the Logos, elevating the mind to God-likeness. The method of iconology, on the other hand, is used to contemplate the providential "actions" or "deeds" (ενέργημα) of the dispensation of God, and, according to St. Maximus the Confessor, it is necessary to know "the difference not only between words, but also among the words 'action' and 'doing,' to understand the meaning of the Scriptures."[37]

In the same sense as it is said that "God is Love" and "Love is in God," it is necessary to mentally distinguish between the concepts "the Logos is Christ" and "the Logos in Christ," because Christ by hypostasis is

---

36 *The Axioms of Religious Experience*, Vol. I, Chapter IX.
37 St. Maximus the Confessor, *Letter* 19.

both the Son and the Logos. According to Maximus the Confessor, He is the *hypostatic Logos of existence* by the dispensation of salvation, but He is the *prosoponic Logos of action* by fulfillment. In the principles of distinction, we can more clearly understand the stages of a single dispensation, involving four mystical meanings of the sacrifice of the Cross: *God — Son — Logos — Man*. The Logos of existence understood as the essential name of the Trinity belongs to and is always directed *to God*, as is said in the Prologue of the Gospel according to St. John [Slavonic text], and the logoi of the world, like seeds, no matter where they may be sown, always remain of uncreated nature.

> In teaching about the logoi, St. Maximus the Confessor has an aspect that is emphasized by Vladimir Lossky: the logoi are identical to uncreated divine "energies." And this "Palamite" interpretation of the theology of St. Maximus drew criticism from some Western scholars.[38]

God said to the prophet Hosea, "I have also spoken by the prophets, and I have *multiplied visions*, and used similitudes, by the ministry of the prophets" (Hos 12:10). John Chrysostom interprets this verse as follows: "I have not revealed the very essence of Mine, but (in a vision) I descend to the weakness of those who see me."[39] This salvational descent of God, inaccessible by nature, makes it possible to see Him in life-giving energies, personifications, and descents, so any divine manifestation has a recognizable ideographic pattern of logos meanings and a vivid, i.e., iconographic, statement of faith, based on the life-giving outpouring of the Icon of God.

The Holy Trinity is a theological example of "unity and distinction in their ineffable union and existence, for the Three Hypostases are both single by essence (because the Logos of existence is one) and different by the image of action."[40] Indescribable by essence, God is knowable to some extent through mental comprehension and through "approximations," and easily knowable by iconographic actions. The Divine Trinity acts outside Itself through processions (πρόοδοι) or powers (δυνάμις),

---

38 Aleksey Sidorov, *Notes to the Works of St. Maximus the Confessor*.
39 St. John Chrysostom, *Against the Anomoeans*.
40 St. Dionysius the Areopagite, *On the Divine Names*.

or directly formed actions (ενέργεια), or indirect deeds (ενέργημα), in which the ways of communion and deification are iconographically depicted. "He is distinguished, remaining simple in everything, and multiplied without losing His unity."[41] God is depicted in Man truly, like an Icon, otherwise Man would not have a model for ascending to Him, and Man, having this contemplation as a basis, paints a true icon modeled on the experience of the knowledge of God. This is the source of the emergence of iconography. "With our dispassionate and immaterial mind (νους), we will partake of His mentally comprehensible illumination and mind-surpassing *unity* — in the radiance of His most brilliant rays in a state similar to the state of heavenly spirits."[42]

In their teaching, the Holy Fathers emphasize the fact that Man can enter into communion with God not only mentally, but also as a whole, which, in fact, is icon-painting, i.e., a *method* of depicting the Divinity in oneself. Perceived by believers as Icons, certain kinds of figurative Revelation, through the mystically endless transfigurations of the soul and the body, are transformed into the reality of an iconographic symbolism of our existence. God's paradigms become visible and truly miraculous icons in Man, and by analogy transfer to some extent into the cosmos of man-made art. According to Vladimir Lossky, "this perichoresis, the energetic interpenetration of created and uncreated things in Christ, finds its analogy in created beings aspiring to become gods by grace."[43] Theology, in its clear and direct meaning, is theoria, contemplation. But the contemplation of what, and in what? It is the contemplation of Theophanies in symbolic images of the uncreated and luminous Icon of the Divinity.

The path of contemplation is revealed to the believer through the principle of "icon-painting" and in the distinction among *perspectives*, *proportions*, and *harmony*, rather than in the differentiation between the "best" and the "worst." The path of iconological statements — cataphatics — reveals God in His actions, with all Divine *ideas*, *eide*, *energies*, and *energemata* becoming depictable in Man and passing through him into man-made icons, while deepening the ontological theme of

---

41 Ibid.
42 Ibid.
43 *The Vision of God.*

icon-painting again and approaching the sensual material always is acting, and we call this a "sacramental action." God—stepping out of His unknowable and indepictable nature, indescribable in the icon of the Logos, or in the religious Idea, or in the beauty of Eidos, or in the anthropomorphic form of the Theophanic Angel—is named Light. However, "God is named Light according to His energy rather than His nature," writes St. Gregory Palamas.[44] Therefore, where there is God's Presence, there is Light; where there is Light, there emerges the phenomenon of Color; and the sacramental action of Light, which "refracts itself" and becomes Color, is the Icon of Revelation and Dispensation, the architectural design of the New Jerusalem in Man. Being the cause of emergence of "life," Divine Light passes through life and unfolds its various properties and shades of color, changing and transforming the "images of the world" into the iconology of the path of deification. Light is the most extraordinary miracle in the life of the universe, and the interpenetrations of its types create a sphere of God's direct participation in the universe, "forming" the *holiness, strength*, and *immortality* of created existence; because "to give birth appertains to nature, and to create appertains to energy."[45] As far as we know, the four planes of existence are the relations among the five types of *light*:

1. Divine Light—the gift and the beginning of the First Day of creation;
2. The light of Cosmos—the light coming from galaxies, suns, and stars.
3. The light of Anthropos—the light of Man's rational soul;
4. The light of the Theocosmos—the noetic light of the angelic Hierarchy;
5. The light of Prosopon—the gracious and life-giving light of the Divinity; the living Light of transformation, resurrection, and deification—the form and content of the future Life of the created world.

The distinction among the types of "light" suggests their inseparability, because integrity is the principle of Life bestowed by the *living*

---

44 *Against Akindynos.*
45 Cyril of Alexandria.

THE ANGEL OF THE COUNTENANCE OF GOD

God. Penetrating into the sensitive or intelligible worlds and becoming imprinted and depicted in them like the Icon, Divine Light becomes easily perceptible and visible. Saying the words "in thy light, O Lord, shall we see the Light of the Father" in their prayers, believers discover the radiance of One Light in themselves. Refracted through the prism of the soul, as if through the facets of a crystal, Light is perceived in the icon as a *figurative* Word (Logos) of God. So, as the prophet Isaiah says, "God forms the Light," i.e., He makes it depictable; insofar as the divine Light is "intelligent," the image becomes meaningful and, being part of the Divine Revelation, iconographically depictable; in other words, the image becomes a Theophanic Icon. "Therefore, the sight and the mind tend to perceive not the same light, but each of them acts in accordance with its nature and within its limits."[46]

Symbolic art can depict the energies of Divine manifestations, portraying them in the iconography of the heart, as on a wooden panel. "If the body, together with the heart, is intended to participate in the ineffable goods of the age to come, it must surely participate in them as far as possible, even at present."[47] Everything that the body feels and sees through the soul can be expressed in icon-painting through the symbolism of lines, light, and color. Anything that can be said through "words" can also be expressed through "images," but sometimes indirectly — through analogies, metaphors, and distinctions, symbolically depicting and embodying them in liturgical actions. This is the determined way of faith, with its symbolic stations "in icons" to "form" the experience of seeing God. This representation resembles the numerous "stations" through which the people of Israel passed on its 40-year journey before they found the sacred dwelling-place of God. The distinction between depictable and indepictable "words" is a theological postulate, without which the reality of communion with God is impossible. Making it possible to establish the harmony of "equivalence" of different parts, we draw attention to the accuracy of the iconological truth of images. "There is, then, a distinction to be observed between the essence, of which no explanatory term has yet been discovered, and the meaning of

---

46 *The Hagiorite Tomos.*
47 Ibid.

the names applied to it."⁴⁸ In fact, we should distinguish between *theological* and *iconographic* names describing God's manifestations: in terms of their accordance with the canon and in terms of how they may be expressed, for example, whether or not the icon's "idea" corresponds to its "eidos," or whether or not the icon "slides down" into decorative historicism or naturalism, to the detriment of the sense of iconological mysticism of God's Presence.

The living Icon, in its basic sense of a "linking element" (which is equivalent to the notion of "symbol"), unites created and uncreated things and has a practical importance of strengthening faith: through reunification faith is *purified*; pure faith passes through the stage of *enlightenment*; strengthened through mystical theology, faith brings believers to *re-unification* with the Divinity. The two opposite forces that help believers on their way to the knowledge of God are "eternal" *fear* and "vehement" *love*. The fear of making a mistake and not recognizing the Logos of one's own Soul causes one to be attentive to iconographic *distinctions*, while the *seed* of Love implanted in the entire creation uncontrollably drives the Soul to look for the Heavenly Bridegroom; and the Soul, rejecting all transitory things and being guided by Love, recognizes the unique features of His Image. "Whereas the mind convinces the reasonable to *love* voluntarily, *fear* (*of God*) compels the unreasonable to endure involuntarily."⁴⁹ In fact, these two moving causes develop the form and content of Theophanies perceived by the mind and heart. For the New Testament person, their content always has the meaning of the Annunciation, determining the vision of God in the Lord's Wisdom and the knowledge of God in the Lord's Love. Summarizing these two areas of faith, it becomes clear that every icon painted according to the style of symbolic realism manifests the Annunciation, and the Soul can hear the voice of the miraculous Angel clothed in His Light and containing the mystical name of the Logos: "O, come My fair one, come and enter into My Chamber, My Bride."

---

48 St. Basil the Great, *The Letter to Eustathius*.
49 Maximus the Confessor, *Letter* 10.

EPILOGUE

Epilogue

We do not know God from His being but from His magnificent works and His Providence for beings. Through these, as through mirrors, we perceive His infinite Goodness and Wisdom and Power.[1]

To those able to follow Him [Christ] as He climbs the high mountain of His Transfiguration, He appears in the form of God, the form in which He existed before the world came to be.[2]

SO, FINISHING OUR STUDY ON THE THEOPHanies of Light in the images of the Angel of Jehovah, the Logos, Emmanuel, or Wisdom and Love; it should primarily be noted that this purely iconological theme is naturally developed (as in the first stage of the painting of icons) in the symbolism of relations between "*light* and *color.*" When positioned as antinomies, two things of different types, or even natures, can be combined through the *symbol*. In everyday life, Man knows and uses sign systems, solves problems through the symbolism of material existence, and practices religion, taking into consideration the symbolism of the noetic world. But the only real Symbol co-natural to God, according to St. Maximus the Confessor, consists in the uncreated energies of the essential Logos of God. St. Dionysius the Areopagite says,

> the initiates of our divine tradition [*iconology*] designate the *undifferenced* attributes of the Transcendently Ineffable and Unknowable Permanence as hidden, incommunicable Ultimates, but the beneficent *Differentiations* of the Supreme Godhead, they call Emanations (πρόοδοι) and Manifestations, because divine things become both united and separated.[3]

---

1 St. Maximus the Confessor, *Chapters on Love, First Century*, 96.
2 St. Maximus the Confessor, *Two Hundred Texts on Theology and the Incarnate Dispensation of the Son of God, Second Century*, 13.
3 *On the Divine Names*.

St. Gregory Palamas explains these expressions as follows: "Therefore, God has different unions and separations, but all of them are divine, i.e., equally *uncreated*. Having generally mentioned 'emanation,' he (Dionysius) divides it into many emanations, saying that they *bestow Being, Life, and Wisdom*."[4]

This triad of "volitions" of the Trihypostatic God can be characterized more clearly as follows:

1. "*bestowal of Being*" — actions of the essential *Light*, or the *Will* gradually fulfilling God's "presence," "incarnation," and "dwelling" in Man and the world;

2. "*bestowal of Life*" — *Love*'s actions kindling life and guiding the Soul from birth to death in its search for the Logos living in the human heart rather than "somewhere outside";

3. "*bestowal of Wisdom*" — *Wisdom*'s actions to prepare and enlighten the Soul on its ways of "reflection," "practice," and "contemplation" of the Divinity.

By the actions of the three energies *bestowing Being, Life, and Wisdom*, the Soul improves and grows to reach the maturity of the Bride; in other words, the Soul is *depicted* in them and becomes an Icon *conformable* to the nature of her divine Bridegroom, unknowable by any other means.

"The God-bearing Fathers say that God's essence is unknowable, while His other attributes are knowable. Everything that surrounds His essence — goodness (love), wisdom, power, etc. — are called Energies."[5] In addition, the Fathers refer to the Divine Energy flowing from the essence of the Divinity in various manifestations as *communications*, *communions*, and *likenesses*. In the Scholia on *The Divine Names*, St. Maximus the Confessor says, "Creative providences and goodnesses are common to the Unity distinguished as the three hypostases."

> The one Providence (Logos) and goodness of God — or, in other words, God's turning towards inferior beings by reason of His goodness — both is, and is thus called by the divinely wise theologians, *many providences* [*logoi*] and

---

4 St. Gregory Palamas, *Treatises*.
5 Ibid.

goodnesses [*images*], for they are indivisibly divided and differentiated among divisible things.

So, according to the God-bearing Fathers, God "in a single action" is indistinguishable and surely indepictable, but owing to "the diversity of His many logoi and modes of action" He can be distinguished and depicted in the symbolic realism of the man-made Icon.

When an iconographical theme is developing and moving toward its embodiment in iconography, it engenders an acting *pair* of primordial divine energies: the *Logos of the Prosopon* (*meaning, content*) and the *Mode of the Logos* (*the method-tropos of existence*). From Theophanies we distinguish and then depict not God's essence or even Hypostases (with the exception of Christ, but only His Face, according to His human nature, is directly depictable), but the things *depictable* through the dispensation of iconography: "creative providences and goodnesses; God's love, wisdom, and power," i.e., the *ideas of divine emanations* that in the Logos and His Image become visible ideas of fulfillment. In the Icon of the Theotokos and Child, for example, Jesus is the Logos, and the Theotokos is His Image. In the Icon of Sophia the Wisdom of God, Sophia is the creative Image, while Christ blessing Her actions is the Logos. The Miraculous "Angel of the Name of God" is the Image (of the actions of Light), while the discos on His chest shows the Logos, the Lamb Emmanuel.

The Fathers discuss not only the "images of actions" of divine powers, but also their movement, which is essential because images are traced by movement. The three iconological movements — *straight*, *spiral*, and *circular-cyclic* — are the three iconological forms of Divine Revelation through which, in practice, the energies of Divine Providence act according to the soul's readiness to perceive specific forms of divine "edification."

> God (*in His providences-logoi*) moves when He brings all things into being and sustains them. *Straightness* we must understand to mean the unswerving emanation of His energies (*in personified images*). His *spiral* movement must be taken to mean the combination of a persistent emanation and a productive stillness. And His *circular* (*cyclic*)

movement is a movement when He makes the things that have gone forth from Him return to Him again.⁶

Expressed iconographically, Theophany is distinguished by the *image* of completeness of action and by the *tropos* (*method*) of movement of fulfillment. Without disturbing the creation and order in the cosmos, Divine fulfillments and providences are transferred through Man into symbols of the man-made icon, and this method of transition from one reality to another may be called "symbolic realism." Taking form in the colorful substance of the icon, the iconological idea does not lose its spiritually affirming "realism" or its ontological correlation with the Icon formed by the color energies of the Divinity. Their correspondence will be by *conformity*, while their distinction will be by *nature*, because the conformity of the created world is in God's Divinity, which contains an essential exemplar of Life of all existent things.

> And we give the name of "Exemplars" to those laws which, preexistent in God as a Unity, produce the essences of things: laws which are called in Divine Science "Pre-ordinations" or Divine and beneficent Volitions, laws which ordain things and create them, laws whereby the Super-Essential pre-ordained and brought into being the whole universe.⁷

Distinguishing the notion "the Image of action of God" in Theophanies, we distinguish *various* names of the single eternal Energy of the Trihypostatic God, of which the most important iconographic sources and examples are: *Will* and *Light* (in the depictions of Christ as the Logos of *Theophanies*), *Wisdom* (in the depictions of the Sophia of Christ as the image of *God-Seeing*), and *Love* (in the depictions of Agape of the Holy Spirit as the Image of *Knowledge of God*). In these distinctions, it should be understood that the Logos of Theophany is a dynamic power and a luminous strength of the Son of God in Man, God-Seeing is the sophianic power of contemplating Him when meeting Him "face to Face" in the future, and the

---

6 Ibid.
7 Dionysius the Areopagite, *On the Divine Names.*

Epilogue

Knowledge of God is the immortal agapean power of deification in His Chamber. St. Gregory of Nyssa says that "every energy which extends from God to the Creation, and is named according to our variable conceptions of it, has its origin from the Father (*by Will*), and proceeds through the Son (*by Wisdom*), and is perfected in the Holy Spirit (*by Love*)."[8] "For energy is a movement of essence rather than essence itself."[9] God became Man, and Man became an iconographic image of God without losing his form. He can see the Light of Theophanies in forms befitting a rational creature, and considers Light to be not a generalized conclusion or abstraction, but a Creature personified in the iconic human image. We have seen an example of this attitude in Symeon the New Theologian's personal opinion of the Agape of God. Indeed, the Fathers say that God, in the economy of salvation, manifoldly *increases* through providential *emanations*, while remaining one in the Hypostatic Trinity, and these emanations are nevertheless "God, although not according to essence," and, being iconographic *images of theology*, they are depictable in icons.

The difficulty of this theme lies in the fact that at present various types of "iconoclasts" — making no detailed spiritual distinctions, like "theomachists" who once ferociously opposed hypostatic distinctions in God — argue against the iconological distinction between the single and saving co-essential Logos of the Trinity and the spermatic and oeconomy-creative Logos of the Divinity, which distinction can be found in the Gospel according to St. John: "The Logos was (turned) TO GOD, and the Logos WAS GOD." And the Logos, who "was in the beginning TO God" [Slavonic text], having become incarnate and man, is now directly, through Jesus Christ, turned to the world. The Most Holy Trinity, as it were, "separates" from Its essential Logos and communicates to Christians the spermatic Logos of the trinitarian saving Communion, because "the Sacred Science (*theology*) sometimes employs a method of non-*differentiation* (*according to the essence*) and sometimes one of *differentiation* (*according to the energies of the Prosopon and their images of communion*)."[10] This is also confirmed

---

8   *To Ablabius*, PG 45.
9   St. Gregory of Nyssa.
10 Dionysius the Areopagite.

THE ANGEL OF THE COUNTENANCE OF GOD

by Gregory Palamas: "the One God inseparably worshiped in Three Hypostases and in one Essence is also inseparably separated into *different energies [communion gifts]*."[11] He is certainly separated in the gracious energies of the Eucharistic Lamb through the Communion of the deifying Logos Emmanuel. St. Cyril of Jerusalem writes: "'Give us this day our superessential bread.' Ordinary bread is not 'superessential'; but this holy bread is superessential in the sense of being ordained for the essence of the soul. Not of this Bread is it said that it 'passes into the stomach and so is discharged into the drain' (Mt 15:17); no, it is absorbed into your whole system to the benefit of both soul and body."[12] And this Bread is an icon-painted Light of Divine creation of the catholic Church and of the church in the soul of every person.

The iconographically visible Light in a variety of ways leads the soul to the recognition of Christ, to the hearing of His providential "word," and to the vision of His dispensation "image." God the Holy Spirit appears in humanly understandable forms and images of Revelation, not only to imprint and vitalize the external image, but also to be embodied in the whole human being, distributing Its energies throughout the body and kindling the heavenly fire of faith in the soul. Through light and color, icon-painting conveys those mystical forms of Revelation that culminate in the experience of a person contemplating icons. Every icon figuratively contains and presents a dialogue between God and Man, revealing all the providences and goodnesses of the dispensation of faith to those who can "read" icons.

After the Holy Communion, the Church sings: "We have seen the true Light, we have received the Heavenly Spirit; we have found the true faith, worshiping the undivided Trinity." We partake of the spermatic Logos of the Son of God, but we worship the whole co-essential Trinity. To elevate and strengthen our faith, we are given the method of the church's distinctions in God: *nature, essence, hypostasis,* and *prosopon*. Among them, the *prosopon* is the main iconological "tool" to depict the reality of Revelation, indicating the need for the iconography of *formation, communication, communion,* and *likeness*. All

---

11 *On the Divine Energies and Their Communion.*
12 *The Mystagogic Catecheses,* V, 15.

of these terms, each in its own way, have to do with specific chords of the soul, because the Soul Bride should appear before the Logos not "monochromatically," but in a polyphonic sound at all the levels of Love, Wisdom, and Light. Indeed, it is true that "those who claim that two names mean the same thing rob their listeners."[13]

The Hypostasis denotes the *existence mode*, hidden and invisible to Man. In Revelation, however, God's specific Hypostasis appears in the *image of action* and becomes iconological, with its own specific features for fulfillment of the faith, meaning, or beauty of Theophany. "Spiritual grace is not nature, but the uncreated energy of the divine Spirit."[14] This is the ontological realism of "God indivisibly known by each of His (*figurative*) energies,"[15] because "every energy is supposed to have its own *name*."[16] As far as the art of icon-painting is concerned, "is supposed to have its own *name*" means that "every energy" is supposed to clothe "God's name" in an appropriate robe of Light and Color, while imprinting an Icon within one's own heart and upon a wooden panel.

Verbal names — i.e., "combinations of words" — depict God in some way, and this depiction, at least partially, can be translated into icon-painting symbols. Inversely, therefore, iconographic images can be read and described in words. This applies not only to icons' visible graphic contents, but also to their invisible dogmatic theology and their liturgical contents related to the Presence of God. Iconologically, it is not in the least strange that on special occasions — for example, during the appearances to Abraham, Jacob, Moses, Peter the Apostle, Paul the Apostle, or the Christian St. Alexander of Svir — God manifests Himself visibly in the form of an anthropomorphic Angel of His essential Light, which is not borrowed from created angels. Together with Gregory Palamas, we can only shrug our shoulders, baffled by some "nominal" Christians' hasty assertions to the effect that there is no, and cannot be any, "uncreated angel" in Christianity. I would like to ask "theologians" of this kind the question asked by St. Gregory

---

13 St. Gregory Palamas, *Treatises*.
14 St. Gregory Palamas, *Antirrhetici*.
15 St. Gregory Palamas.
16 St. Gregory of Nyssa, *On the Divinity of the Son and the Spirit*.

Palamas: "Is it possible that God needs His Creation to replenish His perfection as if before He were deprived of any power?"[17] For, when we hear the church's exclamation "the Holy things unto the Holy" and perceive God's power coming to us, we perceive both the verbal meaning and iconographic beauty of His Divinity while approaching the Chalice as saints by grace.

Reflecting along the lines of simultaneous actions of the "logos-image" of the Lord, we can once again find the answer to the ongoing dispute about the icon of "Paternity." The icon depicts the Lord of Sabaoth (the essential Image and inapproachable Power of the Trinity), Emmanuel (the Logos of the Divinity), and the life-giving Spirit of the Divinity in the form of an Angel (which is similar to the Chalice containing bread and wine representing the Blood and Body of the Logos). The icon of "Paternity" does not express the theology of hypostatic relations of the Trinity, but it expresses the iconological idea — the prayer "Ladder" — leading the way to the Paternity. St. Basil the Great wrote: "The existence (tropos of existence) of the Father reveals to us God as 'fatherhood,' that of the Son, as 'sonship,' and that of the Holy Spirit, as 'sanctity' (or 'sanctification'), i.e., in accordance with the 'characters' or distinctive features (idiomata) of each of them."[18] Considered in terms of the ascetic practice of the philokalia, the Icon of the Paternity expresses three symbolic planes in which a person coming to the Sacrament of Deification can dwell: *Prosopon* (in the depiction of the uniform Image of the Trinity, the Lord of Sabaoth), *Logos* (as a creative and spermatic power of deification), and *Eidos* (the Angel of Light forming the beauty of life in Man). The verbal and conceptual prototype of this iconography is the Lord's Prayer ("Our Father") as interpreted by St. Maximus the Confessor. If we believe and receive baptism "in the name of the Father," we also partake of His Divinity, because "Holy, holy, holy" represents three creative energies of God, but "one Image of the Trinity," "one Lord of Sabaoth" who governs deifying powers.

---

17   St. Gregory Palamas, *Treatises*.
18   See the author's summary of the ideas contained in the treatise *Against Eunomius* in *Letter* 236, as quoted by Basil Lourié in *The History of Byzantine Philosophy*.

Epilogue

For where would many saints come from if they do not partake of His Holiness? In fact, if God is the Lord, we partake of His Lordship, while "paternity" results from the existence of the Lord of Sabaoth, the single Image of the trinitarian Glory, and if we do not partake of the divine powers of the Paternity, how can we acknowledge the Father together with Christ?[19]

Do we paint icons without the liturgical inheritance of grace? The man-made icon is a kind of a man-made *temple*, and, in conformity to the acheiropoetic Icon of God, "all the saints, in whom one *divinity* and one *lordship (and one paternity)* dwell, are the temples of God, and of the Son, and of the Holy Spirit."[20] How can one say that nobody has seen the Heavenly Father if Christ pointed to the little ones and said, "for I say unto you, that in heaven their angels do *always behold* the Face (*prosopon*) of My Father which is in heaven" (Mt 18:10); therefore, the little ones who have not lost their "childishness" can see the *image* of the Father through the angels. The Icon is an expression of childlike—i.e., spontaneous—perception. Everything happens through the Icon of Revelation "when the *image* ascends to the Archetype to whom we now aspire."[21] And again, "we are a particle of God and are called so owing to the *pre-hypostatizedness of our logoi of being in God*."[22] In accordance with them, "God-likeness" is accomplished in Man, and God is depicted in Man in combinations. To achieve a combination, it is necessary to first see that "one thing" can be combined with "another thing." Iconography is a naming of God not only in mineral colors, but also in energies; and "energies and all laudatory theological songs are not exclusively for any particular Person of the divine Trinity, but they are common to the whole Trinity, with the exception of hypostatic features."[23] Therefore, it is said by the Fathers, considering that "there is a time for everything" and "there is a degree for everything," Man can "see the image of

---

19 St. Basil the Great, *Against Eunomius*.
20 Ibid.
21 Maximus the Confessor, *Ambiguum 7*.
22 Ibid.
23 Maximus the Confessor, *Scholia on Dionysius's The Divine Names*.

THE ANGEL OF THE COUNTENANCE OF GOD

God as He is," for "God is He Who sees, and keeps watch, and cares for everything."²⁴

Not only Man can come to know God in Theophanies; angels and intelligent cosmic beings come to know His actions, communing in them with the *logoi, ideas,* and *eide* of emanations of His essential Light. God gave sentient beings the ability to contemplate Him. But to contemplate means to see, understand, and experience to some extent, and the things mystically seen in such a way imply the ability to create dogmatic icons of this intelligent vision. God "saw all things before they were, holding them timelessly in His thoughts; and each one conformably to His voluntary and timeless thought, which constitutes pre-determination and image and pattern, comes into existence at the pre-determined time."²⁵ And when icon painters fully understand the phrase, currently just flying through their minds, "the Icon is theology in colors," it will be possible "at the predetermined time" to depict Theophanies in new forms of "contemplative and liturgical theology."

Coming forward to meet Man, God tests our faith, and the degree and the "starting point" of elevating us to salvation. God contemplates Himself in His Divinity, and in His economy He contemplates the creation, not abstractly, but graciously and iconographically participating in it with His *operations-energemata*. He "wants" to be actually seen and symbolically depicted. "*Energy* is called operation, energema, while *operation* is called energy," says John of Damascus and they (*images of operations*) are contemplated around God and named; and since they are named, they can be iconographically depicted. "God's associated dignities are contemplated according to the number of names, and since the dignities are the same with respect to each of the hypostases, the identity on the score of being of the two subjects of these identical dignities is shown most clearly."²⁶ Naming God, we depict the Icon — inaccessible in its fullness, but possible to contemplate by grace — of divine actions of all Three hypostases. In this Icon, God manifests Himself in His simplicity,

---

24 St. John of Damascus, *Orthodox Faith*.
25 Ibid.
26 Gregory of Nyssa, *To Eunomius*.

"but the small signs manifested in the creation reveal something of what is above it as far as possible; and separating in this way, God remains inseparable in everything."[27]

Theological ideas in the economy of God become Icons of Providence. His actions, enlightenments, and meanings can be realistically rendered in symbolic icon-painting by those who make their art part of the liturgical creativity of the Church. "For everything that has the definable Logos of being is God's *work*, even though the one thing began to be in time, in the sense of creation; while the other thing (*spermatic Logos*) is by grace *incorporated* in creatures like, for example, a certain intrinsic power clearly proclaiming that God exists in all things."[28] Through Christ's essential Logos, Light energemata are depicted and strengthened in us, stabilizing the ontological truth of faith. In fact, the energy of the *Paternity* is transmitted to us from the Father, and we are communed by "some twofold mental (intelligent) grace of the Son (*adoption*) and the Spirit (*spiritualization*) — this *twofold ray* of the Father ministers even unto us the Light of the truth, and also is united to the Father."[29]

Filling the heavens and the earth, the power-dynamis of will of the Heavenly Father becomes the Light of Christ in creatures, and Christ's saving energemata (operations) transform souls by the depiction of the Presence and action of the Holy Spirit. "Don't they (who doubt) know our doctrine of Christ's two *natures, wills, and energies*?" asks Maximus the Confessor. They operate in a person who has discovered the movement of faith, they fill us, and they are symbolically depicted in icon-painting. Isn't the mystical icon-painting being done in our souls through the *"image* of Christ's salvation" according to Paul the Apostle? He is in us together with the Father and the Holy Spirit "like the *image* (εἰκών) which ascended to its Archetype and assumed the divine action."[30] "So, those who are deified (*depicted in Christ, having become an icon of God*) not only improve their nature, but also acquire the divine *Image, the energy* (*of*

---

27   St. Gregory Palamas, *Antirrhetici*.
28   St. Maximus the Confessor, *On Theology*.
29   St. Gregory of Nyssa, *Letter to Evagrius*.
30   St. Maximus the Confessor, *Disputation with Pyrrhus*.

Love) of the Holy Spirit."³¹ Iconology cannot but be reflected in iconography, because the interpenetrations of the five ontological types of the Icon (a man-made icon—a wooden panel; an acheiropoetos icon—Man; a noetic icon—an angel, a prosoponic icon—Divinity; a hypostatic icon—the Trinity) give all levels of consciousness the right to participate, in communion, to the extent of individual perception of Revelation. In terms of this iconological extent, there is a difference between the "processions" (*prosides*) of the hypostatic Holy Spirit of God and the "outpourings" (*proxisis*) of energy of the essential Divine Spirit. The former is really indepictable yet mentally comprehensible to some small degree of theology, while the latter is depictable, nameable, definable, and falls into a category of objectives of creative iconology, thereby solving the problem of the depictability of "theological ideas" in icons.

Theophanies are called uncreated and divine owing to the enhypostatized state of their energies, in which God always dwells, acts, and through them is depicted. They are called the iconic "likenesses" and "communications," transmitting their dignity to the created Icon of Man and, through Man, to the man-made icon. So, God's *indepictable things* are depicted in icons, and act sacramentally in the Divine Spirit's emanations, outpourings, and penetrations into created and even man-made things. In the supreme mystical Icon of the God-Man Christ, a Christian is granted the inheritance and dignity of the "king, priest, prophet, apostle, angel, and God." Having approved Man to be His Icon, the Lord gave those who believe in Him the ability to perceive and commune with His Divinity. The Lord "'rewards those who are obedient to Him with unborn deification,' which is called 'an *enhypostatized* enlightenment, which has no birth, but enjoys an incomprehensible 'appearance in those who are worthy.'"³²

> In fact, the Fathers call these hypostatic properties *enhypostatized*, rather than hypostases, while essential ones they call in the strict sense "enessential" (*enousia*), rather than essence. Even though many natural and hypostatic

---

31 Ibid.
32 Maximus the Confessor's *Questions to Thalassius*, 61 as quoted by St. Gregory Palamas in *Treatises*.

Epilogue

properties merge together in God, none of them exists in a special hypostasis as enhypostatic.[33]

However, they exist as God's *figurative* things determined by His Prosopon. Every enhypostatic property of God is iconographic, manifesting and showing God's presence in it. Depicting the personified properties of God's Dispensation, the prosoponic icon steps back, letting God come forward hypostatically, which the Fathers call an "appearance in those who are worthy."

So, in accordance with the ontological types of the Icon, that which is Invisible by essence becomes Visible by energy. The emergence of unity between visible and invisible things (not by nature, but by the Prosopon of energies) results in the emergence of new Life, which is *conformably* rather than *connaturally* scrutable and contemplatable in various icons. "Therefore," according to St. Gregory of Nyssa, "the name '*divinity*' expresses the *visual power* rather than the nature of the Spirit," making it possible to contemplate spiritual events and, therefore, depict them as latent icon-painting. In addition, Gregory the Theologian calls for iconological practice, saying, "Be illumined [*i.e., icon-painted*] by one essential Light in the sense of divinity." "We do not hold that there are many causes and different Godheads producing different effects, subordinate one to another; but we hold that one God is the universal Source of the *emanations*, and the Possessor of all the Divine *Names* (*logoi*), [*and their icons*] we declare."[34]

> All conceptions and *terms* which regard the divine are of equal dignity one with another, in that they do not vary in regard to the meaning of the subject matter to which they are applied. For some terms denote relations, while others denote dignities or energies; but not a single term denotes *essence*, and it is an utter folly to say that every term does not have a special corresponding meaning.[35]

The *Logos of being*, or the *Image of Existence*, owing to the very term "image," can certainly be depicted in a special aspect and style of

---

33 St. Gregory Palamas, *Treatises*.
34 Dionysius the Areopagite, *On the Divine Names*.
35 St. Basil the Great, *Letter* 189.

symbolic realism in the icon. Quoting Basil the Great, *Letter* 189, St. Gregory Palamas says, "The Lord receives names from His actions." Let us add that from His actions He also receives images divinely manifested in icons through the iconological tradition of the Church, rather than through worldly artists.

"Hypostasis is as different from essence as energy is different from essence, because each of these notions is different in the meaning of its name."[36] A seed planted in the soil is invisible at first; then it grows and not only becomes visible, but also is used in food and in Communion after three modifications: grain, flour, and bread. In the same sense, names, being a movement of cataphatic energy, can develop, expand, and be depicted in icons, descending in their symbolizations closer and closer to the earthly world. It is said, "The whole creation will be saved through the children of God," because the whole creation will know the "images of the Presence" of God. "Those who seek to reach the truth should extend [*increasingly specifying the image*] the meaning of each of the names."[37] This extension of the creative possibilities is the lot of those who want God to be depicted in the soul and body; and, following the artistic tradition, even on the icon panel. The Holy Spirit is simple, but His operations are various, and "His operations come down to us [*and their images are icon-painted in us*], but His essence remains beyond our reach."[38] In fact, by them we "partly commune with God and *see* [*contemplate*] and understand Him vaguely" according to our measure and capacity, but we do not say that it is impossible to see the meaning (ideas) of divine emanations. The problem related to the theology of direct contemplations and indirect symbol-based iconological contemplations is quite complicated. However, it can be solved through the ability to differentiate. Therefore, such issues

> are sometimes self-evident, and sometimes it happens that the mind is invited to learn to consider and research. For example, it is written that the Lord appeared to Abraham and rained fire and brimstone upon Sodom, but at the

---

36 St. Gregory Palamas.
37 Ibid.
38 St. Basil the Great, *Letter* 234 *to Amphilochius*.

same time He appeared to Lot in two Persons. Do we equally [*iconologically*] perceive this with our faith?[39]

Through the grace of *conformity to the Divinity*, we are given Theophanies in one form or another — be it the Angel of the Prosopon, the Fire that came down in Love, the Cloud of Light showing the way, the Voice of Wisdom or the Logos of Light in the Transfiguration, or the Light Itself manifested and visible in the Incarnation — Christ, the Son of God, who does in us His Father's Holy Will, so that we become the "children of His Light." In "Dialogue Between an Orthodox and a Barlaamite," St. Gregory Palamas writes: "In fact, through this communion in the Spirit [*of the Logos and Image*] saints become miraculous *likenesses* of God," or, according to the divine Maximus, "living *icons* of Christ, and even the same as He is, by grace or by assimilation."[40] Every Theophany is the power and beauty acting in the Transfiguration of the soul and in the resurrection of the human spirit. Every mode of existence, and every tropos (method) of revelation that is applicable to creatures for the sake of their salvation, and every divine energy, inseparably reveals God in His entirety. Is not this, consequently, a justification of icon-painting? Therefore, God's manifestations in the images of His own Light are as important for an active and devotional life, and for our understanding, as a direct contemplation of the Divinity of God. And those who have not fully mastered direct contemplation are given iconographic images of God's actions and Presence. According to Dionysius the Areopagite, the *name* of the essence is the divine *emanation* of the One Who Is, while Maximus the Confessor says that "God and saints have one energy, and they are *living icons* of Christ and become like Him by grace."

"God is comprehended from what is *around* Him even before the creation of the world, rather than from what is in Him";[41] and this is something that is useful for the human spirit and depictable in the icon. Therefore, the essential Logos and the essential image of God are the iconographical power and beauty of the Theophanies that have reached us, and "a beauty of the truly Mighty One is His Divinity

---

39 St. Gregory Palamas, *Treatises*.
40 *The Ambigua to John*.
41 St. Gregory the Theologian.

comprehended [in theology] and *contemplated* [in iconology]."[42] If the divine and essential Energy should be called the Divinity, as St. Gregory Palamas says, by multi-distinction of divine names, there will be many intelligible and equally significant Divine energies, "in order by that part of It which we *can comprehend [and depict iconographically]* to draw us to Itself, and by that part of It which we *cannot comprehend* to move our wonder."[43]

So, some iconographic images (for example, the images of the Angel Emmanuel, Sophia, Agape, the Lord of Sabaoth, the Paternity, Motherhood, or other didactic icons of contemplative content) are designed to attract believers' souls to a greater comprehension of the divine Habitation within their lives. Disregard for or rejection of this iconography would exclude from our lives the very *theological* issue concerning the mystical content of faith, whereas the presence of this issue in the Icon forms part of the liturgical iconography of the Church.

In addition, it is often surprising that theologically correct ideas in some icons do not correspond to iconography. This lack of correspondence between "an idea and its eidos" can be found, for example, in icons and paintings depicting the so-called "New Testament Trinity." The goal is quite clear: there should be an icon painted in the New Testament tradition — an icon of the Trinity painted in accordance with the Christian Liturgy and Eucharistic Communion rather than the Old Testament symbolism. But the iconographic versions of the "New Testament Trinity" of the seventeenth to the twentieth centuries, even though they feature the theological *idea* of the basic Christian doctrine of the Tri-hypostatic God, do not correspond to and even contradict the symbolic realism of the ancient-church icon, which means that they are not Orthodox. Firstly, the "depiction" of the Hypostases in this iconography does not correspond to the divine "dignity" in terms of artistic performance; secondly, their style of "naturalistic symbolism" clearly leads to allegorism and a misrepresentation of the mystical theology of the icon. In addition, they misrepresent the dogmas of the Church: the image of God the Holy

---

42 St. Basil the Great.
43 Gregory the Theologian, *Oration* 45, 3.

Spirit "in the form of a dove" is not appropriate, because it does not belong to the field of theological speculation; in addition, the "dove" "flies" somewhere above the heads of Christ and the Father, which completely distorts the Orthodox theology of the Spirit's "procession" from the Father.

In accordance with the ancient Christian tradition, the iconography of the Trinity is permissible only with regard to appearances of the miraculous Angels of the essential and unapproachable Light. "For it is proclaimed that God's Face [*Prosopon, Icon*] *can be seen* by the worthy—our angels can always see the Face [*not the Hypostasis*] of our Heavenly Father, and we have been promised that we will contemplate the Trinity, which is called the seventh stage of prayer." It is possible that the contemplation of the Trinity, as in the case of the saving Theophanies, is similar to the contemplations of the Trinity by Abraham in the Old Testament or by the Christian St. Alexander of Svir, to whom the Trinity appeared in the likeness of Angels for the purpose of dispensation. In addition, St. Gregory Palamas says that "Both the Spirit and the Son descended upon the Virgin Mary, the Latter did so by Hypostasis and the Former by Energy, because only the Son became man, not the Spirit."[44] Only Christ was manifested hypostatically in the Divine-human form, while the other two Hypostases are visible and can have iconographic forms only by the *symbolism of Their action*—for example, in the likeness of the Angel of the Divinity or the form-making Light, or in an approximate form of a specific "light formation" corresponding to a specific symbol or metaphor ("in the form" of a cloud, fire, a sphere or a dove, etc.). "In Him is no darkness at all," but diverse are the light formations of ideas and eide, with very specific forms and even enhypostatized iconographic personifications.

In connection with the discussion of the theme of Theophanies, which is a quite serious theme for spiritual education, it is necessary to repeatedly assert the truth that Man contemplates the *actions* that God *forms* (*iconographically depicts*) in accordance with His providence of salvation and deification of the faithful. Divine images are not just spatially scattered actions of cosmic powers, or quickly and

---

44   St. Gregory Palamas, *Treatises*.

easily alternating pictures of phenomena, like ones in our world; instead, they are *enhypostatized* energies, which means that they are firmly connected to one or another Hypostasis of God, strengthening and elevating Man's faith. This *priceless gift* of the gracious Light is enhypostatized in the hypostasis of Man, preparing him for complete deification with flashes of enlightenment and illumination. A person of this kind can see the *image* of God's Presence within himself and *realize* the mystical *logos* of His likeness. According to the Fathers, this experience is called "communion" and "likening." Given in Theophanies, the Tri-radiant Light reunites with Man's triad inside him, because energy and the body of its habitation are always reunited for interaction in this case—for example, Will—body, Wisdom—soul, Love—spirit; and this reunited "likening" is the beginning of Man's Path to transformation, resurrection, and deification.

> According to the Fathers, the Light of deifying grace is *enhypostatic*. However, since *enhypostatic* (ἐνυπόστατον) is a word having many meanings, just like the word *non-hypostatic* (ἀνυπόστατον), they call the grace of deification hypostatic not as *self-hypostatic*, but as the one dwelling in those into whom it comes to dwell. For "it gives constant and continuous Light to those upon whom it comes to shine," says Gregory of Nyssa.[45]

For a person of this kind, God's image becomes visible, recognizable, and communionable in the enhypostatic energies of Light. As God has a personal character in Christianity, which determines Him as Three Hypostases, His appearances in Light images are absolutely personal, iconographic and iconic, and recognizable by the actions of relations among the *ideas* and *eide* of His *uncreated* Icon and the icon-painted created world.

Discussing the term "enhypostatic" in relation to human nature and the flesh of the Lord, St. John of Damascus, in his *Dialectic*, says that this term, as used by Christian writers, means something that exists or participates in some other thing's hypostasis and, "having received its existence in the given hypostasis," means an *enhypostatized*

---

45 Ibid.

(i.e., actually existing) property that has its own "image" within, while having its own independent attributes other than those pertaining to the hypostasis. Such enhypostatic *images* can be found in icon-painting: for example, Emmanuel — the Angel of the Blessed Silence, Sophia — the Wisdom of Christ, or Agape — the Love of the Holy Spirit. In addition, there is the hard-to-comprehend *uniform image* of the Lord of Sabaoth, which is interpreted by the Fathers as an enhypostatized Trinitarian Energy of the *power and lordship* of the One God. This is the idea understood not in the hypostatic theological sense, but in the prosoponic iconological sense, because iconography is a certain figurative form of naming. The "triad of holiness" chanted by the cherubim contains the idea of the mystical iconology of dispensation, while the "oneness" of the Lord contains the idea of the theology of deification. Both ideas are distinguishable in the experience of *action and contemplation*, but they are inseparable in the sacrament of deification.[46] "For thy Maker is thine husband; the Lord of Sabaoth is his name; and thy Redeemer [Logos-Christ] the Holy One of Israel; the God of the whole earth shall he be called" (Is 54:5). "The Divinity indivisibly unfolds in the trinitarity without division";[47] and "unfolding" just as in the first stage of painting of icons, He manifests the images (recognizable for salvation) of volitions of the consubstantial Holy Trinity, because the unfolding church-creating energies of the Divinity is the iconological and enhypostatic Power of God: "Holy God is the Father; Holy Mighty is the incarnate Son; Holy Immortal is the Holy Spirit."[48]

"In fact, even those who refer to the Hypostasis itself and the Spirit's grace [energy] as the *Spirit*, also referring to the Spirit's energies as the *seven spirits*, do not worship two or many spirits."

> For we theologize — according to Athanasius of Alexandria — about one God in Three Hypostases who has one essence, power, energy, and everything else that is *seen* as being theologized and glorified (icon-painted) around the essence — everything that is *said* about God apophatically

---

46 See St. John of Damascus, *On the Trisagion*.
47 Ibid.
48 Ibid.

(uncreated, timeless, eternal, etc.) and everything that is *seen* and *named* cataphatically (Light, Life, Goodness, Love, etc.). According to the Tradition, all this is called *all the fullness of the Godhead.*[49]

In terms of depictability, this "fullness" is clearly revealed in that icon which is dogmatically correct in style and compositional interpretation.

The purpose of icon-painting is not to express the essential aspect of Theophanies, because that is unknowable, but to "glorify [*in paint and light patterns*] God's essentially creative emanations to all beings." Unlocking the potential of icon-painting even more and making it possible for the human spirit to creatively and freely reflect on the legacy of the Tradition, the icon can and should glorify not only the manifested community of saints, but, according to St. Athanasius the Great, "the *beneficial* Providence manifested in existent things as pre-eminently goodness and cause of all good things" as well. St. Gregory Palamas expresses the same idea more precisely: "Providence is the natural and essential energy of God."[50] God manifoldly manifested in the *form* of Light (Christ — "I am the Light descended from Heaven"), or the Light repeatedly taking the form of the Miraculous Angel, is the mystic iconography of the constantly reuniting prayer and the manifestation of God's "Gift bestowing both Goodness and Deity."

The Bible gives us examples of prophetic references to the *word and image* operating in Theophanies, because "the prophetic word in such *praises* shows [*iconographically depicts*] some part of the divine energy without naming or even considering the very (essential) power from which the energy comes, lest the nature of that power be mentioned."[51] Invisible by nature, God is iconographically depicted by various actions of the Divinity (otherwise, where would the principles of the Icon come from?) and, according to the providence of salvation and deification, becomes visible in the symbolic realism of the Icon, the Cross, and the Gospels. "His emanations are definitely capable of contemplation as energy in some essential distinctive properties

---

49 St. Gregory Palamas, *Treatises*.
50 As quoted from *On the Divine Names* by Dionysius the Areopagite.
51 St. Gregory of Nyssa, *On the Beatitudes*.

Epilogue

around Him."⁵² The essential Logos of the Divinity manifests Himself in the likeness of deifying and creative energies, and "just as artworks serve as an indication of the power and wisdom of art rather than its essence itself, so God becomes visible through figurative and intelligent Light," because the term "divinity" expresses the *"visual power"* of the Trinity rather than the nature of the Spirit (the Father, and the Son).⁵³ This "dispensational, visual, and providential power was communed with by the prophets too." This power consistently impresses itself upon the soul through the visual power of the New Testament Cross, is theologized through the faith of the Gospel, and penetrates into the spheres of iconographic depiction, impressing itself into the paint of the Icon. "For what kind of *nature* is it without its natural power [*Logos*] and beauty [*Image*]?" exclaims St. Gregory Palamas. Following his idea, we can say, "What kind of icon is it if it has no images of God's Presence or Theophanic radiance?"

The fact that God may appear visibly in a certain form is evidenced even by saints' lives. For example, many saints appeared in their own *form* hundreds of kilometers away from the place where they were actually located. According to the Acts of the Apostles (8:39–40), Philip the Deacon was "caught away" by the Spirit of the Lord and "found at Azotus." Let us also recall the prophet Habakkuk whom the Angel of the Lord carried to Babylon to feed the prophet Daniel and then "set Habakkuk in his own place (*in Judea*) again immediately" (Dan 14:33–39). And here is a story from the life of a Christian saint who lived in the eighteenth to the nineteenth centuries: while staying in a cell, St. Seraphim of Sarov appeared at night to a sick woman who lived forty kilometers away from him, and on the following morning some visitors saw him as usual in his cell. An interesting example of "figurative" appearance can be found in the life story of Abba George, Hegumen of Sinai. Once on a Paschal Saturday, he wished that he would celebrate Pascha in Jerusalem and prayed all day long. On the holy day of Pascha, he was caught away and set in the Jerusalem Church of the Resurrection. He partook of the Body and Blood of the Lord from the Chalice offered by the patriarch Peter. When invited

---

52   Ibid.
53   Ibid.

by the patriarch to a meal, Abba George answered, "The will of the Lord be done!" But when Abba George bowed to the Holy Sepulcher, he became invisible and saw himself in his cell again. Saddened by the absence of Abba George at the meal, the patriarch sent him a letter, to which the old man replied, describing the miracle that had happened to him and predicting that the patriarch would die in six months. When the patriarch's messengers returned, they said that Abba George had never left the Sinai Monastery for seventy years. Meanwhile, all the bishops, priests, and deacons who saw the old man during the Pascha service at Jerusalem's Church of the Resurrection testified as follows: "We all kissed him." This is how the saints' all-pervading "figurative" power operates, making it possible to "form," instantly transfer over all distances, and make visible the presence of the Soul of a person who is away from a particular place. And science confirms this fact: "The scientific community seriously discusses the possibility of existence of (created) objects beyond time and space."[54]

When the divine Image (*Icon*) *in us* returns to the Archetype (*Divinity*), God answers the Lord Jesus's miraculous prayer for us, "that all may be one" (Jn 17:21). The mysterious "Providence is God's natural and essential Energy," leading the believer from the *image of fulfillment* to the *logos of ever-being*; "truly, the *mystery* of uniting and blending two bodies into one flesh is great, for the seal gives its entire self to wax, although wax is not the seal."[55] The Kingdom of God, which should be distinguished from the "Kingdom of Heaven," is not only a *place of deification*, but also a *state* of the Glory of reunification of the Image and the Logos, because "the Kingdom of God is the communication by grace of what is naturally inherent in God."[56]

So, indepictable apophatic theology "does not contradict cataphatic [*iconological*] theology, according to which God moves [*showing Himself in images*] and, having the Power (*Logos*), is theologized and accepts our worship as the One and as the Self-Truth."[57] Revealed in the iconography of Theophanies, the uncreated Icon animates created

---

54 Alexander Belinsky, *Christianity and Science*.
55 St. Gregory Palamas, *On the Divine and Deifying Participation*.
56 St. Maximus the Confessor, *Two Hundred Texts on Theology*.
57 St. Gregory Palamas, *Treatises*.

Epilogue

icons — the people have communion with the image and likeness of Christ; while the people, in their iconographic works, animate substance to form man-made icons to contemplate the Presence of God. St. Basil the Great says, "the beauty of the truly Mighty One is His Divinity *comprehended* [*in theology*] and *contemplated* [*in iconology*]."[58]

* * *

> If anything had existed before the formation of this sensible and perishable world, no doubt we conclude it *would have been in Light*. The orders of angels, the heavenly hosts, all intellectual natures, named or unnamed, all the ministering spirits, did not live in darkness, but enjoyed a condition fit for them in Light and spiritual joy. No one will contradict this; least of all he who looks for celestial Light as one of the rewards promised to the virtuous, the Light which, as Solomon says, is always a Light to the righteous, the Light which made the Apostle say "Giving thanks unto the Father, which hath made us meet to be partakers of the inheritance of the saints in Light."[59]

But if the Light of the First Day of Creation is infinite in the manifestations of the divine and hypostatic Light nourishing the angels, equally great is its "embodiment" in Color in which all existent things can contemplate the Image of God, His uncreated and visual Icon of the image of eternal Life. He who looks at It will not die, but be alive; he who contemplates this holy Icon experiences an internal transition from an "imitative" *image* to *likeness*. This is evidenced by St. Diadochos of Photiki:[60]

> When the intellect (*nous*) begins to perceive the Holy Spirit with full consciousness, we should realize that grace is beginning to *paint the divine likeness over the divine image within us*. Our power of perception shows us that we are being formed into the divine likeness; but the perfecting

---

58 St. Basil the Great, *Homily on Psalm* 45.
59 Basil the Great, *On the Hexaemeron*, Homily II, 5.
60 Chapter 89.

THE ANGEL OF THE COUNTENANCE OF GOD

of this likeness we shall know only by the *light* of grace. But no one can acquire spiritual Love (*Agape*) unless he experiences fully and clearly the *illumination* [*after the likeness*] of the Holy Spirit.

But indeed, this requires benevolent, infallible, and substantial hearing [*and sight*]. For as the Divinity is distinguished by both hypostasis and energy, every distinction shows a [*iconographic*] difference, because they intersect with each other. For the proper names of the divine hypostases are common to the energies, while those common to the Hypostases are the proper names of the divine energies. God is divided by Hypostasis, being united by energy: for the Father, the Son, and the Holy Spirit have the same energies. God is divided by energy, being united by hypostasis: for each energy (*by the mode of existence*) is the Father, the Son, and the Holy Spirit. Therefore, theologians add the word "all" to the energies and hypostases. Therefore, it is always said that existent things partake of *all* of God.[61]

The Icon is painted in accordance with Theophanic energies and shows not only one hypostasis, but "all" of them as a trinitarian Theophany. The Angel of the Countenance of God, described in the Bible and discussed in this book following the Church Fathers' teachings of the divine Light, is the image of Theophany of the *whole* Trinity. "The truth is the Angel of Light, the good ('miraculous,' according to the Bible) Angel. What kind of Light other than the Light of God is heralded by the Angel of Light Whose (uncreated) Angel he is?"[62] Because, according to Gregory the Theologian,[63] "God Himself is the Light for eternal creatures, and there is no other [for why would those who possessed the greatest of lights need a second one?]"

The Icon is painted according to the *image of action* of divine Energy, rather than according to the Hypostasis, but the whole Hypostasis happens to be manifested through the "ideographic image,"

---

61 St. Gregory Palamas, *Antirrhetici*.
62 St. Gregory Palamas, *Antirrhetici*, VIII, 21.
63 *Oration* 44.

Epilogue

"for never can any essence be contemplated without *stillness* or *movement*; in other words, without energy or power."[64] Explaining the difference between "essence" and "energy," Gregory the Theologian says that no one "ever stood before the Council and Essence of God, as it is written, or saw, or proclaimed the Nature of God."[65] Gregory Palamas, referring to Maximus the Confessor, adds that "the source of uncreated energy and will is the essence of God," because "God" refers to the *actor*, while "divinity" refers to *action*, according to Gregory of Nyssa.

* * *

> This is how you should understand and preserve divine simplicity; but do not dismiss His natural (diverse) *emanations* as non-existent, and do not consider the unfading, immutable, and essential Light to have a beginning; and do not talk about two Divinities or two Thearchies — the created [energy] and the uncreated [essence], because there will really be two in the division. As essence and energy are uncreated, nothing prevents them from being one, just like a sun ray and the Sun are one light. And do not consider the divinity of God and the Kingdom of God [*Prosopon*] to be created, because they are God's natural energies. And do not reduce the deifying grace to the status of a creature. And do not make yourself so miserable that you could not have the divine and deifying communion or even hope for it. In addition, do not make God so powerless that He could not send His holy communion into His intelligent creatures. And do not consider God's names [*revealed in Theophanies, and their images*] to have no essential content as denoting the same thing, thinking that they are names [*and images*] for essence only [*rather than energies*]. But believe in One and the Same [*just as in the icons of the Three Angels, so in the icons of the Lord of Sabaoth, His Logos, and His divine Spirit*] divisible and

---

64 St. Gregory Palamas, *Treatises*.
65 *Oration* 28, 19.

THE ANGEL OF THE COUNTENANCE OF GOD

indivisible God, united in *distinction* and divided in *unity*, never going out of Himself in [*iconological*] *emanations* and eternally moving in *immobility*, indivisibly divisible [*in the Image of action*], and fully communicable in the image of a sun ray.[66]

Amen, and "Glory to Him who has shown us the Light!"

---

66 St. Gregory Palamas, *Treatises*.

www.ingramcontent.com/pod-product-compliance
Lightning Source LLC
Chambersburg PA
CBHW020349170426
43200CB00005B/113